DIALOGUES AND ADDRESSES

THE
OTHER VOICE
IN
EARLY MODERN
EUROPE

A Series Edited by Margaret L. King and Albert Rabil Jr.

RECENT BOOKS IN THE SERIES

Madame de Maintenon

DIALOGUES AND ADDRESSES

‿

Edited and Translated by
John J. Conley, S.J.

THE UNIVERSITY OF CHICAGO PRESS
Chicago & London

Madame de Maintenon, 1635–1719

John J. Conley, S.J., is professor of philosophy at Fordham University.
He is the author of *The Suspicion of Virtue: Women Philosophers in Neoclassical France*, coeditor of *Prophecy and Diplomacy: The Moral Doctrine of John Paul II*, and the editor and translator of Jacqueline Pascal's *A Rule for Children and Other Writings*.

The University of Chicago Press, Chicago 60637
The University of Chicago Press, Ltd., London
© 2004 by The University of Chicago
All rights reserved. Published 2004
Printed in the United States of America

13 12 11 10 09 08 07 06 05 04   1 2 3 4 5

ISBN: 0-226-50241-4 (cloth)
ISBN: 0-226-50242-2 (paper)

Library of Congress Cataloging-in-Publication Data

Maintenon, Madame de, 1635–1719.
[Selections. English. 2004]
Dialogues and addresses / Madame de Maintenon ; edited and translated by John J. Conley.
p.   cm. — (The other voice in early modern Europe)
Includes bibliographical references and index.
ISBN 0-226-50241-4 (cloth : alk. paper) — ISBN 0-226-50242-2 (pbk. : alk. paper)
1. Women—Education—Europe—Early works to 1800.   2. Women—Europe—
Conduct of life—Early works to 1800.   I. Conley, John J.   II. Title.   III. Series.
LC1422.M27513 2004
370'.82—dc22
2004001298

Dedicated to the memory of my beloved father,
Peter Thomas Conley (1920–2001)

CONTENTS

PREFACE

When I first began to read Madame de Maintenon, I thought I had discovered the Miss Jean Brodie of French literature. Here was a dedicated teacher, but an overwhelming one. She orders us to sit up straight, to close doors quietly, and to speak proper French. She hands us precise rules on everything from writing a letter to praying the Pater Noster. She is a determined tutor, but how much moral improvement can we take?

Only further reading unveiled another Madame de Maintenon. She not only wants us to be virtuous; she systematically redefines the virtues to conform with the experience of women. She counsels us to endure the duties of our state in life, but she warns us of the stony edges of these duties, especially for impoverished women. Even as she hectors us on our moral obligations, she advises us to be reasonable in trying to live the good life on a tight budget. This Maintenon, with her taste for virtue theory and her tragic sense of freedom's limits, differs from the pious martinet of first impressions. It is my hope that this translation of her dialogues and addresses will introduce this philosophical Maintenon to an Anglophone public.

I owe a debt to many institutions and individuals for their assistance on this project. I thank the staffs of the libraries where I conducted much of my research: Fordham University Library, New York Public Library, Bibliothèque nationale de France, Bibliothèque Mazarine, Bibliothèque de la Société de Port-Royal, and Bibliothèque municipale de Versailles. I thank the National Endowment for the Humanities for a research grant in 2002 that enabled me to study the manuscripts of Maintenon at Versailles. I am grateful to the Office of the Vice President for Academic Affairs at Fordham University for its assistance in the publication of this volume. I thank Albert Rabil Jr. and Margaret King, co-editors of the Other Voice series, for their encouragement and assistance. I thank my graduate assistant Daniel Fincke for his proofreading of the original manuscript.

Like all students of Maintenon, I owe a particular debt to the nineteenth-century French scholars who managed to salvage the works and the reputation of Maintenon against hostile caricatures. The biographer Madame de Genlis and the editor Théophile Lavallée can still teach us how to take Maintenon seriously.

John J. Conley, S.J.

THE OTHER VOICE IN
EARLY MODERN EUROPE:
INTRODUCTION TO THE SERIES

Margaret L. King and Albert Rabil Jr.

THE OLD VOICE AND THE OTHER VOICE

In western Europe and the United States, women are nearing equality in the professions, in business, and in politics. Most enjoy access to education, reproductive rights, and autonomy in financial affairs. Issues vital to women are on the public agenda: equal pay, child care, domestic abuse, breast cancer research, and curricular revision with an eye to the inclusion of women.

These recent achievements have their origins in things women (and some male supporters) said for the first time about six hundred years ago. Theirs is the "other voice," in contradistinction to the "first voice," the voice of the educated men who created Western culture. Coincident with a general reshaping of European culture in the period 1300–1700 (called the Renaissance or early modern period), questions of female equality and opportunity were raised that still resound and are still unresolved.

The other voice emerged against the backdrop of a three-thousand-year history of the derogation of women rooted in the civilizations related to Western culture: Hebrew, Greek, Roman, and Christian. Negative attitudes toward women inherited from these traditions pervaded the intellectual, medical, legal, religious, and social systems that developed during the European Middle Ages.

The following pages describe the traditional, overwhelmingly male views of women's nature inherited by early modern Europeans and the new tradition that the "other voice" called into being to begin to challenge reigning assumptions. This review should serve as a framework for understanding the texts published in the series the Other Voice in Early Modern Europe. Introductions specific to each text and author follow this essay in all the volumes of the series.

TRADITIONAL VIEWS OF WOMEN, 500 B.C.E.–1500 C.E.

Embedded in the philosophical and medical theories of the ancient Greeks were perceptions of the female as inferior to the male in both mind and body. Similarly, the structure of civil legislation inherited from the ancient Romans was biased against women, and the views on women developed by Christian thinkers out of the Hebrew Bible and the Christian New Testament were negative and disabling. Literary works composed in the vernacular of ordinary people, and widely recited or read, conveyed these negative assumptions. The social networks within which most women lived—those of the family and the institutions of the Roman Catholic Church—were shaped by this negative tradition and sharply limited the areas in which women might act in and upon the world.

GREEK PHILOSOPHY AND FEMALE NATURE. Greek biology assumed that women were inferior to men and defined them as merely childbearers and housekeepers. This view was authoritatively expressed in the works of the philosopher Aristotle.

Aristotle thought in dualities. He considered action superior to inaction, form (the inner design or structure of any object) superior to matter, completion to incompletion, possession to deprivation. In each of these dualities, he associated the male principle with the superior quality and the female with the inferior. "The male principle in nature," he argued, "is associated with active, formative and perfected characteristics, while the female is passive, material and deprived, desiring the male in order to become complete."[1] Men are always identified with virile qualities, such as judgment, courage, and stamina, and women with their opposites—irrationality, cowardice, and weakness.

The masculine principle was considered superior even in the womb. The man's semen, Aristotle believed, created the form of a new human creature, while the female body contributed only matter. (The existence of the ovum, and with it the other facts of human embryology, was not established until the seventeenth century.) Although the later Greek physician Galen believed there was a female component in generation, contributed by "female semen," the followers of both Aristotle and Galen saw the male role in human generation as more active and more important.

In the Aristotelian view, the male principle sought always to reproduce itself. The creation of a female was always a mistake, therefore, resulting

---

1. Aristotle, *Physics* 1.9.192a20–24, in *The Complete Works of Aristotle*, ed. Jonathan Barnes, rev. Oxford trans., 2 vols. (Princeton, 1984), 1:328.

from an imperfect act of generation. Every female born was considered a "defective" or "mutilated" male (as Aristotle's terminology has variously been translated), a "monstrosity" of nature.[2]

For Greek theorists, the biology of males and females was the key to their psychology. The female was softer and more docile, more apt to be despondent, querulous, and deceitful. Being incomplete, moreover, she craved sexual fulfillment in intercourse with a male. The male was intellectual, active, and in control of his passions.

These psychological polarities derived from the theory that the universe consisted of four elements (earth, fire, air, and water), expressed in human bodies as four "humors" (black bile, yellow bile, blood, and phlegm) considered, respectively, dry, hot, damp, and cold and corresponding to mental states ("melancholic," "choleric," "sanguine," "phlegmatic"). In this scheme the male, sharing the principles of earth and fire, was dry and hot; the female, sharing the principles of air and water, was cold and damp.

Female psychology was further affected by her dominant organ, the uterus (womb), *hystera* in Greek. The passions generated by the womb made women lustful, deceitful, talkative, irrational, indeed—when these affects were in excess—"hysterical."

Aristotle's biology also had social and political consequences. If the male principle was superior and the female inferior, then in the household, as in the state, men should rule and women must be subordinate. That hierarchy did not rule out the companionship of husband and wife, whose cooperation was necessary for the welfare of children and the preservation of property. Such mutuality supported male preeminence.

Aristotle's teacher Plato suggested a different possibility: that men and women might possess the same virtues. The setting for this proposal is the imaginary and ideal Republic that Plato sketches in a dialogue of that name. Here, for a privileged elite capable of leading wisely, all distinctions of class and wealth dissolve, as, consequently, do those of gender. Without households or property, as Plato constructs his ideal society, there is no need for the subordination of women. Women may therefore be educated to the same level as men to assume leadership. Plato's Republic remained imaginary, however. In real societies, the subordination of women remained the norm and the prescription.

The views of women inherited from the Greek philosophical tradition became the basis for medieval thought. In the thirteenth century, the supreme Scholastic philosopher Thomas Aquinas, among others, still echoed

2. Aristotle, *Generation of Animals* 2.3.737a27–28, in *The Complete Works*, 1 : 1144.

Aristotle's views of human reproduction, of male and female personalities, and of the preeminent male role in the social hierarchy.

ROMAN LAW AND THE FEMALE CONDITION. Roman law, like Greek philosophy, underlay medieval thought and shaped medieval society. The ancient belief that adult property-owning men should administer households and make decisions affecting the community at large is the very fulcrum of Roman law.

About 450 B.C.E., during Rome's republican era, the community's customary law was recorded (legendarily) on twelve tablets erected in the city's central forum. It was later elaborated by professional jurists whose activity increased in the imperial era, when much new legislation was passed, especially on issues affecting family and inheritance. This growing, changing body of laws was eventually codified in the *Corpus of Civil Law* under the direction of the emperor Justinian, generations after the empire ceased to be ruled from Rome. That *Corpus*, read and commented on by medieval scholars from the eleventh century on, inspired the legal systems of most of the cities and kingdoms of Europe.

Laws regarding dowries, divorce, and inheritance pertain primarily to women. Since those laws aimed to maintain and preserve property, the women concerned were those from the property-owning minority. Their subordination to male family members points to the even greater subordination of lower-class and slave women, about whom the laws speak little.

In the early republic, the *paterfamilias*, or "father of the family," possessed *patria potestas*, "paternal power." The term *pater*, "father," in both these cases does not necessarily mean biological father but denotes the head of a household. The father was the person who owned the household's property and, indeed, its human members. The *paterfamilias* had absolute power—including the power, rarely exercised, of life or death—over his wife, his children, and his slaves, as much as his cattle.

Male children could be "emancipated," an act that granted legal autonomy and the right to own property. Those over fourteen could be emancipated by a special grant from the father or automatically by their father's death. But females could never be emancipated; instead, they passed from the authority of their father to that of a husband or, if widowed or orphaned while still unmarried, to a guardian or tutor.

Marriage in its traditional form placed the woman under her husband's authority, or *manus*. He could divorce her on grounds of adultery, drinking wine, or stealing from the household, but she could not divorce him. She could neither possess property in her own right nor bequeath any to her children upon her death. When her husband died, the household property passed not to her but to his male heirs. And when her father died, she had no claim to any family inheritance, which was directed to her brothers or more remote male relatives. The effect of these laws was to exclude women from civil society, itself based on property ownership.

In the later republican and imperial periods, these rules were significantly modified. Women rarely married according to the traditional form. The practice of "free" marriage allowed a woman to remain under her father's authority, to possess property given her by her father (most frequently the "dowry," recoverable from the husband's household on his death), and to inherit from her father. She could also bequeath property to her own children and divorce her husband, just as he could divorce her.

Despite this greater freedom, women still suffered enormous disability under Roman law. Heirs could belong only to the father's side, never the mother's. Moreover, although she could bequeath her property to her children, she could not establish a line of succession in doing so. A woman was "the beginning and end of her own family," said the jurist Ulpian. Moreover, women could play no public role. They could not hold public office, represent anyone in a legal case, or even witness a will. Women had only a private existence and no public personality.

The dowry system, the guardian, women's limited ability to transmit wealth, and total political disability are all features of Roman law adopted by the medieval communities of western Europe, although modified according to local customary laws.

CHRISTIAN DOCTRINE AND WOMEN'S PLACE. The Hebrew Bible and the Christian New Testament authorized later writers to limit women to the realm of the family and to burden them with the guilt of original sin. The passages most fruitful for this purpose were the creation narratives in Genesis and sentences from the Epistles defining women's role within the Christian family and community.

Each of the first two chapters of Genesis contains a creation narrative. In the first "God created man in his own image, in the image of God he created him; male and female he created them" (Gn 1:27). In the second, God created Eve from Adam's rib (2:21–23). Christian theologians relied principally on Genesis 2 for their understanding of the relation between man and woman, interpreting the creation of Eve from Adam as proof of her subordination to him.

The creation story in Genesis 2 leads to that of the temptations in Genesis 3: of Eve by the wily serpent and of Adam by Eve. As read by Christian theologians from Tertullian to Thomas Aquinas, the narrative made Eve responsible for the Fall and its consequences. She instigated the act; she deceived her husband; she suffered the greater punishment. Her disobedience made it necessary for Jesus to be incarnated and to die on the cross. From the pulpit, moralists and preachers for centuries conveyed to women the guilt that they bore for original sin.

The Epistles offered advice to early Christians on building communities of the faithful. Among the matters to be regulated was the place of women. Paul offered views favorable to women in Galatians 3:28: "There is neither Jew nor Greek, there is neither slave nor free, there is neither male nor female; for you are all one in Christ Jesus." Paul also referred to women as his coworkers and placed them on a par with himself and his male coworkers (Phlm 4:2–3; Rom 16:1–3; 1 Cor 16:19). Elsewhere, Paul limited women's possibilities: "But I want you to understand that the head of every man is Christ, the head of a woman is her husband, and the head of Christ is God" (1 Cor 11:3).

Biblical passages by later writers (although attributed to Paul) enjoined women to forgo jewels, expensive clothes, and elaborate coiffures; and they forbade women to "teach or have authority over men," telling them to "learn in silence with all submissiveness" as is proper for one responsible for sin, consoling them, however, with the thought that they will be saved through childbearing (1 Tm 2:9–15). Other texts among the later Epistles defined women as the weaker sex and emphasized their subordination to their husbands (1 Pt 3:7; Col 3:18; Eph 5:22–23).

These passages from the New Testament became the arsenal employed by theologians of the early church to transmit negative attitudes toward women to medieval Christian culture—above all, Tertullian (*On the Apparel of Women*), Jerome (*Against Jovinian*), and Augustine (*The Literal Meaning of Genesis*).

THE IMAGE OF WOMEN IN MEDIEVAL LITERATURE. The philosophical, legal, and religious traditions born in antiquity formed the basis of the medieval intellectual synthesis wrought by trained thinkers, mostly clerics, writing in Latin and based largely in universities. The vernacular literary tradition that developed alongside the learned tradition also spoke about female nature and women's roles. Medieval stories, poems, and epics also portrayed women negatively—as lustful and deceitful—while praising good housekeepers and loyal wives as replicas of the Virgin Mary or the female saints and martyrs.

There is an exception in the movement of "courtly love" that evolved in southern France from the twelfth century. Courtly love was the erotic love between a nobleman and noblewoman, the latter usually superior in social rank. It was always adulterous. From the conventions of courtly love derive modern Western notions of romantic love. The tradition has had an impact disproportionate to its size, for it affected only a tiny elite, and very few women. The exaltation of the female lover probably does not reflect a higher evaluation of women or a step toward their sexual liberation. More likely it gives expression to the social and sexual tensions besetting the knightly class at a specific historical juncture.

The literary fashion of courtly love was on the wane by the thirteenth century, when the widely read *Romance of the Rose* was composed in French by two authors of significantly different dispositions. Guillaume de Lorris composed the initial four thousand verses about 1235, and Jean de Meun added about seventeen thousand verses—more than four times the original—about 1265.

The fragment composed by Guillaume de Lorris stands squarely in the tradition of courtly love. Here the poet, in a dream, is admitted into a walled garden where he finds a magic fountain in which a rosebush is reflected. He longs to pick one rose, but the thorns prevent his doing so, even as he is wounded by arrows from the god of love, whose commands he agrees to obey. The rest of this part of the poem recounts the poet's unsuccessful efforts to pluck the rose.

The longer part of the *Romance* by Jean de Meun also describes a dream. But here allegorical characters give long didactic speeches, providing a social satire on a variety of themes, some pertaining to women. Love is an anxious and tormented state, the poem explains: women are greedy and manipulative, marriage is miserable, beautiful women are lustful, ugly ones cease to please, and a chaste woman is as rare as a black swan.

Shortly after Jean de Meun completed *The Romance of the Rose*, Mathéolus penned his *Lamentations*, a long Latin diatribe against marriage translated into French about a century later. The *Lamentations* sum up medieval attitudes toward women and provoked the important response by Christine de Pizan in her *Book of the City of Ladies*.

In 1355, Giovanni Boccaccio wrote *Il Corbaccio*, another antifeminist manifesto, although ironically by an author whose other works pioneered new directions in Renaissance thought. The former husband of his lover appears to Boccaccio, condemning his unmoderated lust and detailing the defects of women. Boccaccio concedes at the end "how much men naturally surpass women in nobility" and is cured of his desires.[3]

WOMEN'S ROLES: THE FAMILY. The negative perceptions of women expressed in the intellectual tradition are also implicit in the actual roles that

---

3. Giovanni Boccaccio, *The Corbaccio, or The Labyrinth of Love*, trans. and ed. Anthony K. Cassell, rev. ed. (Binghamton, N.Y., 1993), 71.

women played in European society. Assigned to subordinate positions in the household and the church, they were barred from significant participation in public life.

Medieval European households, like those in antiquity and in non-Western civilizations, were headed by males. It was the male serf (or peasant), feudal lord, town merchant, or citizen who was polled or taxed or succeeded to an inheritance or had any acknowledged public role, although his wife or widow could stand as a temporary surrogate. From about 1100, the position of property-holding males was further enhanced: inheritance was confined to the male, or agnate, line—with depressing consequences for women.

A wife never fully belonged to her husband's family, nor was she a daughter to her father's family. She left her father's house young to marry whomever her parents chose. Her dowry was managed by her husband, and at her death it normally passed to her children by him.

A married woman's life was occupied nearly constantly with cycles of pregnancy, childbearing, and lactation. Women bore children through all the years of their fertility, and many died in childbirth. They were also responsible for raising young children up to six or seven. In the propertied classes that responsibility was shared, since it was common for a wet nurse to take over breast-feeding and for servants to perform other chores.

Women trained their daughters in the household duties appropriate to their status, nearly always tasks associated with textiles: spinning, weaving, sewing, embroidering. Their sons were sent out of the house as apprentices or students, or their training was assumed by fathers in later childhood and adolescence. On the death of her husband, a woman's children became the responsibility of his family. She generally did not take "his" children with her to a new marriage or back to her father's house, except sometimes in the artisan classes.

Women also worked. Rural peasants performed farm chores, merchant wives often practiced their husbands' trades, the unmarried daughters of the urban poor worked as servants or prostitutes. All wives produced or embellished textiles and did the housekeeping, while wealthy ones managed servants. These labors were unpaid or poorly paid but often contributed substantially to family wealth.

WOMEN'S ROLES: THE CHURCH. Membership in a household, whether a father's or a husband's, meant for women a lifelong subordination to others. In western Europe, the Roman Catholic Church offered an alternative to the career of wife and mother. A woman could enter a convent, parallel in function to the monasteries for men that evolved in the early Christian centuries.

In the convent, a woman pledged herself to a celibate life, lived according to strict community rules, and worshiped daily. Often the convent offered training in Latin, allowing some women to become considerable scholars and authors as well as scribes, artists, and musicians. For women who chose the conventual life, the benefits could be enormous, but for numerous others placed in convents by paternal choice, the life could be restrictive and burdensome.

The conventual life declined as an alternative for women as the modern age approached. Reformed monastic institutions resisted responsibility for related female orders. The church increasingly restricted female institutional life by insisting on closer male supervision.

Women often sought other options. Some joined the communities of laywomen that sprang up spontaneously in the thirteenth century in the urban zones of western Europe, especially in Flanders and Italy. Some joined the heretical movements that flourished in late medieval Christendom, whose anticlerical and often antifamily positions particularly appealed to women. In these communities, some women were acclaimed as "holy women" or "saints," whereas others often were condemned as frauds or heretics.

In all, although the options offered to women by the church were sometimes less than satisfactory, they were sometimes richly rewarding. After 1520, the convent remained an option only in Roman Catholic territories. Protestantism engendered an ideal of marriage as a heroic endeavor and appeared to place husband and wife on a more equal footing. Sermons and treatises, however, still called for female subordination and obedience.

THE OTHER VOICE, 1300–1700

When the modern era opened, European culture was so firmly structured by a framework of negative attitudes toward women that to dismantle it was a monumental labor. The process began as part of a larger cultural movement that entailed the critical reexamination of ideas inherited from the ancient and medieval past. The humanists launched that critical reexamination.

THE HUMANIST FOUNDATION. Originating in Italy in the fourteenth century, humanism quickly became the dominant intellectual movement in Europe. Spreading in the sixteenth century from Italy to the rest of Europe, it fueled the literary, scientific, and philosophical movements of the era and laid the basis for the eighteenth-century Enlightenment.

Humanists regarded the Scholastic philosophy of medieval universities as out of touch with the realities of urban life. They found in the rhetorical discourse of classical Rome a language adapted to civic life and public speech. They learned to read, speak, and write classical Latin and, eventually, classical Greek. They founded schools to teach others to do so, establishing the pattern for elementary and secondary education for the next three hundred years.

In the service of complex government bureaucracies, humanists employed their skills to write eloquent letters, deliver public orations, and formulate public policy. They developed new scripts for copying manuscripts and used the new printing press to disseminate texts, for which they created methods of critical editing.

Humanism was a movement led by males who accepted the evaluation of women in ancient texts and generally shared the misogynist perceptions of their culture. (Female humanists, as we will see, did not.) Yet humanism also opened the door to a reevaluation of the nature and capacity of women. By calling authors, texts, and ideas into question, it made possible the fundamental rereading of the whole intellectual tradition that was required in order to free women from cultural prejudice and social subordination.

A DIFFERENT CITY. The other voice first appeared when, after so many centuries, the accumulation of misogynist concepts evoked a response from a capable female defender: Christine de Pizan (1365–1431). Introducing her *Book of the City of Ladies* (1405), she described how she was affected by reading Mathéolus's *Lamentations*: "Just the sight of this book . . . made me wonder how it happened that so many different men . . . are so inclined to express both in speaking and in their treatises and writings so many wicked insults about women and their behavior."[4] These statements impelled her to detest herself "and the entire feminine sex, as though we were monstrosities in nature."[5]

The rest of *The Book of the City of Ladies* presents a justification of the female sex and a vision of an ideal community of women. A pioneer, she has received the message of female inferiority and rejected it. From the fourteenth to the seventeenth century, a huge body of literature accumulated that responded to the dominant tradition.

The result was a literary explosion consisting of works by both men and

4. Christine de Pizan, *The Book of the City of Ladies*, trans. Earl Jeffrey Richards, foreword by Marina Warner (New York, 1982), 1.1.1, pp. 3–4.

5. Ibid., 1.1.1–2, p. 5.

women, in Latin and in the vernaculars: works enumerating the achievements of notable women; works rebutting the main accusations made against women; works arguing for the equal education of men and women; works defining and redefining women's proper role in the family, at court, in public; works describing women's lives and experiences. Recent monographs and articles have begun to hint at the great range of this movement, involving probably several thousand titles. The protofeminism of these "other voices" constitutes a significant fraction of the literary product of the early modern era.

THE CATALOGS. About 1365, the same Boccaccio whose *Corbaccio* rehearses the usual charges against female nature wrote another work, *Concerning Famous Women*. A humanist treatise drawing on classical texts, it praised 106 notable women: ninety-eight of them from pagan Greek and Roman antiquity, one (Eve) from the Bible, and seven from the medieval religious and cultural tradition; his book helped make all readers aware of a sex normally condemned or forgotten. Boccaccio's outlook nevertheless was unfriendly to women, for it singled out for praise those women who possessed the traditional virtues of chastity, silence, and obedience. Women who were active in the public realm—for example, rulers and warriors—were depicted as usually being lascivious and as suffering terrible punishments for entering the masculine sphere. Women were his subject, but Boccaccio's standard remained male.

Christine de Pizan's *Book of the City of Ladies* contains a second catalog, one responding specifically to Boccaccio's. Whereas Boccaccio portrays female virtue as exceptional, she depicts it as universal. Many women in history were leaders, or remained chaste despite the lascivious approaches of men, or were visionaries and brave martyrs.

The work of Boccaccio inspired a series of catalogs of illustrious women of the biblical, classical, Christian, and local pasts, among them Filippo da Bergamo's *Of Illustrious Women*, Pierre de Brantôme's *Lives of Illustrious Women*, Pierre Le Moyne's *Gallerie of Heroic Women*, and Pietro Paolo de Ribera's *Immortal Triumphs and Heroic Enterprises of 845 Women*. Whatever their embedded prejudices, these works drove home to the public the possibility of female excellence.

THE DEBATE. At the same time, many questions remained: Could a woman be virtuous? Could she perform noteworthy deeds? Was she even, strictly speaking, of the same human species as men? These questions were debated over four centuries, in French, German, Italian, Spanish, and English, by authors male and female, among Catholics, Protestants, and Jews, in ponderous volumes and breezy pamphlets. The whole literary genre has been called the *querelle des femmes,* the "woman question."

The opening volley of this battle occurred in the first years of the fifteenth century, in a literary debate sparked by Christine de Pizan. She exchanged letters critical of Jean de Meun's contribution to *The Romance of the Rose* with two French royal secretaries, Jean de Montreuil and Gontier Col. When the matter became public, Jean Gerson, one of Europe's leading theologians, supported de Pizan's arguments against de Meun, for the moment silencing the opposition.

The debate resurfaced repeatedly over the next two hundred years. *The Triumph of Women* (1438) by Juan Rodríguez de la Camara (or Juan Rodríguez del Padron) struck a new note by presenting arguments for the superiority of women to men. *The Champion of Women* (1440–42) by Martin Le Franc addresses once again the negative views of women presented in *The Romance of the Rose* and offers counterevidence of female virtue and achievement.

A cameo of the debate on women is included in *The Courtier,* one of the most widely read books of the era, published by the Italian Baldassare Castiglione in 1528 and immediately translated into other European vernaculars. *The Courtier* depicts a series of evenings at the court of the duke of Urbino in which many men and some women of the highest social stratum amuse themselves by discussing a range of literary and social issues. The "woman question" is a pervasive theme throughout, and the third of its four books is devoted entirely to that issue.

In a verbal duel, Gasparo Pallavicino and Giuliano de' Medici present the main claims of the two traditions. Gasparo argues the innate inferiority of women and their inclination to vice. Only in bearing children do they profit the world. Giuliano counters that women share the same spiritual and mental capacities as men and may excel in wisdom and action. Men and women are of the same essence: just as no stone can be more perfectly a stone than another, so no human being can be more perfectly human than others, whether male or female. It was an astonishing assertion, boldly made to an audience as large as all Europe.

THE TREATISES. Humanism provided the materials for a positive counterconcept to the misogyny embedded in Scholastic philosophy and law and inherited from the Greek, Roman, and Christian pasts. A series of humanist treatises on marriage and family, on education and deportment, and on the nature of women helped construct these new perspectives.

The works by Francesco Barbaro and Leon Battista Alberti—*On Mar-*

riage (1415) and *On the Family* (1434–37)—far from defending female equality, reasserted women's responsibility for rearing children and managing the housekeeping while being obedient, chaste, and silent. Nevertheless, they served the cause of reexamining the issue of women's nature by placing domestic issues at the center of scholarly concern and reopening the pertinent classical texts. In addition, Barbaro emphasized the companionate nature of marriage and the importance of a wife's spiritual and mental qualities for the well-being of the family.

These themes reappear in later humanist works on marriage and the education of women by Juan Luis Vives and Erasmus. Both were moderately sympathetic to the condition of women without reaching beyond the usual masculine prescriptions for female behavior.

An outlook more favorable to women characterizes the nearly unknown work *In Praise of Women* (ca. 1487) by the Italian humanist Bartolommeo Goggio. In addition to providing a catalog of illustrious women, Goggio argued that male and female are the same in essence, but that women (reworking the Adam and Eve narrative from quite a new angle) are actually superior. In the same vein, the Italian humanist Mario Equicola asserted the spiritual equality of men and women in *On Women* (1501). In 1525, Galeazzo Flavio Capra (or Capella) published his work *On the Excellence and Dignity of Women*. This humanist tradition of treatises defending the worthiness of women culminates in the work of Henricus Cornelius Agrippa *On the Nobility and Preeminence of the Female Sex*. No work by a male humanist more succinctly or explicitly presents the case for female dignity.

THE WITCH BOOKS. While humanists grappled with the issues pertaining to women and family, other learned men turned their attention to what they perceived as a very great problem: witches. Witch-hunting manuals, explorations of the witch phenomenon, and even defenses of witches are not at first glance pertinent to the tradition of the other voice. But they do relate in this way: most accused witches were women. The hostility aroused by supposed witch activity is comparable to the hostility aroused by women. The evil deeds the victims of the hunt were charged with were exaggerations of the vices to which, many believed, all women were prone.

The connection between the witch accusation and the hatred of women is explicit in the notorious witch-hunting manual *The Hammer of Witches* (1486) by two Dominican inquisitors, Heinrich Krämer and Jacob Sprenger. Here the inconstancy, deceitfulness, and lustfulness traditionally associated with women are depicted in exaggerated form as the core features of witch behavior. These traits inclined women to make a bargain with the devil—sealed by sexual intercourse—by which they acquired unholy powers. Such bizarre claims, far from being rejected by rational men, were broadcast by intellectuals. The German Ulrich Molitur, the Frenchman Nicolas Rémy, and the Italian Stefano Guazzo all coolly informed the public of sinister orgies and midnight pacts with the devil. The celebrated French jurist, historian, and political philosopher Jean Bodin argued that because women were especially prone to diabolism, regular legal procedures could properly be suspended in order to try those accused of this "exceptional crime."

A few experts such as the physician Johann Weyer, a student of Agrippa's, raised their voices in protest. In 1563, he explained the witch phenomenon thus, without discarding belief in diabolism: the devil deluded foolish old women afflicted by melancholia, causing them to believe they had magical powers. Weyer's rational skepticism, which had good credibility in the community of the learned, worked to revise the conventional views of women and witchcraft.

WOMEN'S WORKS. To the many categories of works produced on the question of women's worth must be added nearly all works written by women. A woman writing was in herself a statement of women's claim to dignity.

Only a few women wrote anything before the dawn of the modern era, for three reasons. First, they rarely received the education that would enable them to write. Second, they were not admitted to the public roles—as administrator, bureaucrat, lawyer or notary, or university professor—in which they might gain knowledge of the kinds of things the literate public thought worth writing about. Third, the culture imposed silence on women, considering speaking out a form of unchastity. Given these conditions, it is remarkable that any women wrote. Those who did before the fourteenth century were almost always nuns or religious women whose isolation made their pronouncements more acceptable.

From the fourteenth century on, the volume of women's writings rose. Women continued to write devotional literature, although not always as cloistered nuns. They also wrote diaries, often intended as keepsakes for their children; books of advice to their sons and daughters; letters to family members and friends; and family memoirs, in a few cases elaborate enough to be considered histories.

A few women wrote works directly concerning the "woman question," and some of these, such as the humanists Isotta Nogarola, Cassandra Fedele, Laura Cereta, and Olympia Morata, were highly trained. A few were professional writers, living by the income of their pens; the very first among them was Christine de Pizan, noteworthy in this context as in so many others. In addition to *The Book of the City of Ladies* and her critiques of *The Romance of the Rose*, she wrote *The Treasure of the City of Ladies* (a guide to social decorum for women), an advice book for her son, much courtly verse, and a full-scale history of the reign of King Charles V of France.

WOMEN PATRONS. Women who did not themselves write but encouraged others to do so boosted the development of an alternative tradition. Highly placed women patrons supported authors, artists, musicians, poets, and learned men. Such patrons, drawn mostly from the Italian elites and the courts of northern Europe, figure disproportionately as the dedicatees of the important works of early feminism.

For a start, it might be noted that the catalogs of Boccaccio and Alvaro de Luna were dedicated to the Florentine noblewoman Andrea Acciaiuoli and to Doña María, first wife of King Juan II of Castile, while the French translation of Boccaccio's work was commissioned by Anne of Brittany, wife of King Charles VIII of France. The humanist treatises of Goggio, Equicola, Vives, and Agrippa were dedicated, respectively, to Eleanora of Aragon, wife of Ercole I d'Este, duke of Ferrara; to Margherita Cantelma of Mantua; to Catherine of Aragon, wife of King Henry VIII of England; and to Margaret, duchess of Austria and regent of the Netherlands. As late as 1696, Mary Astell's *Serious Proposal to the Ladies, for the Advancement of Their True and Greatest Interest* was dedicated to Princess Anne of Denmark.

These authors presumed that their efforts would be welcome to female patrons, or they may have written at the bidding of those patrons. Silent themselves, perhaps even unresponsive, these loftily placed women helped shape the tradition of the other voice.

THE ISSUES. The literary forms and patterns in which the tradition of the other voice presented itself have now been sketched. It remains to highlight the major issues around which this tradition crystallizes. In brief, there are four problems to which our authors return again and again, in plays and catalogs, in verse and letters, in treatises and dialogues, in every language: the problem of chastity, the problem of power, the problem of speech, and the problem of knowledge. Of these the greatest, preconditioning the others, is the problem of chastity.

THE PROBLEM OF CHASTITY. In traditional European culture, as in those of antiquity and others around the globe, chastity was perceived as woman's quintessential virtue—in contrast to courage, or generosity, or leadership, or rationality, seen as virtues characteristic of men. Opponents of women charged them with insatiable lust. Women themselves and their defenders—without disputing the validity of the standard—responded that women were capable of chastity.

The requirement of chastity kept women at home, silenced them, isolated them, left them in ignorance. It was the source of all other impediments. Why was it so important to the society of men, of whom chastity was not required, and who more often than not considered it their right to violate the chastity of any woman they encountered?

Female chastity ensured the continuity of the male-headed household. If a man's wife was not chaste, he could not be sure of the legitimacy of his offspring. If they were not his and they acquired his property, it was not his household, but some other man's, that had endured. If his daughter was not chaste, she could not be transferred to another man's household as his wife, and he was dishonored.

The whole system of the integrity of the household and the transmission of property was bound up in female chastity. Such a requirement pertained only to property-owning classes, of course. Poor women could not expect to maintain their chastity, least of all if they were in contact with high-status men to whom all women but those of their own household were prey.

In Catholic Europe, the requirement of chastity was further buttressed by moral and religious imperatives. Original sin was inextricably linked with the sexual act. Virginity was seen as heroic virtue, far more impressive than, say, the avoidance of idleness or greed. Monasticism, the cultural institution that dominated medieval Europe for centuries, was grounded in the renunciation of the flesh. The Catholic reform of the eleventh century imposed a similar standard on all the clergy and a heightened awareness of sexual requirements on all the laity. Although men were asked to be chaste, female unchastity was much worse: it led to the devil, as Eve had led mankind to sin.

To such requirements, women and their defenders protested their innocence. Furthermore, following the example of holy women who had escaped the requirements of family and sought the religious life, some women began to conceive of female communities as alternatives both to family and to the cloister. Christine de Pizan's city of ladies was such a community. Moderata Fonte and Mary Astell envisioned others. The luxurious salons of the French *précieuses* of the seventeenth century, or the comfortable English drawing rooms of the next, may have been born of the same impulse. Here women not only might escape, if briefly, the subordinate position that life in the family entailed but might also make claims to power, exercise their capacity for speech, and display their knowledge.

THE PROBLEM OF POWER. Women were excluded from power: the whole cultural tradition insisted on it. Only men were citizens, only men bore arms, only men could be chiefs or lords or kings. There were exceptions that did not disprove the rule, when wives or widows or mothers took the place of men, awaiting their return or the maturation of a male heir. A woman who attempted to rule in her own right was perceived as an anomaly, a monster, at once a deformed woman and an insufficient male, sexually confused and consequently unsafe.

The association of such images with women who held or sought power explains some otherwise odd features of early modern culture. Queen Elizabeth I of England, one of the few women to hold full regal authority in European history, played with such male/female images—positive ones, of course—in representing herself to her subjects. She was a prince, and manly, even though she was female. She was also (she claimed) virginal, a condition absolutely essential if she was to avoid the attacks of her opponents. Catherine de' Medici, who ruled France as widow and regent for her sons, also adopted such imagery in defining her position. She chose as one symbol the figure of Artemisia, an androgynous ancient warrior-heroine who combined a female persona with masculine powers.

Power in a woman, without such sexual imagery, seems to have been indigestible by the culture. A rare note was struck by the Englishman Sir Thomas Elyot in his *Defence of Good Women* (1540), justifying both women's participation in civic life and their prowess in arms. The old tune was sung by the Scots reformer John Knox in his *First Blast of the Trumpet against the Monstrous Regiment of Women* (1558); for him rule by women, defects in nature, was a hideous contradiction in terms.

The confused sexuality of the imagery of female potency was not reserved for rulers. Any woman who excelled was likely to be called an Amazon, recalling the self-mutilated warrior women of antiquity who repudiated all men, gave up their sons, and raised only their daughters. She was often said to have "exceeded her sex" or to have possessed "masculine virtue"—as the very fact of conspicuous excellence conferred masculinity even on the female subject. The catalogs of notable women often showed those female heroes dressed in armor, armed to the teeth, like men. Amazonian heroines romp through the epics of the age—Ariosto's *Orlando Furioso* (1532) and Spenser's *Faerie Queene* (1590–1609). Excellence in a woman was perceived as a claim for power, and power was reserved for the masculine realm. A woman who possessed either one was masculinized and lost title to her own female identity.

THE PROBLEM OF SPEECH. Just as power had a sexual dimension when it was claimed by women, so did speech. A good woman spoke little. Excessive speech was an indication of unchastity. By speech, women seduced men. Eve had lured Adam into sin by her speech. Accused witches were commonly accused of having spoken abusively, or irrationally, or simply too much. As enlightened a figure as Francesco Barbaro insisted on silence in a woman, which he linked to her perfect unanimity with her husband's will and her unblemished virtue (her chastity). Another Italian humanist, Leonardo Bruni, in advising a noblewoman on her studies, barred her not from speech but from public speaking. That was reserved for men.

Related to the problem of speech was that of costume—another, if silent, form of self-expression. Assigned the task of pleasing men as their primary occupation, elite women often tended toward elaborate costume, hairdressing, and the use of cosmetics. Clergy and secular moralists alike condemned these practices. The appropriate function of costume and adornment was to announce the status of a woman's husband or father. Any further indulgence in adornment was akin to unchastity.

THE PROBLEM OF KNOWLEDGE. When the Italian noblewoman Isotta Nogarola had begun to attain a reputation as a humanist, she was accused of incest—a telling instance of the association of learning in women with unchastity. That chilling association inclined any woman who was educated to deny that she was or to make exaggerated claims of heroic chastity.

If educated women were pursued with suspicions of sexual misconduct, women seeking an education faced an even more daunting obstacle: the assumption that women were by nature incapable of learning, that reasoning was a particularly masculine ability. Just as they proclaimed their chastity, women and their defenders insisted on their capacity for learning. The major work by a male writer on female education—that by Juan Luis Vives, *On the Education of a Christian Woman* (1523)—granted female capacity for intellection but still argued that a woman's whole education was to be shaped around the requirement of chastity and a future within the household. Female writers of the following generations—Marie de Gournay in France, Anna Maria van Schurman in Holland, and Mary Astell in England—began to envision other possibilities.

The pioneers of female education were the Italian women humanists who managed to attain a literacy in Latin and a knowledge of classical and Christian literature equivalent to that of prominent men. Their works implicitly and explicitly raise questions about women's social roles, defining problems that beset women attempting to break out of the cultural limits that had bound them. Like Christine de Pizan, who achieved an advanced education through her father's tutoring and her own devices, their bold questioning makes clear the importance of training. Only when women were educated to the same standard as male leaders would they be able to raise that other voice and insist on their dignity as human beings morally, intellectually, and legally equal to men.

THE OTHER VOICE. The other voice, a voice of protest, was mostly female, but it was also male. It spoke in the vernaculars and in Latin, in treatises and dialogues, in plays and poetry, in letters and diaries, and in pamphlets. It battered at the wall of prejudice that encircled women and raised a banner announcing its claims. The female was equal (or even superior) to the male in essential nature—moral, spiritual, and intellectual. Women were capable of higher education, of holding positions of power and influence in the public realm, and of speaking and writing persuasively. The last bastion of masculine supremacy, centered on the notions of a woman's primary domestic responsibility and the requirement of female chastity, was not as yet assaulted—although visions of productive female communities as alternatives to the family indicated an awareness of the problem.

During the period 1300–1700, the other voice remained only a voice, and one only dimly heard. It did not result—yet—in an alteration of social patterns. Indeed, to this day they have not entirely been altered. Yet the call for justice issued as long as six centuries ago by those writing in the tradition of the other voice must be recognized as the source and origin of the mature feminist tradition and of the realignment of social institutions accomplished in the modern age.

We thank the volume editors in this series, who responded with many suggestions to an earlier draft of this introduction, making it a collaborative enterprise. Many of their suggestions and criticisms have resulted in revisions of this introduction, although we remain responsible for the final product.

PROJECTED TITLES IN THE SERIES

Maria Gaetana Agnesi, Giussepa Eleonora Barbapiccola, Diamante Medaglia Faina, and Aretafila Savini de' Rossi, *The Contest for Knowledge: Debates over Women's Learning in Eighteenth-Century Italy*, edited and translated by Rebecca Messbarger and Paula Findlen

Isabella Andreini, *Mirtilla*, edited and translated by Laura Stortoni

Tullia d'Aragona, *Complete Poems and Letters*, edited and translated by Julia Hairston

Tullia d'Aragona, *The Wretch, Otherwise Known as Guerrino*, edited and translated by Julia Hairston and John McLucas

Francesco Barbaro et al., *On Marriage and the Family*, edited and translated by Margaret L. King

Laura Battiferra, *Selected Poetry, Prose, and Letters*, edited and translated by Victoria Kirkham

Giulia Bigolina, *"Urania" and "Giulia,"* edited and translated by Valeria Finucci

Francesco Buoninsegni and Arcangela Tarabotti, *Menippean Satire: "Against Feminine Extravagance" and "Antisatire,"* edited and translated by Elissa Weaver

Rosalba Carriera, *Letters, Diaries, and Art*, edited and translated by Shearer West

Madame du Chatelet, *Selected Works*, edited by Judith Zinsser

Vittoria Colonna, *Sonnets for Michelangelo*, edited and translated by Abigail Brundin

Vittoria Colonna, Chiara Matraini, and Lucrezia Marinella, *Marian Writings*, edited and translated by Susan Haskins

Princess Elizabeth of Bohemia, *Correspondence with Descartes*, edited and translated by Lisa Shapiro

Isabella d'Este, *Selected Letters*, edited and translated by Deanna Shemek

Fairy-Tales by Seventeenth-Century French Women Writers, edited and translated by Lewis Seifert and Domna C. Stanton

Moderata Fonte, *Floridoro*, edited and translated by Valeria Finucci

Moderata Fonte and Lucrezia Marinella, *Religious Narratives*, edited and translated by Virginia Cox

Francisca de los Apostoles, *Visions on Trial: The Inquisitional Trial of Francisca de los Apostoles*, edited and translated by Gillian T. W. Ahlgren

Catharina Regina von Greiffenberg, *Meditations on the Life of Christ*, edited and translated by Lynne Tatlock

In Praise of Women: Italian Fifteenth-Century Defenses of Women, edited and translated by Daniel Bornstein

Louise Labé, *Complete Works*, edited and translated by Annie Finch and Deborah Baker

Lucrezia Marinella, *L'Enrico, or Byzantium Conquered*, edited and translated by Virginia Cox

Lucrezia Marinella, *Happy Arcadia*, edited and translated by Susan Haskins and Letizia Panizza

Chiara Matraini, *Selected Poetry and Prose*, edited and translated by Elaine MacLachlan

Eleonora Petersen von Merlau, *Pietism and Women's Autobiography*, edited and translated by Barbara Becker-Cantarino

Alessandro Piccolomini, *Rethinking Marriage in Sixteenth-Century Italy*, edited and translated by Letizia Panizza

Christine de Pizan et al., *Debate over the "Romance of the Rose,"* edited and translated by Tom Conley with Elisabeth Hodges

Christine de Pizan, *Life of Charles V*, edited and translated by Charity Cannon Willard

Christine de Pizan, *The Long Road of Learning*, edited and translated by Andrea Tarnowski

Madeleine and Catherine des Roches, *Selected Letters, Dialogues, and Poems*, edited and translated by Anne Larsen

Oliva Sabuco, *The New Philosophy: True Medicine*, edited and translated by Gianna Pomata

Margherita Sarrocchi, *La Scanderbeide*, edited and translated by Rinaldina Russell

Justine Siegemund, *The Court Midwife*, edited and translated by Lynne Tatlock

Gabrielle Suchon, *"On Philosophy" and "On Morality,"* edited and translated by Domna Stanton with Rebecca Wilkin

Sara Copio Sullam, *Sara Copio Sullam: Jewish Poet and Intellectual in Early Seventeenth-Century Venice*, edited and translated by Don Harrán

Arcangela Tarrabotti, *Convent Life as Inferno: A Report*, introduction and notes by Francesca Medioli, translated by Letizia Panizza

Laura Terracina, *Works*, edited and translated by Michael Sherberg

Katharina Schütz Zell, *Selected Writings*, edited and translated by Elsie McKee

ABBREVIATIONS

BMV	Bibliothèque municipale de Versailles
LC	*Les conversations de Madame de Maintenon*
LE	*Lettres édifiantes de Madame de Maintenon*
LMM	*Les loisirs de Madame de Maintenon*
MRSC	*Madame de Maintenon et la maison royale de Saint-Cyr* (1686–1793)

Louis Elle (1648–1717), portrait of Françoise d'Aubigné, marquise de Maintenon, with her niece, Françoise-Amable d'Aubigné, the future duchesse de Noailles (c. 1688). Photograph by Gerard Blot. Châteaux de Versailles et de Trianon, Versailles, France. Photograph: Copyright Réunion des Musées Nationaux/Art Resource, NY.

VOLUME EDITOR'S
INTRODUCTION

THE OTHER VOICE

Hating Madame de Maintenon is a durable French pastime. Starting with her contemporaries, the Duc de Saint-Simon[1] and the Duchesse d'Orléans,[2] opponents have denounced Maintenon as a political schemer. Even when they recognize her pioneering role in the education of women, critics lament her emphasis on piety over science. Patricia Mazuy's recent film *Saint-Cyr* (2000) only confirms the standard portrait of Maintenon as a religious fanatic opposed to the social emancipation of women.

Detecting the "other voice" in such a champion of social convention might appear to be a daunting task. But Maintenon qualifies on several counts. As founder and director of the Institution royale de Saint-Louis at Saint-Cyr, Maintenon established a curriculum and a pedagogical method that made the school the premier European academy for women for over a century. If they reject egalitarian feminism, her voluminous writings diagnose the typical oppressions facing women as nuns and as wives. In her dialogues and addresses Maintenon systematically alters the definition of the various virtues so that they might reflect the gendered experience of women.

More than a personal testament, the works of Maintenon express the

---

1. In his memoirs Saint-Simon repeatedly depicted Mme de Maintenon as a shadowy counselor who systematically pushed Louis XIV's government in the direction of religious intolerance. See Saint-Simon, *Mémoires et additions au Journal de Dagneau.*

2. Charlotte-Élisabeth de Bavière, duchesse d'Orléans (1652–1722), the sister-in-law of Louis XIV, was a German princess who underwent a nominal conversion to Catholicism in order to marry into the French royal family. Opposed to the anti-Protestant policies of the French throne, she criticized Maintenon's alleged undue influence over the ministers of Louis XIV in her posthumously published letters. See Charlotte-Élisabeth de Bavière, duchesse d'Orléans, *Lettres de Madame, duchesse d'Orléans, née princesse Palatine.*

aspirations of a specific class of women, French aristocrats of the late seventeenth century, to a more scientific education and personal culture. Often written in dialogical form, Maintenon's writings reflect in particular the cultural ambitions of women who participated in the literary salons of Paris. In both style and content they echo the polite conversation of the salon. On many substantive salon disputes, Maintenon defends comparatively conventional views toward the status of women. She criticizes, for example, contemporary efforts to champion the vocation of the single professional woman as superior to that of the wife-mother. But even when she defends social custom, her dialogical texts faithfully present the voices of students, faculty, and fictitious characters who demand a more substantial change in the social position of women. Throughout her canon Maintenon constructs an apology for the right of women to their own culture: an ensemble of artistic, moral, and vocational practices that differ from the norms of male society. For Maintenon the authentic advancement of women must recognize and institutionalize precisely what makes woman other than man.

LIFE

Born on November 24, 1635, Françoise d'Aubigné entered the world in the prison of Niort, where her father was imprisoned for counterfeiting money. The disowned son of the Huguenot poet Agrippa d'Aubigné, Constant d'Aubigné had previous criminal convictions for abduction, for treason, and for the murder of his first wife. Françoise d'Aubigné's mother was Jeanne de Cardilhac, the daughter of the prison's warden, whom Constant had married in 1627.

Françoise's childhood became a drama of poverty and abandonment. Although baptized a Catholic at her mother's insistence, she was first raised by a Huguenot aunt, Madame de Villette, who converted her to Protestantism. In 1645 her father, liberated from prison, took Françoise and the rest of the family to Martinique in the mistaken belief that he had been appointed the governor of the island colony. After several months he abandoned his family, leaving them without resources. In 1647 the impoverished family returned to La Rochelle, where her mother forced Françoise to beg in the streets. In 1648, armed with a royal order to save Françoise from the Protestant influence of Madame de Villette, a distant Catholic relative, Madame de Neuillant, received legal custody of the child. Treated as a domestic servant, Françoise rebuffed efforts to convert her to Catholicism by the parish priest and by the Ursulines at Niort. Finally converted during her stay at the Ursuline convent in Paris in 1649, Françoise became a devout Catholic but maintained a lifelong disdain for convent education.

Despite her tormented childhood, the education of Françoise d'Aubigné was not completely neglected. At the insistence of her mother, she read and memorized substantial portions of Plutarch's *Lives*, an exercise that whetted her taste for the genre of morally edifying biography. Her studies under the Ursulines at Niort and at Paris helped to shape the clear and concise literary style evident in her later writings. They also probably introduced her to Latin, since she demonstrated some knowledge of this language during her later years in the salons of Paris.

Penniless and orphaned, the adolescent Françoise faced a grim social future. In 1652 she accepted a proposal of marriage from the poet Paul Scarron.[3] Twenty-five years her senior, crippled by arthritis, impotent, sarcastic, and nearly bankrupt himself, Scarron was an unlikely prospect for a happy marriage. Françoise openly admitted that she had married Scarron in order to escape the alternative of the convent. Despite its poor prospects, the marriage proved to be a reasonably successful one, with Françoise patiently nursing a disabled husband who visibly esteemed his wife's beauty and intelligence.

The young Madame Scarron suddenly found herself the hostess of Scarron's literary salon, a hub for Parisian intellectuals, many of whom adhered to the religious skepticism of the libertines. Prominent salon members included the writers Vivonne,[4] Costar,[5] Benserade,[6] Chapelain,[7] Ménage,[8] Saint-Aignan,[9] and Madame de Sévigné.[10] During this period she was per-

---

3. Paul Scarron (1610–60) was a novelist, dramatist, and poet. He achieved fame through his various comic works, often satirical in nature. Major works include *Quelques vers burlesques* (1643) and *Le Virgile travesti* (1648–53).

4. A military officer and essayist, Louis-Victor de Rochechouart, duc de Mortemart et de Vivonne (1636–88), defended the superiority of the Greco-Roman classics in the literary quarrel between the ancients and the moderns.

5. A literary controversialist, Pierre Costar (1603–60) defended the works of several writers, notably Vincent Voiture, accused of impiety.

6. A lyric poet and a member of the Académie française, Isaac de Benserade (1613–91) defended the controversial skeptical theories of Pierre Bayle.

7. An essayist and dramatic poet, Jean Chapelain (1585–1674) defended the value of classical literature in the quarrel between the ancients and the moderns.

8. A lexicographer and grammarian, Gilles Ménage (1613–92) authored an influential etymological dictionary and in 1690 published the first major history of modern female philosophers.

9. A military officer and poet, François Beauvillier, duc de Saint-Aignan (1610–87), was elected a member of the Académie française in 1663.

10. A central figure in the intellectual salons of Paris, Marie de Rabutin-Chantal, marquise de Sévigné (1626–96), established her literary reputation with the posthumous publication of her letters.

sonally tutored by the Chevalier de Méré,[11] who proposed the *honnête homme*, the temperate and prudent gentleman, as a moral ideal to replace the older aristocratic figure of the warrior. Under the tutelage of her husband she also acquired the rudiments of Spanish and Italian.

Celebrated for her literary taste, Madame Scarron was soon lionized in salon circles as the perfect *précieuse*.[12] Among the *salonnières* Scarron befriended, Madame de Sévigné became an especially close friend. In numerous letters Sévigné praised Scarron's mastery of the learned conversation that constituted the heart of salon culture. Widely admired was Scarron's ability to discuss the salon's favorite topic, the nature of love:

> Madame Scarron has a pleasant and a wonderfully logical mind. It is a pleasure to hear her reflect on a certain country [love] she knows so well. . . . These speeches sometimes go quite far, from one moral issue to another, sometimes from a Christian perspective, sometimes from a political one.[13]

Sévigné's encomium indicates that Scarron's impressive salon performance involved more than rhetorical skill and literary erudition. It revealed her capacity as a *moraliste*, a commentator on the recesses of the human heart and on the religious and political problems related to this complex human psychology.

Despite its literary glory, the Scarron salon never resolved its financial precariousness. Dinner rarely followed the literary banter at the *Hôtel de l'impécuniosité*. The death of her husband in 1660 left Madame Scarron in debt. She rented a room in the convent of the Hospitaller Sisters of Our Lady and through the intervention of old salon acquaintances obtained a pension of 2,700 pounds from the Queen-Mother Anne d'Autriche. During this ob-

---

11. An essayist attentive to the details of aristocratic politeness, Georges Brossin, chevalier de Méré (1610–85), defended *honnêteté*, a type of skeptical prudence, as the ethical ideal of the salon aristocrat. Published posthumously, his major works include *De l'éloquence et de l'entretien* and *De la vraie honnêteté*.

12. Derived from the Latin adjective *pretiosus*, the term *précieux* originally referred to whatever is costly, worthy, or venerable. In seventeenth-century literary culture the term referred specifically to what is refined or cultivated. By the middle of the seventeenth century, women who made an effort to adopt a more refined speech and to acquire a greater artistic and scientific culture were hailed as *précieuses*. The literary salon was their site of predilection. The term soon acquired a negative connotation; *précieux* now referred to what was overly refined and excessively cultivated. The *précieuse* became a woman whose elaborate speech and pseudo-erudition provoked derision. Among other works Molière's *Les précieuses ridicules* (1659) contributed to this semantic change and to its concomitant dismissal of salon culture.

13. Madame de Sévigné, "Letter of January 13, 1672, to Madame de Grignan," in *Correspondance*, 1 : 414.

scure period she continued to participate in the salon life of Paris and to deepen her ties to the aristocratic elite of the city.

In 1669 Madame Scarron accepted a position that introduced her into the heart of the court itself. Madame de Montespan had become the mistress of Louis XIV and found herself pregnant with his child. To avoid scandal, the king and his mistress sought a discreet, cultivated woman to raise the child away from the gaze of court gossips. A friend of Montespan through her salon contacts, Madame Scarron accepted the delicate post and began to raise the first and subsequent children from the affair at a secluded chateau. In 1673, when Louis XIV publicly acknowledged and legitimized these children, she moved with them to the court and assumed the position of governess. Impressing the couple by her pedagogical skill, she appeared to work miracles in helping their ailing son, the Duc du Maine, recover his health. In 1674 Louis XIV awarded her services with an endowment, which permitted her to purchase the chateau of Maintenon. In 1675 he conferred the titles of the estate upon her. Independently wealthy and ennobled by an aristocratic title, Madame de Maintenon now assumed her own role in court society and quickly proved herself a trusted confidante of Louis XIV.

As the relationship between the king and Madame de Montespan deteriorated, Madame de Maintenon urged the monarch to attempt a reconciliation with his estranged wife, Queen Marie-Thérèse d'Autriche. Her efforts at reconciliation, applauded by Church officials long disturbed by Louis's infidelities, proved reasonably successful. If the royal couple favored Maintenon with even greater social privileges, Madame de Montespan's court allies began a campaign of denigration against the woman they considered a schemer who had brusquely turned on her former benefactress.

Queen Marie-Thérèse's sudden death on July 30, 1683 drew the widowed king and Maintenon even closer. Later in the year, probably on October 8, 1683, Archbishop Harlay de Champvallon of Paris presided at their marriage in a private ceremony held late at night. Morganatic, the marriage conferred neither the title nor the prerogatives of queen on Maintenon. No relation of Maintenon could claim succession to the throne. The marriage was also secret. Throughout their lives neither party would publicly acknowledge that the marriage had occurred.

The secrecy probably stemmed from two considerations. First, the marriage of the Sun King to a governess of impoverished, indeed criminal, origin assaulted the aristocratic propriety of the period. Maintenon's enemy Saint-Simon was not the only courtier to denounce the marriage as an insult to the dignity of the French throne. Second, Louis XIV had insisted that all the marriages contracted by members of the French royal family were to be determined by dynastic motives. The decision to marry a governess baldly contradicted the policy of using royal marriage to forge political alliances with other sovereign states.

If never publicly acknowledged, the existence of the marriage was soon apparent to the members of the court. Both the king and Maintenon wryly alluded to the marriage in informal remarks. The king's religious counselors privately praised a marriage they had quietly encouraged to foster the repentance of a heretofore adulterous monarch. Louis XIV regularly visited Maintenon's apartments in the late afternoon for conversation and conjugal relations. Madame de Maintenon began to assume the hosting, advisory, and philanthropic duties usually reserved to the queen. Surviving documentary evidence, such as a series of letters from Paul Godet des Marais, bishop of Chartres, to Maintenon and Louis XIV in 1697, confirmed the existence and the approximate date of the marriage.

Throughout her long marriage to Louis XIV, Maintenon served as a key advisor to the king. Her major influence was religious. Her personal example prodded the king to return to a more regular practice of the Catholic faith and fostered a more austere, pious atmosphere in the court of Louis's later years. She sponsored candidates for major ecclesiastical appointments to dioceses and abbeys. On the whole, her nominees were men of moral probity and of evangelical zeal. For centuries, critics condemned Maintenon as the major architect of Louis XIV's Revocation of the Edict of Nantes (1685), which abolished the freedoms and rights of French Protestants. Several of the eighteenth-century documents alleging such influence, however, have been unmasked as forgeries, and most contemporary commentators argue that Maintenon had little influence on the anti-Protestant measures that the king and his ministers had long envisioned.[14] Indisputably, however, Maintenon encouraged Louis XIV's campaign against the Catholic dissident movements of Jansenism and of Quietism.

Maintenon's greatest achievements during her marriage to Louis XIV occurred in the field of education. In the early 1680s she had already helped to design and direct schools for working girls at Montmorency and at Rueil. Later in the decade she began her most ambitious educational venture: a boarding school for daughters of the impoverished aristocracy, which opened its permanent location at Saint-Cyr in 1686. Louis XIV financed the project, providing dowries for the school's 250 students as well as endowing

---

14. A key scholarly document debunking the myth of Maintenon as the secret author of the Revocation of the Edict of Nantes was Alfred Rosset's *Madame de Maintenon et la révocation de l'Édit de Nantes.*

the palatial buildings and grounds designed by Hardouin-Mansart. Maintenon personally supervised the educational program from the details of the
curriculum to the design of the school uniforms.

The students of Saint-Cyr were divided into four classes: "reds" (7–11
years old), "greens" (11–14), "yellows" (14–17), and "blues" (17–20). Carefully planned by Maintenon, the educational program followed a strict gra-
dation as the students passed from one class to another. Older students followed courses (history, Latin, painting) unavailable to younger students.
The material used in the staple courses of reading, writing, arithmetic, and
religion became progressively more difficult as the students advanced in age.

Even more innovative was Maintenon's organization of the classroom
and formation of her professorial corps. Assisted by apprentice teachers, the
head teacher of each class directed course work from the center of the classroom. Each class was divided into smaller groups, directed by a mature student who would guide the group in discussion and review of the material
presented by the teacher. Saint-Cyr's pedagogical method stressed the importance of dialogue between teacher and student, as well as dialogue among
students, as the key to successful communication of knowledge and formation of character.

To instruct the pupils, Maintenon formed a community of laywomen,
the Dames de Saint-Louis. Although bound by a vow of celibacy and committed to a communal life on the premises of the school, the Dames neither
wore a habit nor belonged to any religious order. The original lay status of
the Dames de Saint-Louis reflected the aversion of Maintenon and Louis XIV
to convent education. Both believed that the education provided by convent
schools did not suit the demands of the typical laywoman and that its level
rarely surpassed that of bare literacy. Not only did Maintenon personally
instruct and supervise her teachers in her dialogical method of education;
she insisted that they acquire a personalized knowledge of each student's
temperament and history so that they might assist students in discerning
and preparing for their particular vocation in life. The bulk of the surviving
works of Maintenon derives from the countless lectures and conferences
she presented to the faculty and students at Saint-Cyr over more than three
decades.

The early history of Saint-Cyr is customarily divided into three distinct
periods. In its "worldly" era (1686–89), the school stressed cultural achievement. Students performed elaborate plays, concerts, and liturgical services.
The school's premiere of Jean Racine's *Esther* on January 26, 1689 was an
artistic triumph, earning the acclaim of the courts of Europe. Maintenon,
however, was soon convinced that the emphasis on cultural sophistication

had been an educational mistake. The rehearsals and performances seriously reduced the time spent in class. The adulation of a libertine public fostered the vices of pride and envy among the students. At the end of this period Maintenon revised the curriculum to stress moral formation. She banned licentious literature from the premises and dismissed the original head-mistress, Madame de Brinon, who was considered too imbued by the worldly spirit of the salons.

In its "mystical" era (1690–97), Saint-Cyr fell under the spell of the Quietist movement. Madame Guyon,[15] head of the movement in France, in-structed the students and faculty in the movement's doctrine of passive aban-donment to God's providence. She trained them in her method of simple meditation, which rejected all recourse to vocal prayer, to the use of the imagination, or to discursive reflection. At first impressed by the movement's austerity, Maintenon slowly turned against it. The stress on radical passivity discouraged the acquisition of the moral virtues. Spiritual illusion became rife. Pupils who barely understood the Decalogue boasted of their experi-ences of mystical marriage. Alarmed by the effects of Quietism, Maintenon gradually eliminated the movement's influence at Saint-Cyr through a series of stern measures: the ecclesiastical condemnation of Quietism in 1694; the arrest of Guyon in 1695; the dismissal of faculty sympathetic to the move-ment; anti-Quietist lectures at the school by Bossuet in 1696 and by Louis XIV himself in 1698.

In the "normal" era (starting in 1698), Saint-Cyr acquired the academic profile it would maintain for the remaining century of its existence. Chas-tened by the earlier excesses of aestheticism and of mysticism, Maintenon placed greater emphasis on the practical skills needed by the majority of the students, who were destined to become the wives of the straitened provin-cial aristocracy. Home economics and embroidery reduced the earlier em-phasis on painting, singing, and dancing.

If the school still stressed the cultivation of piety, Maintenon insisted

---

15. Jeanne-Marie Bouvier de La Motte-Guyon (1648–1717) propagated her "quietist" methods of meditation among the French aristocracy in the last two decades of the seventeenth-century. Her Quietism stressed the centrality of passive abandonment to God in prayer and criticized the recourse to imaginative and intellectual meditation. Published in 1685, her *Le moyen court de faire l'oraison* popularized her methods among the courtiers of Versailles, including Mme de Maintenon. Suspicious of all mystical movements as potentially treasonous, Louis XIV had Guyon arrested in 1688, but Mme de Maintenon intervened to secure her release. At the height of her influence in the early 1690s, Guyon saw her theories condemned by an ecclesiastical committee in 1694 and suffered imprisonment from 1695 until 1703. After her release she re-frained from all public theological comment until her death in 1717.

that it must be a "reasonable" piety, centered on moral duties and opposed to mystical fancy. Despite Maintenon's disdain for the convent, Saint-Cyr increasingly assumed the characteristics of the convent school of the period. The Dames de Saint-Louis incorporated themselves as a canonical religious order following the rule of Saint Augustine.[16] Although a majority of the alumnae pursued careers as wives and mothers in provincial manor houses, a substantial minority entered the cloister after graduation.

In the eighteenth century Maintenon showed even greater attention to the direction of Saint-Cyr. Her lectures, conferences, and classroom visitations became a daily routine at the school. In her various speeches Maintenon elaborated her philosophy of education for women and detailed her moral philosophy of the virtues to be prized and the vices to be shunned by aristocratic women. Upon the death of Louis XIV in 1715, Maintenon retired permanently to her apartments at the school. Repulsed by the libertine morals of the court under the Regent, Philippe, duc d'Orléans, Maintenon transformed her retirement into a religious retreat. Among other dignitaries, Tsar Peter I visited Maintenon in retirement and toured what had become Europe's model academy for the education of women.

Madame de Maintenon died on April 15, 1719. The academy at Saint-Cyr survived until 1793, when it was closed by order of the revolutionary government in Paris. In 1794 a Jacobin mob desecrated Maintenon's tomb and scattered her remains in the environs of the school. During the demolition of the old Saint-Cyr buildings in 1945, workers discovered a box containing Madame de Maintenon's remains. They were later interred in the Palace of Versailles, providing tacit official recognition of France's hidden queen.

WORKS

The literary corpus of Madame de Maintenon has an unusual origin. With the exception of the letters, her written works began as a type of oral communication. During her long tenure as the director of Saint-Cyr, Maintenon delivered hundreds of talks to the school's teachers and pupils. The Dames

16. Widely used by new women's congregations in seventeenth-century France, the Rule of Saint Augustine was considered the most flexible of the constitutions approved by the Catholic Church for use by religious orders. With its minimal rules of cloister, governance, and communal prayer, the Rule of Saint Augustine permitted Maintenon to retain practical control of the Dames de Saint-Louis and to maintain their focus on educational work rather than contemplation.

de Saint-Louis were assigned to make thorough transcriptions of these conferences, which were subsequently reviewed and corrected by Maintenon
herself. The approved final text would then be copied and circulated in manuscript form by the Dames. Maintenon also composed a series of dramatic
dialogues to be performed by the students as part of their classroom exercises. Extolling various virtues proper to aristocratic women and exploring
the social vicissitudes faced by the typical Saint-Cyr alumna, the dialogues
are miniatures of the morally edifying narratives that Maintenon considered
central to education. Collecting the various addresses and dialogues, the
Dames produced and expanded manuscript collections of Maintenon's works
(1688, 1693, 1713, 1721, 1740). The later editions added letters from Maintenon's correspondence, especially letters dealing with pedagogical issues.

The Dames de Saint-Louis's manuscript collections constituted the
principal source for subsequent editions of Maintenon's works. In the eighteenth century, Archbishop Languet de Gergy of Sens commissioned a new
seven-volume manuscript edition of Maintenon's works, copied from the archives of the Dames. Still extant in the archives of the Bibliothèque municipale de Versailles, the Sens manuscript edition has been used as a primary
source for the works translated in this book.

The eighteenth century also witnessed the first print editions of Maintenon's works. La Beaumelle (1752) published an edition of Maintenon's letters that attracted a wide readership, including the exiled Napoleon Bona-
parte, who claimed to prefer them to the letters of Madame de Sévigné. A
militant Protestant opposed to the religious policies of the French throne, La
Beaumelle had expertly mixed forged letters of his own fabrication with authentic letters of Maintenon in this influential edition. The forged letters
helped to create the prejudicial image of Maintenon as a religious fanatic,
devoted to the persecution of Protestants. Anonymously edited, *Les loisirs de
Madame de Maintenon* (1757) presented many of her Saint-Cyr dramatic dialogues and revealed Maintenon as an innovative educational reformer.

In the nineteenth century Théophile Lavallée published a substantial
portion of Maintenon's writings in a series of multivolume works (1854–
70). More critical in its use of manuscript sources than earlier editions,
Lavallée's edition introduced the French public to the wide range of literary
genres mastered by Maintenon. It became and remains the standard source
for subsequent anthologies of Maintenon's work and scholarly studies on
Maintenon.

At the end of the nineteenth century, several experts in public education published anthologies of Maintenon's writings. Octave Gréard (1884),
Émile Faguet (1884), and Paul Jacquinet (1888) compiled the scholastic edi-

tions of Maintenon's works. Assuring a large diffusion of Maintenon's works among faculty and pupils in French public schools, especially in lycées for women, these anthologies bear the stamp of the anticlericalism of the educational establishment of the Third Republic. Maintenon's religious concerns are systematically suppressed—entire religious passages are simply excised from different texts—and the "lay" inspiration behind Saint-Cyr is given an anti-Catholic flavor foreign to Maintenon herself. Even the recent Maintenon anthology by Jacques Prévot (1981) continues the tradition of this secularist recasting of Maintenon's pedagogical theory.

Maintenon's work divides into five principal literary genres. Addressed to the faculty at Saint-Cyr, the *Entretiens* (conferences) treat pedagogical concerns raised in question-and-answer sessions between Maintenon and the Dames. Presented to the students themselves, the *Instructions* (addresses) extol the virtues essential to the pupils and discuss current problems in the student body. Morality plays composed to be performed by older students, the *Conversations* (dialogues) frequently attempt to clarify the nature of a particular virtue to be cultivated by the pupils. Written for younger pupils, the *Proverbes* (proverb plays) are humorous skits, often with a simple moral lesson, based on popular French maxims. The massive correspondence of Maintenon, comprising more than five thousand letters, contains numerous passages presenting her educational philosophy and discussing the major figures of Louis XIV's court. Allied to her pedagogical principles, the works of Maintenon employ cultured dialogue as the privileged means to explore ethical issues and to shape moral character.

Not only do the works of Maintenon stress her concern for education; they also express her concern for the pedagogical and moral issues proper to women alone. Convinced that the education of women should be conducted differently from that of men, Maintenon repeatedly addresses the specific vocations that her impoverished, aristocratic pupils will face and the need to provide an education adapted to these gendered ends. A number of her addresses to students soberly depict the moral duties and the constraints on freedom that they will endure as provincial aristocratic mothers or as nuns assigned to impoverished convents. Many of her dramatic dialogues attempt to wrest the moral virtues from their male-biased origins and to transform them in light of the typical experiences of women. Accordingly, the glory of the warrior is transposed into the glorious patience of the homemaker; the wit of the courtier into the shrewd management of the provincial countess; the political eminence of nobles into the eminent integrity of working-class women.

Among the varied works of Maintenon, this book contains translations of works from three genres: the *Conversations* (dialogues), the *Instructions* (addresses given to students), and the *Entretiens* (addresses to faculty). These genres provide complementary examples of Maintenon's dialogical method: the fictitious dialogues designed for performance by students and the actual dialogues between Maintenon and the students and the faculty at Saint-Cyr. They reflect the primacy of the conversational method employed in the school's instruction and incorporate Maintenon's cherished genre of the morally edifying tale. Not the most endearing of her traits, Maintenon repeatedly uses Louis XIV and herself as flattering illustrations of the moral point she is trying to prove.

The dialogues and addresses also manifest the gendered concerns of Maintenon. In her addresses she insists that her pupils recognize the particular forms of social constraint they will face as women, especially as impoverished women. In her dramatic dialogues she invites her pupils to embrace a world of virtue designed for women, a world sensibly different from the standard world of virtue designed by and for men.

Despite their volume, their crystalline style, and their significance for the education of women, the writings of Madame de Maintenon have received comparatively little attention. Two principal factors account for this oblivion. First, the controversial life of Maintenon has diverted attention from her written works and her social theories. Commentators have long focused on the novelistic incidents in Maintenon's life: the sudden marriage with Scarron; the battle with the royal mistress, Madame de Montespan; the secret marriage with Louis XIV; her role in the persecution of Madame Guyon; her political influence on Louis XIV. Certain treatments of Maintenon betray a sexual obsession: Was the marriage with Scarron consummated? Was she the mistress of Louis XIV before their marriage? Reduced to the status of a character in a romance novel, Maintenon the author and the philosopher is easily neglected.

Second, ideological factors have tended to marginalize the writings of Maintenon. In the seventeenth-century struggle to unmask the oppression of women and to construct emancipatory alternatives, Maintenon holds a comparatively conservative position. Like other reformers, she frankly depicts the social oppression endured by women. She recognizes that educational reform is the key to women's advancement. In her ideas for reform, however, she does not envision major changes in the social roles ascribed to the sexes. On the contrary, the amelioration of the status of women requires the maintenance of a separate social sphere for women, in which the vocation as wife and mother holds pride of place. While recognizing her signal contribution to the emancipation of women by her educational projects, recent critics have tended to dismiss her writings because their insistence on sexual difference so clearly departs from the current social norm of equal access to educational and occupational opportunities.

The ideological obstacles to an appreciation of Maintenon's works emerge more clearly in a comparison between Maintenon and Marie de Gournay, a seventeenth-century French author who is currently attracting substantial scholarly attention.[17] The disciple and editor of Montaigne, Gournay wrote a series of essays in which she argued that women had the right to occupy the same social positions men did. Outside strictly biological differences, the gender differences in social roles were based upon prejudice and were designed to subjugate women. Given her theory of the strict equality between men and women, Gournay insisted that education in the arts and sciences be opened to all qualified students, regardless of gender. Her own lifestyle, that of a single professional woman making a living through writing and editing, embodied the demand for gender equality that characterized her tracts. Maintenon explicitly rejects the egalitarian theories of Gournay and her circle. Her writings insist on the psychological complementarity, rather than identity, between the sexes, thus requiring a differentiated system of education.

It is hardly surprising that contemporary academe has championed the works of Gournay,[18] so close to its dominant creed of egalitarian feminism, and has treated with suspicion the writings of Maintenon, so clearly opposed to this version of women's emancipation. But Maintenon's works cannot be dismissed simply as relics of sexual subordination. If they reject the demands for civic and educational equality of a Gournay, they transfer the empowerment of women to another terrain: the right of women to their own distinctive culture. Maintenon's works defend the thesis that the authentic development of women must engender a language, a code of virtue, an ensemble of practical skills, and a method of education that bear the irre-

---

17. Marie Le Jars de Gournay (1565–1645) authored two influential feminist treatises, *L'égalité des hommes et des femmes*, which defends equality between the sexes, and *Grief des dames*, which defends the equal access of the sexes to education and to work. Both of these have appeared in this series: see Gournay, *Apology for the Woman Writing*. Her edition of Montaigne's essays also established her literary reputation.

18. At least twelve French editions of Gournay's works have been published since 1980. At least two English translations of Gournay have appeared since 1998 (see the citation in note 17, above). The Modern Language Association lists more than one hundred recent articles devoted to the analysis of Gournay's thought.

ducible stamp of the feminine sex. If such a vision of sexual difference rejects liberal egalitarian feminism, it parallels certain concerns of contemporary gender feminism in the effort to identify and promote certain patterns of thought and action more proper to women than to men.

INFLUENCES

Given her spotty education, it is difficult to identify the precise texts and ideas influencing Maintenon's philosophy of education, of gender, and of virtue. The adolescent study of Plutarch clearly shaped her preference for the morally edifying portrait in literature and in education. Chevalier Méré's ideal of the *honnête homme* influenced her insistence that temperance, rather than justice or courage, constituted the paramount moral virtue.

Indisputably the major influence on her design for education was Fénelon, the tutor to the dauphin's eldest son and the archbishop of Cambrai.[19] In his *Traité de l'éducation des filles* (1687), Fénelon had proposed a scheme of education for women. Like Maintenon, Fénelon sought to form an elite corps of women who would revivify French Christendom through their maternal, religious, and charitable work as wives of the provincial nobility. Also like Maintenon, Fénelon disdained the then current convent education as too narrow in its curriculum, too disorganized in its methods, and too distant from the practical concerns of the typical laywoman. Until their bitter split over the issue of Quietism, Fénelon preached regularly in the school chapel. In some key respects, however, Maintenon's theory and practice of education for women differed from that championed by Fénelon. She stressed artistic rather than scientific formation. Especially after the Quietist debacle, she insisted on a "reasonable" piety opposed to the mystical aspirations of Fénelon. Her pedagogical innovations, such as the systematic use of drama and discussion groups in the classroom, remain largely her personal inspiration.

Theologically Saint Francis de Sales's *Introduction to the Devout Life* [*Intro-*

---

19. François de Salignac de La Mothe-Fénelon (1651–1715) rose quickly in French court circles to become the tutor to Louis XIV's grandson, Louis, the duke of Burgundy, in 1689 and the archbishop of Cambrai in 1696. A close ally of Mme de Maintenon in the early 1690s, he collaborated with her on writing the Constitutions of Saint-Cyr in 1694. The author of numerous educational treatises, he composed the *Treatise for the Education of Girls* at the request of the duchess of Beauvilliers, a devout Versailles courtier with eight daughters. The Quietist controversy drew Fénelon and Maintenon apart when Fénelon refused to subscribe to the 1694 condemnation of Mme Guyon. His own *Explication des maximes des saints*, a defense of mitigated Quietism during his pamphlet war with Bossuet, was itself condemned by the Holy Office in 1699. Forbidden by Louis XIV to leave the confines of his diocese, Fénelon devoted his last years to pastoral work in the Cambrai region.

duction à la vie dévote] constitutes a major influence on Maintenon.[20] Except for the Bible itself, the *Introduction* is the most cited work in the addresses of Maintenon. The Salesian approach to spirituality appealed to Maintenon on several levels. First, it insisted that the pious laywoman must develop a distinctively lay, not a monastic, method for integrating prayer and work in her life. Second, all ascetical efforts must be undertaken with moderation. Personal mortification must respect the needs of the body and the requirements of one's social station. Third, Christian asceticism must be adapted to one's personal vocation in life. Against rigorists of the period, de Sales argued that an aristocratic woman could properly attend balls and engage in artistic work, as long as these activities were practiced with discretion. Maintenon's repeated insistence on moderation in spiritual exercises and on attention to one's social duties carries many Salesian echoes.

In multiple ways, the salons frequented by the young Madame Scarron also shaped Maintenon's concept of virtue and gender. The elaborate attention to politeness and to the proper conduct of conversation in many of her works reflects the etiquette of the salon, which she attempted to impart to her pupils. The style of Maintenon's moral arguments echoes the popular genres of the salon. Her pithy moral aphorisms often resemble the *maxime*.[21] Her edifying narratives of virtuous personages often use the techniques of the *portrait moral*.[22] In her analysis of the virtues, she often wields the arms of the *distinguo*, in which she establishes minute distinctions among the dif-

20. First published in 1608, *Introduction to the Devout Life* [*Introduction à la vie dévote*] by Saint François de Sales (1567–1622) became the most popular spiritual book for French Catholics throughout the seventeenth century. A manual for meditation and for the acquisition of virtues proper to the Christian, the book was especially influential among aristocratic and bourgeois women. Addressed to a fictitious female reader ("Philothea"), the work attempted to foster a piety adapted to the circumstances of socially prominent laywomen rather than to nuns living in a cloister.

21. Derived from the Latin noun *maxima*, the word *maxime* originally referred to any sentence expressing a general principle. In seventeenth-century French the term *maxime* referred more narrowly to sentences expressing a general rule of conduct or of judgment. In salons of the period, especially in the salon of Madame de Sablé (1598–1678), where the genre was widely practiced, the term denoted more specifically sentences distinguished by their literary concision and by their focus on moral psychology (virtues, vices, passions). The *Réflexions: ou, Sentences et maximes morales* (1682) by La Rochefoucauld, a member of Sablé's salon, set the standard for the genre.

22. Widely practiced in the salons of the period, the *portrait moral* was a literary depiction of the moral personality of a particular individual. It often focused on that individual's particular mix of virtues and vices. Often published anonymously with the individual under analysis described through a neoclassical pseudonym, the *portrait moral* became a popular literary diversion in aristocratic society. The salon of Anne-Marie-Louise d'Orléans, duchesse de Montpensier (1627–93), enjoyed particular renown for its production of literary portraits.

ferent senses of a particular trait.[23] If indebted to salon culture, Maintenon maintains a patent originality in her work. Her efforts to redefine the moral virtues in terms of the experience of women, especially impoverished women, diverge from the usual concerns of the novels and etiquette books avidly read by aristocratic *salonnières* of the period.

In their dialogical form Maintenon's works reflect the primacy accorded the art of conversation among salon activities. As Elizabeth Goldsmith argues,[24] conversational skill had become the central social ornament for an aristocracy attempting to impose itself on an expanded court society, and the salon had emerged as the privileged locus to polish this refined speech. Not confined to its oral expression, polite conversation encouraged the production of a burgeoning literature: etiquette books, manuals of model letters, novels, portraits, and written conversations. It also fostered the revival of an ancient genre, the literary dialogue, suited to the tastes and preoccupations of the French salon and court.

Among female practitioners of the literary dialogue, Mademoiselle de Scudéry holds a central place.[25] A close friend of Maintenon, Scudéry published six collections of dialogues from 1680 until 1692.[26] Maintenon used the earlier dialogues of Scudéry for classroom instruction at Saint-Cyr until 1691, when Maintenon reformed the school's curriculum and eliminated Scudéry's sketches as too redolent of the worldliness of salon society. Echoing the concerns of the new court society at Versailles, Scudéry's dialogues explore the major virtues and vices of the aristocracy: magnanimity, politeness, pride, discretion, avarice. They discuss and model the art of conversation: when to speak and when to be silent, how to maintain a correspondence. They examine intellectual topics: the philosophy of Confucius, the history of French poetry, and the life-cycle of butterflies. In the freewheeling debates, the speakers are often evenly matched; the conversations

23. Derived from the Latin verb *distinguere*, the term *distinguo* referred to the act of subdividing a term to indicate what part of the term one accepted and what part one rejected. In the seventeenth century *distinguo* acquired a positive connotation. It now also referred to the finesse and the subtlety with which a speaker could make such a distinction. Among many examples Maintenon's distinction between *bonne gloire* (true glory) and *mauvaise gloire* (false glory) illustrates her mastery of the *distinguo*.

24. See Goldsmith, *"Exclusive Conversations."*

25. Madeleine de Scudéry (1607–1701) was noted for the literary salon (*les samedis littéraires*) that she hosted in Paris. One of her most famous literary achievements was her heroic novel, *Artamène: ou, Le Grand Cyrus* (1649–53), the story of Sapho in part 10 of which has been published in this series. Maintenon regularly attended the sessions of Scudéry's salons.

26. For a representative selection of these dialogues, see Mademoiselle de Scudéry, *Choix de conversations de Mlle de Scudéry.*

frequently end inconclusively. Written in a refined prose, not completely free of the preciosity for which Scudéry was criticized, the dialogues are constructed as a model of polite conversation for the intellectually curious *salonnière*.

Maintenon's dialogues bear clear resemblances to the models she found in Scudéry. Both authors use a refined, occasionally stilted, rhetoric to epitomize polite speech. Dedicated moralists, both analyze a common set of aristocratic virtues, such as glory and magnanimity. Both study in detail the nuances of courteous behavior essential for an aristocratic woman of the period. But the differences between the authors are even more striking. Unlike Scudéry, Maintenon exhibits little enthusiasm for the arts and sciences. On the contrary, Maintenon's dialogues repeatedly warn pupils of the vanity fostered by erudition and of the moral lapses caused by intellectual curiosity. Maintenon's exploration of the aristocratic virtues is complemented by a new emphasis on more bourgeois virtues: diligence, thrift, industriousness, and entrepeneurship. The worldly atmosphere of Scudéry's conversations is countered by the strict moral order of Maintenon's, where piety is a central virtue, and sexual license an omnipresent threat. Where Scudéry's characters breezily engage in fantasy or philosophical speculation, Maintenon's firmly face their practical duties in straitened circumstances and in a pitiless social hierarchy. There is little uncertainty in Maintenon's dialogues. While she may present multiple conflicting viewpoints, the correct position is usually unmistakable as Maintenon guides the reader to embrace a certain virtue or to reject a particular illusion.

In her practice of verbal and literary dialogue Maintenon draws upon the conventions of the salon culture she had known and mastered. But in her later years she transforms these conventions in an educational program that opposes the *salonnière* as an ideal for women. Moral certitude, allied to religious and political orthodoxy, replaces the cultured skepticism of a Scudéry. Industrious devotion trumps speculative brio. The polite conversation of the salon continues to govern the form of Maintenon's dialogues, but their ideal of the pious, practical woman rejects the earlier salon ideal of the intellectual virtuoso.

Maintenon's works are also marked by an aversion to certain influential philosophical and theological movements of the period. Often polemical in nature, her educational writings warn her audience against the perils of several intellectual currents that had gained the sympathy of aristocratic women. Three movements in particular aroused Maintenon's ire: libertinism, Jansenism, and Quietism.

A diffuse movement among the French aristocracy of the period, libertinism combined religious skepticism with sexual licentiousness. In philosophy the libertine scoffed at the Christian claims of revelation. In practice the libertine defied Christian morality by the open conduct of extramarital affairs. During her years as hostess of the Scarron salon, Maintenon had acquired an intimate knowledge of libertine intellectuals like Isaac de Benserade, with their dismissal of the miraculous and their skepticism about human immortality. She had also witnessed the strategies of seduction that structured the romantic lives of salon libertines. In many of Maintenon's educational pieces the libertine assumes male form. He attempts to destroy both the piety and the chastity of vulnerable women by a combination of sarcasm and sentimentality imported from the arsenal of libertine arguments.

Not confined to men, libertinism also attracted numerous influential women in the salons of the late seventeenth century. Personal acquaintances of Maintenon, both Madame Deshoulières[27] and Ninon de Lenclos[28] conducted salons renowned for their religious skepticism and for their amorous intrigue. In several of Maintenon's works the libertine assumes female form. The character Celestine in the dialogue *On True Wit* and the lady-in-waiting in the address *Of Avoiding the Occasions of Sin* are both figures of the libertine woman endangering her reputation by respectively dabbling in astrology and engaging in an adulterous affair. Maintenon's polemic against the emergence of a single, professional life as a vocational option for women springs in part from her antilibertine perspective. For Maintenon the independent woman, neither wife nor nun, easily deteriorates into the female libertine, alienated from religious orthodoxy by skeptical speculation and from moral propriety by sexual transgression.

Situated at the antipodes of libertinism, Jansenism was an austere religious movement that had bitterly divided French Catholicism in the seventeenth century. Disciples of the Belgian theologian Cornelius Jansenius,[29]

---

27. Antoinette du Ligier de La Garde, Madame Deshoulières (1638–94) was a leading poet of the period. A disciple of Gassendi, she defended a philosophical naturalism in which all actions, even the most spiritual, are caused by material agents. Her salon become celebrated for the religious skepticism of its prominent members. See Deshoulières, *Oeuvres*.

28. A prominent courtesan in Parisian society, Ninon de Lenclos (1616–1705) achieved fame in cultivated society through her musical and linguistic skills. Her salon acquired notoriety for its sexual licence and its opposition to religious orthodoxy. Molière and the young Voltaire were distinguished members of her skeptical coterie.

29. Cornelius Jansenius (1585–1638) was a leading theologian at the Catholic University of Louvain who became the bishop of Ypres. His posthumously published work *Augustinus* (1640) argued that Saint Augustine's position on grace insisted on total human depravity and strongly emphasized predestination in its account of salvation. In an earlier work, *Mars Gallicus* (1635), Jansenius had condemned the cynicism of the foreign policy of Louis XIII and his prime minister, Cardinal Richelieu.

the Jansenists contested ecclesiastical and political authorities on several fronts. Theologically they insisted on humanity's complete dependence on God's grace for salvation. Divine sovereignty, predestination, and radical human depravity became central themes in their theology. They condemned mainstream Catholicism, especially the Jesuits, for exaggerating the goodness of human nature and the role of human freedom in salvation. Morally, they insisted on a rigorist interpretation of the ethical demands of the gospel. Usury, dueling, gambling, and attendance at theatrical performances were categorically condemned. They denounced the widespread practice of causistry as an adulteration of the moral law to suit the vices of the age.[30] Politically they insisted that religious ideals rather than national prestige govern foreign policy. They condemned the French throne's policy of alliance with Protestant, Orthodox, and Islamic powers and of warfare against Catholic Spain. Louis XIV's bitter persecution of the Jansenist movement was rooted in his conviction that the movement's sympathy for greater religious democracy—enhanced power for local pastors and bishops, greater active lay participation in the liturgy, tolerance of dissent in theological disputes— encouraged political dissidents opposed to monarchial absolutism.

As Maintenon recognized, Jansenism had a particular appeal for educated women. From 1630 until its destruction by royal command in 1710, the Cistercian convent of Port-Royal served as the center of Jansenism in the Parisian region. Port-Royal nuns led a decades-long resistance to royal and episcopal commands to submit to church condemnations of Jansenius. The publication of their theological writings and the successful operation of their convent school assured a wide diffusion of their theories.[31] A coterie of laywomen, led by influential aristocrats such as Madame de Longueville,[32]

---

30. Widely practiced by the Jesuits, casuistry was a method of moral reasoning that attempted to develop flexible rules of moral conduct by noting the similarity and dissimilarity among "cases" of conduct in a similar area. Jesuit casuistry was closely tied to probabilism, a moral theory that argued that a moral agent only needed "probable reasons" (that is, good or sound reasons approved by at least one major Catholic authority) to engage in a course of action when several paths of action seemed possible. Among other Jansenist authors, Blaise Pascal in his *Provincial Letters* (1656–59) denounced Jesuit casuistry as a dangerously lax moral system that eviscerated the moral demands of the gospel and discouraged authentic religious conversion.

31. Four Port-Royal nuns distinguished themselves as authors: Mère Angélique Arnauld (1591–1661), Mère Agnès Arnauld (1593–1671), Mère Angélique de Saint-Jean Arnauld d'Andilly (1624–84), and Soeur Jacqueline de Saint-Euphémie Pascal (1625–61). Often published posthumously, these works were usually published clandestinely by presses located in the Lowlands. For a recent English translation, see, in this series, Jacqueline Pascal, *A Rule for Children*.

32. Anne Geneviève de Bourbon, duchesse de Longueville (1619–79) distinguished herself by her opposition to the religious and political orthodoxies of the day. A partisan of the Fronde (1648–53), a coalition of aristocrats and parliamentarians opposed to royal absolutism, Madame de Longueville took a central role in the military and political campaigns against the

defended the convent during time of persecution and disseminated Jansenist views among the laity. In their voluminous writings and in their educational work the Port-Royal nuns, echoed by their lay associates, underscored the right of women to a sophisticated theological culture and the related right to engage in theological controversy, even when that controversy entailed criticism of papal, episcopal, or royal positions.

Maintenon opposed Jansenism on doctrinal, moral, and political grounds. Its extreme emphasis on grace seemed to destroy human freedom and responsibility. Its moral rigorism assaulted the temperance Maintenon considered central in the cultivation of virtue. Its religious "spirit of faction" inevitably fostered political factions, threatening social harmony. For Maintenon as for Louis XIV, religious dissidence was the close relative of political treason. As the address *Against Religious Innovations* attests, Maintenon also opposed Jansenism on specifically gendered grounds. She believed that part of Jansenism's allure was its status as an elite, persecuted group. This appealed to an alleged attraction of cultivated women to any controversial movement of the moment. Not only opposed to its specific doctrines, Maintenon opposed Jansenism simply because it drew women into doctrinal controversies. Maintenon insisted that religious education should provide women with a generic Catholicism and should avoid engagement in theological controversies, a realm reserved for male clerics. As certain critics have long alleged, this disdain for women's theological reflection, sharply divergent from Jacqueline Pascal's model of education for women at Port-Royal, manifests the anti-intellectual streak in Maintenon's educational experiment. But it also reveals Maintenon's own version of Christianity, which she is more than willing to defend by her own theological arguments. This version of the gospel insists that the test of discipleship is the daily practice of virtues appropriate to one's state of life. Too great an insistence on grace can destroy a woman's determination to use her personal freedom for moral improvement. Too ardent an interest in theological speculation only distracts her from the practical duties at hand. Typically Maintenon insists that religious meditation must generate practical resolutions for future conduct. Allied to the muscular Christianity of the Jesuits, Maintenon condemns Jansenism as a dangerous diversion from the pragmatic gospel she considers central to a woman's education and to a woman's successful pursuit of a laborious vocation.

French prime minister, Cardinal Mazarin. A close friend of the Jansenists, Longueville used her political and religious connections to soften the persecution of the nuns at Port-Royal and to bring about the "Clementine peace" (the lifting of sanctions against the nuns by Pope Clement IX) in 1669.

Intimately connected with Saint-Cyr, the Quietist movement enjoyed a complicated relationship with Maintenon. Devoted primarily to the practice of prayer, the Quietists insisted that Christian prayer should be as passive or "quiet" as possible. Meditation methods using the imagination or discursive reflection were shunned. The praying subject should simply await the action of the Holy Spirit. This spiritual posture of quiet should be accompanied by a moral posture of complete abandonment to God's will. Unreserved acceptance of the divine will, rather than practical resolutions to perform good works, was now the hallmark of religious maturity. Appealing to a section of devout lay Catholics at court and in salons, Quietism exercised a pronounced attraction for certain aristocratic women. Its simple methods of prayer made it eminently practical for busy women unable to engage in more elaborate meditation. Its emphasis on personal religious experience privileged the mystical aspirations of women. As attested by the prominence of its leader Madame Guyon on the lecture circuit, Quietism lent women a new religious authority, derived from individual spiritual experience rather than from sacramental ordination or ecclesiastical mandate.

Attracted by Quietism in the late 1680s, Maintenon decisively turned against the movement in the mid 1690s. The deleterious effect of the movement on the behavior of the Saint-Cyr pupils, especially their reluctance to engage in hard work, convinced Maintenon of the doctrinal unsoundness of the Quietists. The emphasis on passivity had undercut the effort to cultivate practical virtues, the keystone of Maintenonian education. The insistence on the primacy of the divine will had destroyed the determination of the human will to persist in the combat against vice. In *Against Religious Innovations* Maintenon also reveals her gendered concerns regarding the damage caused by Quietism. More prone to mystical experience than men, women were more easily led into illusion by the movement's repeated exhortations to spiritual exaltation. Maintenon's opposition to Quietism sprang from the primacy she accorded the practical virtues, such as courage and temperance, and the value she placed on personal cultivation of the will. But it also sprang from her enthusiasm for such bourgeois virtues as industriousness and personal enterprise. The address *Portrait of a Reasonable Person* is an exuberant celebration of the perfectly organized day, uniting work, prayer, and fellowship in a timetable of military precision. Before such a practical and activist interpretation of female discipleship, Quietism could only be condemned as an assault on moral earnestness veiled in a mystical glow.

The major influence of the works of Maintenon has been practical rather than theoretical. Her prestigious experiment at Saint-Cyr inspired hundreds of modest imitations in academies for women throughout Europe. At the end of the nineteenth century, new editions of her works flooded the lycées of

France. Extracts from Maintenon were used to shape the moral character of adolescent women, but the anticlerical editors of these editions systematically omitted her religious concerns. A strangely secularized Maintenon became a pedagogical tool to foster moderation, diligence, and courtesy in the female citizens of the republic.

Madeleine Daniélou restored the theological foundation of Maintenon's concept of education in her magisterial study of Maintenon's pedagogical methods in 1946. A prominent educational administrator herself, Daniélou explicitly cited Maintenon as her inspiration in the founding and direction of a Catholic institute for the formation of teachers that challenged the educational hegemony of the secularist École Normale Supérieure in Paris. During the same period, several doctoral dissertations and master's theses at American Catholic universities attempted to apply Maintenon's educational principles to contemporary education. The works of Cudmore (1945) and of Molphy (1955) are illustrative of this Catholic retrieval of Maintenon.

No discussion of the influence of Maintenon can ignore the "black legend" that has made her an object of opprobrium for centuries. In the eighteenth century, critics depicted Maintenon as a religious fanatic who personally goaded Louis XIV into violent anti-Protestant persecutions. The forgeries of La Beaumelle strongly contributed to this image of Maintenon as a manipulative bigot. Having largely absolved her of these charges, contemporary critics tend to lambast Maintenon on other grounds. While recognizing her importance in the education of women, they lament the limited access provided to the arts and sciences at Saint-Cyr. They often denounce her conventional views on the virtue of submission to husband, priest, and king. Carlo François offers a typical condemnation:

> To the desire to be free and emancipated, she [Madame de Maintenon] substitutes the traditional precepts of devotion and of submission. As in the past, it is masculine power that takes up its rights; however, this time the patriarchal power is exercised through a matriarchy that is its accomplice . . . Madame de Maintenon made her girls into the slaves of privilege.[33]

Such criticism accords little recognition to the sober analysis of the social oppression of women that emerges in many of Maintenon's works. Nor does it recognize how the Maintenonian pedagogy of dialogue valorized the conversation of women themselves, rather than the recitation of works written by men, as the norm for the instruction of women.

33. François, *Précieuses et autres indociles*, 100–1.

One often has the impression that the dismissal of Maintenon's educational philosophy derives from the religious nature of the education she champions. It is her emphasis on piety and the Christian cast of the virtues she defends that arouse the ire of her critics. Still mired in religious polemics, the ancient legend of Maintenon as a Torquemada in lace has yet to recede. Maintenon the moral and educational philosopher remains to be discovered.

A NOTE ON THE TRANSLATION

This translation of Maintenon's works is based primarily on two manuscripts housed in the archives of the Bibliothèque municipale de Versailles. The first is the seven-volume edition of Maintenon's works, entitled *Lettres édifiantes*, commissioned by the archbishop of Sens in the eighteenth century. The second is the single volume of Maintenon's writings, entitled *Les conversations*, also composed in the eighteenth century. I have also consulted the Lavallée (1854) and the Leroy-Loyau (1998) print editions of these works. *Les loisirs de Madame de Maintenon* (1757) has provided the text for several of the dramatic dialogues.

The translation emphasizes clarity and accuracy in its rendering of the French. In order to represent more clearly the dialogical structure of these works, I have added colons, quotation marks, and paragraph indentations when deemed appropriate. The addresses have been presented in the order of genre and theme rather than that of chronology. For the identification of the students who serve as Maintenon's interlocutors in the addresses, I have consulted the appendices in Théophile Lavallée's *Madame de Maintenon et la maison royale de Saint-Cyr* (1862).

In this translation I have used inclusive language to render anthropological terms, such as *l'homme*. However, I have maintained traditional gendered language for religious terms, out of respect for the integrity of the text and for Maintenon's theology. In the Maintenonian universe God the Father and Mother Church enjoy inalienable rights.

The works I have chosen for this volume present a particular challenge for translation into contemporary English. Although composed in dialogical form, Maintenon's dramatic sketches and addresses are written in a formal rather than a colloquial French. Students, faculty, and dramatic characters address each other by proper titles. Stiff formulae of politeness punctuate the discussions. The frequent use of conditional clauses and rhetorical questions lends the debates a certain aloofness. This formal prose reflects the unusual culture of the Saint-Cyr academy. Educating an exclusively aristocratic audience, Maintenon insisted that every educational exercise perfectly embody the key aristocratic virtues of politeness, civility, and courtesy. She composed her dialogues and revised the transcripts of her addresses to make them exemplars of literary refinement and moral propriety. The formality of these works never prevents Maintenon from speaking candidly. Her remarks on sexuality, politics, and religion can be blunt. But a faithful translation of these works requires some maintenance of their starched rhetoric, which expresses the conventions of a vanished aristocratic culture Maintenon wished to purify.

I have also added etymological notes to clarify certain abstract terms frequently used by Maintenon. Words like *esprit* and *raison* possessed certain meanings in seventeenth-century French, especially in the argot of literary salons, that differ from their primary meanings in contemporary French.

FOR FURTHER READING

We are far from a complete, let alone a critical, edition of Maintenon's works in the original French. Several recent anthologies provide a solid introduction to her works. Leroy and Loyau (*Comment la sagesse vient aux filles,* 1998) present the major writings on education. Prévot (*La première institutrice de France,* 1981) provides a more eclectic selection. The earlier anthologies by Gréard (*Extraits de ses lettres,* 1885), Faguet (*Madame de Maintenon, institutrice,* 1885), and Jacquinet (*Choix de ses lettres,* 1888) distort her educational theory but accurately represent the "lay" Madame de Maintenon diffused throughout the public schools of the Third Republic. The massive editions of the works of Maintenon by Théophile Lavallée (1854–70) remain a standard reference for students of Maintenon, but they are incomplete, and their presentation of her letters is unreliable. The four-volume edition of her letters by Langlois (1935–39) is critical in nature but incomplete.

Given her unusual life and social ascent, Maintenon has never lacked for biographers. The recent studies of André Castelot (*Madame de Maintenon*) and Eric Le Nabour (*La porteuse d'ombre*) explore the power exercised by Maintenon in her secret marriage to Louis XIV. Louis Mermaz (*Madame de Maintenon*) places a greater focus on the religious mission of Maintenon. Charlotte Haldane (*Madame de Maintenon*) provides a solid account of her life in English. Although fictionalized, Françoise Chandernagor's *L'allée du roi* provides a penetrating study of the motives of Maintenon, based on her actual writings.

Numerous books on pioneers of women's education contain chapters recognizing Maintenon's contributions. Daniélou (*Madame de Maintenon éducatrice*) and Lougee (*Le paradis des femmes*) provide contrasting judgments on the success of Maintenon's educational ventures and the extent to which they contributed to the emancipation of women. Daniélou praises Maintenon's commitment to moral formation and her effort to provide a practical education suited to the typical duties of provincial aristocratic women. Lougee criticizes Maintenon's emphasis on social subordination and its concomitant limitation of the access of women to the arts and sciences.

To situate the writings and theories of Maintenon, it is important to grasp the broader seventeenth-century cultural background from which her work emerged. Gibson (*Women in Seventeenth-Century France*) and Timmermans (*L'accès des femmes à la culture*) provide detailed overviews of the status of women in this period. DeJean (*Tender Geographies*), Stephens (*History of Women's Writing in France*), and Wilson (*Encyclopedia of Continental Women Writers*) explore the writings of Frenchwomen during this era. Analyses of the Parisian salon culture that shaped Maintenon are provided by Goldsmith (*"Exclusive Conversations"*) and Pekacz (*Conservative Tradition*). Broad (*Women Philosophers*), Conley (*Suspicion of Virtue*), and Harth (*Cartesian Women*) study the philosophical currents typical of the period's educated women. Rapley (*The Dévotes*) examines the new schools for women generated by the religious orders and the lay movements of the Counter-Reformation in France. Adam on libertinism (*Les libertins*), Doyle on Jansenism (*Jansenism*), and Armogathe on Quietism (*Le Quiétisme*) sketch the central religious movements opposed by Maintenon.

VOLUME EDITOR'S
BIBLIOGRAPHY

PRIMARY SOURCES

Manuscripts

Maintenon, Françoise d'Aubigné, Madame de. *Les conversations*. Ms. F. 729. Bibliothèque municipale de Versailles.

——. *Lettres édifiantes*. 7 vols. Ms. P.62–68. Bibliothèque municipale de Versailles.

Printed Sources

Editions of Lavallée

Maintenon, Françoise d'Aubigné, Madame de. *Conseils et instructions aux demoiselles pour leur conduite dans le monde*. Éd. Théophile Lavallée. 2 vols. Paris: Charpentier, 1857.

——. *Correspondance générale de Madame de Maintenon*. Éd. Théophile Lavallée. 2 vols. Paris: Charpentier, 1865, 1866.

——. *Entretiens sur l'éducation des filles*. Éd. Théophile Lavallée. Paris: Charpentier, 1854.

——. *Lettres et entretiens sur l'éducation des filles*. Éd. Théophile Lavallée. 2 vols. Paris: Charpentier, 1861.

——. *Lettres historiques et édifiantes adressées aux dames de Saint Louis*. Éd. Théophile Lavallée. 2 vols. Paris: Charpentier, 1856.

——. *Lettres sur l'éducation des filles*. Éd. Théophile Lavallée. Paris, Charpentier, 1854.

Other Editions

Maintenon, Françoise d'Aubigné, Madame de. *Choix de ses lettres et entretiens avec une introduction et des notes historiques et litteraires*. Éd. Paul Jacquinet. Paris: Belin, 1888.

——. *Comment la sagesse vient aux filles*. Éd. Pierre-E. Leroy et Marcel Loyau. Etrepilly: Bartillat, 1998.

——. *Extraits de ses lettres, avis, entretiens, conversations et proverbes sur l'éducation*. Éd. Octave Gréard. Paris: Hachette, 1885.

——. *Lettres*. Éd. Marcel Langlois. 4 vols. Paris: Letouzey et Ané, 1935–45.

——. *Lettres de Madame de Maintenon*. Éd. Laurent Angliviel de La Beaumelle. Nancy: Chez Deilleau, 1752.

——. *Les loisirs de Madame de Maintenon*. Londres: n.p., 1757.

——. *Madame de Maintenon d'après sa correspondance authentique: Choix de ses lettres et entretiens*. Éd. Auguste Geffroy. Paris: Hachette, 1887.

————. *Madame de Maintenon: Éducation et morale; choix de lettres, entretiens et instructions.* Éd. Félix Cadet et Eugène Darin. Paris: Delagrave, 1885.

————. *Madame de Maintenon, institutrice: Extraits de ses lettres, avis, entretiens, conversations et proverbes sur l'éducation.* Éd. Émile Faguet. Paris: Librairie classique H. Oduin, 1885.

————. *La première institutrice de France: Madame de Maintenon.* Éd. Jacques Prévot. Paris: Belin, 1981.

SECONDARY SOURCES

Autour de Françoise d'Aubigné, marquise de Maintenon: actes des Journées de Niort, 23–25 mai 1996. Éd. Alain Niderst. Paris: Champion, 1996.

Barnard, Howard Clive. *Madame de Maintenon and Saint-Cyr.* London: A. & C. Black, 1934.

Cambier, Maurice. *Racine et Madame de Maintenon.* Brussels: Durendal, 1949.

Castelot, André. *Madame de Maintenon: La reine secrète.* Paris: Perrin, 1996.

Chandernagor, Françoise. *L'allée du roi: Souvenirs de Françoise d'Aubigné, marquise de Maintenon, épouse du Roi de France.* Paris: Julliard, 1981.

Cordelier, Jean. *Madame de Maintenon: Une femme au grand siècle.* Paris: Éditions du Seuil, 1955.

Cudmore, Muriel Frances. "Madame de Maintenon and the Education of girls in seventeenth-century France." Unpublished M.A. thesis: Fordham University, 1945.

Daniélou, Madeleine. *Madame de Maintenon, éducatrice.* Paris: Bloud & Gay, 1946.

Derrida, Jacques. "Given Time: The Time of the King." *Critical Inquiry* 18 (1992): 161–87.

Guelfi, Julien. *Madame de Maintenon, 1635–1719.* Lyon: L'Hermès, 1986.

Haldane, Charlotte. *Madame de Maintenon: Uncrowned Queen of France.* Indianapolis: Bobbs-Merrill, 1970.

Hastier, Louis. *Louis XIV et Madame de Maintenon.* Paris: Fayard, 1957.

Langlois, Marcel. *Madame de Maintenon.* Paris: Plon, 1932.

Lavallée, Théophile. *La famille d'Aubigné et l'enfance de Mme de Maintenon.* Paris: Plon, 1863.

————. *Madame de Maintenon et la maison royale de Saint-Cyr (1686–1793).* Paris: Plon, 1862.

Le Nabour, Eric. *La Porteuse d'ombre: Madame de Maintenon et le Roi-Soleil.* Paris: Tallandier, 1999.

Lougee, Carolyn. *Le paradis des femmes: Women, Salons, and Social Stratification in Seventeenth-Century France.* Princeton, NJ: Princeton University Press, 1976.

Mermaz, Louis. *Madame de Maintenon; ou, L'amour dévot.* Lausanne: Éditions Rencontre, 1965.

Molphy, Rosemary Therese. "Fénelon, Madame de Maintenon, and the Education of Women." Unpublished M.A. thesis: St. John's University, 1955.

Niderst, Alain. "L'Enjouée Plotine, Madame de Maintenon, Madame de Scudéry, et Ninon de Lenclos," *Papers on French Seventeenth-Century Literature* 27, no. 53 (2000): 501–8.

Rosset, Alfred. *Madame de Maintenon et la révocation de l'Édit de Nantes: Essai historique.* Aud-incourt: C. Jacot, 1897.

Rowan, Mary M. "Seventeenth-Century French Feminism: Two Opposing Attitudes," *International Journal of Women's Studies* 3 (1980): 273–91.

TERTIARY SOURCES

Adam, Antoine. *Les libertins au XVIIe siècle.* Paris: Buchet/Chastel, 1986.

Armogathe, Jean-Robert. *Le Quiétisme.* Paris: Presses universitaires de France, 1973.

Bertière, Simone. *Les femmes du Roi-Soleil.* Paris: Éditions de Fallois, 1998.

Broad, Jacqueline. *Women Philosophers of the Seventeenth Century.* Cambridge: Cambridge University Press, 2003.

Cognet, Louis. *Le Jansénisme.* Paris: Presses universitaires de France, 1961.

Conley, John J. *The Suspicion of Virtue: Women Philosophers in Neoclassical France.* Ithaca, NY: Cornell University Press, 2002.

DeJean, Joan E. *Tender Geographies: Women and the Origins of the Novel in France.* New York: Columbia University Press, 1991.

De Sales, Saint François. *Introduction à la vie dévote.* Ed. Étienne-Marie Lajeunie. Paris: Éditions du Seuil, 1995.

Deshoulières, Antoinette du Ligier de La Garde. *Oeuvres.* 2 vols. Paris: Stéréotype d'Hernan, 1803.

Doyle, William. *Jansenism: Catholic Resistance to Authority from the Reformation to the French Revolution.* New York: St. Martin's Press, 2000.

François, Carlo. *Précieuses et autres indociles: Aspects du féminisme dans la littérature française du XVIIe siécle.* Birmingham, AL: Summa Publications, 1987.

Gibson, Wendy. *Women in Seventeenth-Century France.* New York: St. Martin's Press, 1989.

Goldsmith, Elizabeth C. *"Exclusive Conversations": The Art of Interaction in Seventeenth-Century France.* Philadelphia: University of Pennsylvania Press, 1988.

Gournay, Marie Le Jars de. *"Apology for the Woman Writing" and Other Works.* Trans. and ed. Richard Hillman and Colette Quesnel. Chicago: University of Chicago Press, 2002.

Guyon, Jeanne Marie Bouvier de La Motte. *Le moyen court et autres écrits spirituels: Une simplicité subversive.* Ed. Marie-Louis Gondal. Grenoble: J. Millon, 1995.

Harth, Erica. *Cartesian Women: Versions and Subversions of Rational Discourse in the Old Regime.* Ithaca, NY: Cornell University Press, 1992.

La Rochefoucauld, François, duc de. *Oeuvres complètes.* Ed. Louis Martin-Chauffier. Paris: Gallimard-Pléiade, 1950.

Méré, Antoine Gombaud, chevalier de. *Oeuvres complètes du chevalier de méré.* Ed. Charles H. Boudhors. 3 vols. Paris: F. Roches, 1930.

Orléans, Charlotte-Élisabeth de Bavière, duchesse de. *Lettres de Madame, duchesse d'Orléans, née princesse Palatine.* Ed. Olivier Amiel. Paris: Mercure de France, 1999.

Pascal, Jacqueline. *A Rule for Children and Other Writings.* Trans. and ed. John J. Conley, S.J. Chicago: University of Chicago Press, 2003.

Pekacz, Jolanta K. *Conservative Tradition in Pre-Revolutionary France.* New York: Peter Lang, 1999.

Rapley, Elizabeth. *The Dévotes: Women and Church in Seventeenth-Century France.* Kingston, Ontario: McGill-Queen's University Press, 1989.

Reynier, Gustave. *La femme au XVIIe siècle.* Paris: Plon, 1933.

Sablé, Madeleine Souvré, marquise de. *Maximes de Madame la Marquise de Sablé: Suivies de pensées de M.L.D.* Ed. Nicolas d'Ailly. Paris: Mabre-Cramoisy, 1678.

Saint-Simon, *Mémoires et additions au Journal de Dagneau.* Ed. Yves Coirault. 8 vols. Paris: Gallimard-Pléiade, 1983–88.

Scudéry, Madeleine de. *Choix de conversations de Mlle de Scudéry.* Ed. Philip J. Wolfe. Ravenna: Longo Editore, 1977.

Sévigné, Marie de Rabutin-Chantal, marquise de. *Correspondance.* Ed. Roger Duchêne. 3 vols. Paris: Gallimard-Pléiade, 1972–78.

Stephens, Sonya, ed. *A History of Women's Writing in France.* Cambridge: Cambridge University Press, 2000.

Timmermans, Linda. *L'accès des femmes à la culture.* Paris: Champion, 1993.

Wilson, Katharina M., ed. *An Encyclopedia of Continental Women Writers.* 2 vols. New York: Garland, 1991.

DIALOGUES

Composed for classroom performance by older pupils at Saint-Cyr, Maintenon's dramatic dialogues constitute one of the theatrical genres used by Maintenon in her schema of education. At the beginning of instruction at the academy, Maintenon had used written dialogues composed by the headmistress Madame de Brinon and by the novelist Mademoiselle de Scudéry. But in her reaction against the worldliness of the original Saint-Cyr curriculum, Maintenon had eliminated the neoclassical sketches as too pagan and too frivolous. As a substitute, she wrote dozens of her own dramatic dialogues, miniature morality plays designed to inculcate a particular virtue deemed essential for the students.

Most of the dialogues attempt to clarify a moral quality to be cultivated by the student audience. Justice, courage, prudence, temperance, piety, wit, and glory are among the virtues debated in the following dialogues. Maintenon's presentation of the virtues follows certain patterns of argumentation. Attentive to the gender of her audience, Maintenon repeatedly transforms the meaning of a virtue from its traditional masculine associations to traits specific to the experience of women. *On True Glory* presents glory as the endurance of the homemaker. *On True Wit* celebrates authentic wit as a capacity to serve others in different situations. Refuting the theory that only men can acquire courage, *On Courage* illustrates the nonmartial exercise of the virtue by women in the school and in the home.

On True Glory typifies Maintenon's technique in the gendered transposition of virtue. Rooted in the Greek classics, the virtue of glory (*gloire*) was commonly interpreted in the Renaissance as the attribute of a person who had achieved renown through public service. So frequently was the service of a military nature that the term *gloire militaire* had become a standard phrase. Banned from the military and most sectors of civic life, women were not

considered proper subjects for the possession of *gloire*. In *On True Glory* Maintenon contests the male bias surrounding the virtue by redefining it and by
providing a new narrative for it, rooted in the distinctive experience of
women. Maintenonian glory is the courage to maintain one's honor against
the temptation to moral compromise. The exemplars of glory are no longer
warriors and statesmen. They are the maid who refuses a bribe and the spin-
ster who refuses an immoral suitor. Against the traditional patriarchal cast
of the virtues, Maintenon reconceptualizes the virtues in terms of the history of women, especially impoverished women. But rather than insisting
that women pursue virtue by entering traditionally male domains of action,
Maintenon chronicles how women pursue the virtues differently in a sphere
of action proper to their gender alone.

Maintenon's dialogues also frankly depict the typical constraints faced
by women. *On the Necessity of Dependence* skewers the adolescent fantasy of the
freedom that beckons after the end of studies. It details the social demands
that will severely limit the freedom of any woman, whether single, or married, or widowed. *On the Drawbacks of Marriage* similarly studies the constraints
governing both the convent and marriage, the destinations of the vast majority of women. For Maintenon, the experience of dependence and restriction is not limited to women alone. As she argues in *On Constraint*, the king
himself, like all men and women, must suffer the painful limitations on his
personal freedom created by religion, law, custom, and the daily demands of
his state in life.

Maintenon's dialogues reflect her ambiguity on ethical issues related to
social class. If many of the dialogues celebrate a hierarchical social order by
their emphasis on deference, many of them also insist that moral value is distinct from, indeed often opposed to, material wealth and social rank. *On Eminence* exalts the moral worth of a commoner who becomes a general on the
basis of merit while it mocks the aristocrat who flatters himself on account
of his birth. This hesitation on the value of social hierarchy reflects Maintenon's own embittered relationship with a blood aristocracy who despised
her as a low-born upstart. It also reflects Louis XIV's controversial policy of
ennobling commoners who had served the throne meritoriously and in re-
ducing the privileges of the ancient French nobility, defined by its ancestry.

The dialogues follow a similar structure. Several female characters discuss a moral dilemma of obvious concern to adolescent women of aristocratic background. Part of the effectiveness of the plays lies in Maintenon's
skillful use of her characters as projections of her adolescent audience's typical beliefs, questions, and anxieties about the future. The dialogues usually
debate the meaning of a specific virtue essential for women of such a social

rank. Maintenon often employs the *distinguo* to explore subtle gradations of meaning behind an abstract term. *On True Glory*, for example, carefully studies different meanings of the term as it establishes the opposition between "true" and "false" glory.

To illustrate her moral point, Maintenon frequently uses an edifying narrative, often the tale of an impoverished person who overcomes social obstacles through mastery of the virtue under discussion. In numerous dialogues the edifying tale becomes thinly disguised autobiography. In *On Privilege*, the mysterious "Lady" with a hidden role in court affairs is obviously Maintenon herself. In *On Constraint*, Louis XIV's daily routine is depicted as a type of genteel martyrdom, lovingly recounted by a court insider. Several of the dialogues are little more than royalist propaganda. *On Current Discussions*, for example, baldly defends Louis XIV's policy of economic protectionism and condemns political dissent.

If the dialogues present opposing viewpoints on a moral question, Maintenon rarely leaves in doubt what constitutes the proper perspective on the issue in question. *On True Wit*, for example, clearly prefers the industriousness of the homemaker over the erudition of the scholar as the higher form of intelligence. Maintenon inevitably leads the student to the traditional moral and religious virtues as the key to facing the social demands she must endure. Maintenon's moralism, however, refuses fanaticism. The dialogues insist that all virtues, even piety, must be "reasonable." It is sober temperance, not ecstatic charity, that occupies the apex of Maintenon's edifice of virtue.

ON THE CARDINAL VIRTUES [1]

VICTORIA: In order to be faithful to the project they have of making us capable of holding refined conversations, I thought that for today's conversation we should turn to the subject of the cardinal virtues. Each one of us could say whatever comes to mind about this subject.

PAULINE: Since that's decided, I'll take the role of Justice.

VICTORIA: I'll take Fortitude.

EUPHRASIA: I'll take Prudence.

AUGUSTINA: You don't leave me any choice. But I'm happy with my part and I'm delighted to play the role of Temperance.

JUSTICE: I don't think that any of you even pretends to be my equal.

---

1. This translation is based on Madame de Maintenon, *Sur les vertus cardinales*, in LC, BMV, Ms. F. 729, 198–204.

Nothing is as beautiful as Justice. She always has Truth beside her. She judges without prejudice. She puts everything in order. She knows how to condemn her friend and how to find on behalf of her enemy. She even condemns herself. She only respects what truly merits respect.

FORTITUDE: All of that is true, but you need me. If I didn't support you, you would grow weary.

JUSTICE: Why would I grow weary?

FORTITUDE: Because you have a rather gloomy personality. People have little affection for you. They fear you. People have to be exceptionally meritorious to get along with you.

PRUDENCE: It's my responsibility to set some limits to her projects, to prevent her from going overboard, to make her take her time. Without me, both of you would soon spoil everything.

JUSTICE: But shouldn't we always be just?

PRUDENCE: Of course. But you shouldn't always be at court avid to hand out a sentence. You should do everything in its own due time.

FORTITUDE: It's true that you might in fact offer certain services to Justice, but my services are just as important to help you. You tend to paralyze rather than to encourage action, unless I give both of you some of my boldness.

JUSTICE: I don't understand you. What? Do you think that I need your help just to see that my friend is wrong and my enemy is right?

FORTITUDE: No, you can figure that out by yourself. But you need me to help you render that judgment loud and clear, since your friendship makes you find it so difficult to upset your friend.

JUSTICE: It's enough for me to see that something is just in order for me to do it.

FORTITUDE: Yes, I agree with you. But you just don't want to see that what you attribute to Justice alone actually belongs to Fortitude. That is where you are being unjust.

TEMPERANCE: Ladies, I can only marvel at how you think that you can do without me and that I count for nothing since I'm in no rush to speak.

PRUDENCE: Do you also want to claim that you are necessary?

TEMPERANCE: I'm so powerful that I challenge all three of you to try to operate without my influence.

FORTITUDE: And how can your coolness help me?

TEMPERANCE: I will prevent you from exhausting everyone by your fervor.

JUSTICE: And how would you help me?

TEMPERANCE: I would moderate your justice, because it is often too bitter and inflexible.

PRUDENCE: I don't think you have any claim on me.

TEMPERANCE: I will oppose your indecisiveness. Your timidity often goes much too far.

FORTITUDE: Very well. To listen to you, one would have the impression that you are more important than all of us.

TEMPERANCE: Undoubtedly you all lean to certain extreme positions if I don't moderate you. I'm the one who places the limits to everything. I'm the one who takes this middle position, so necessary but so difficult to find. I'm the one who must oppose all excess.

PRUDENCE: I always thought of you as something opposed to gluttony and nothing more.

TEMPERANCE: That's because you didn't know me. In effect I destroy gluttony and lust. I suffer no exaggeration. Not only do I oppose all evil, but I have to put reasonable limits to the good. Without me Justice would be unbearable to human weakness, Fortitude would drive humanity to despair, and Prudence would often prevent people from making necessary decisions and would waste too much time weighing every option. But with me Justice becomes capable of adaptation, Fortitude becomes softer, Prudence starts to give advice without too much weakness, without being either too slow or too quick to judge. In other words, I'm the remedy to all the extremes.

JUSTICE: I'm astonished at what I'm hearing. Now, wouldn't you agree that wisdom can do without you?

TEMPERANCE: You can answer that question yourself, because you're well aware that to be wise you must be sober. Don't look for further arguments, Miss. You can't do anything good without me.

PRUDENCE: Well, can't we at least achieve our salvation without you?

TEMPERANCE: Only with great difficulty. I calm the religious zeal that is too combative, too angry, too aggressive. I have to help religious faith conduct itself in a way that avoids excess. I moderate the desire to give alms as well as the desire to keep them. I limit the time for prayer, penances, retreat, silence, good works. I abbreviate a sermon. I shorten a session of spiritual direction or an examination of conscience. Finally, I have to soften even the flames of religious fervor.

JUSTICE: You certainly keep busy.

TEMPERANCE: My personality doesn't permit me to feel fatigue. I intervene gently and serenely.

FORTITUDE: All this leads to the conclusion that we very much need you. But don't you need someone in particular?

TEMPERANCE: No, I'm quite self-sufficient.

FORTITUDE: But can't someone be too moderate?

TEMPERANCE: But that would no longer be moderation, because it tolerates neither too much nor too little.

PRUDENCE: You make me unhappy with my own condition. I now desire yours.

TEMPERANCE: That's because you had too high an opinion of yourself. Still, you are all very worthy qualities. Is there anything more magnificent than Justice? Always founded on truth, free of prejudice, incorruptible, disinterested, capable of ruling against herself despite her self-love?

JUSTICE: But even with all of that, you say that I am hated.

TEMPERANCE: That's because you refuse to flatter others, and they want to be flattered.

FORTITUDE: And you still think that I would ruin everything without you?

TEMPERANCE: Yes, but with me, you do wonders. You enliven all the virtues, you follow through on all your projects until they are finished, and you never surrender to fatigue.

PRUDENCE: And I'm still just someone who hesitates.

TEMPERANCE: You know how to choose the right time. You're accommodating. You foresee possible dangers. You know how to take the measure of a situation. You're absolutely indispensable as long as I can prevent you from falling into an excess of caution.

FORTITUDE: You're just trying to cheer us up. In the end, our role is less important than yours.

TEMPERANCE: But what would I be without you? Used only and often uselessly to oppose excess and human passion? My true value is to be necessary for the moderation of all the other virtues.

FORTITUDE: But are we really virtues, if we often need you to avoid some extreme action? A virtue, after all, is supposed to hold always to the middle.

TEMPERANCE: It's up to me to make this middle position known. Now, I'm not saying that you might do some great evil, but there's still the danger that you might go too far.

JUSTICE: Is it possible for me to be too just?

TEMPERANCE: No, but to judge too often and to be constantly on everyone's back helps no one. When the ardor of Fortitude is joined with the aridity of Justice, the situation becomes even more dangerous.

PRUDENCE: I could try to remedy that situation.

TEMPERANCE: Often enough you try to do so. We need each other. We should live together serenely and without jealousy. Let's unite ourselves against the corruption of the world. If it weren't for the assistance of grace, it would be stronger than all the virtues together.

ON COURAGE[2]

FAUSTINE: I am really tired of being preached to every day about courage. I truly would like to know in what exactly courage consists.

ELEANOR: Courage is not having any fear. This kind of achievement is not for our sex. It's acceptable for us to be afraid of ghosts, of thunder, and of all kinds of danger.

SOPHIE: It has to be acceptable, because I would not be able to avoid it.

VICTORIA: Certainly courage is opposed to fear. But there is more than one kind of fear. It's not necessary for us to cultivate the courage that makes someone go to war or be willing to risk his life. But I would certainly want to eliminate the weaknesses our friend just discussed.

SOPHIE: Oh! Just how could I eliminate these?

VICTORIA: First of all, by opposing them. The weaknesses we pick up in our youth—and which we think are so charming—became illnesses later on that make us suffer and that we can no longer abandon. I've seen some people really oppressed by this sort of thing.

FAUSTINE: Nothing seems more excusable to me.

EMILY: We will continue to have enough weaknesses that must be excused without keeping some voluntarily.

FAUSTINE: But let's return to the topic of courage.

VICTORIA: I am convinced that our friend probably knows more than us about the subject.

EMILY: If that's true, it's because she has more frequently sought out the one who makes these reproaches[3] and listened to her counsels.

SOPHIE: Miss, whatever the case may be, tell us what you have learned about the subject.

EMILY: I've heard it said that courage is surmounting the obstacles we find in ourselves and in others. It is pursuing our projects without permitting ourselves to be discouraged.

SOPHIE: And what projects can we pursue here, since we only have to obey and to observe a rule of life?

VICTORIA: Courage is required to obey and to observe such a rule.

FAUSTINE: Then all of us must have courage, since we don't see a single person among us who is dispensed from the rule.

---

2. This translation is based on Madame de Maintenon, *Sur le courage* in *LC*, BMV, Ms. F.729, 293–301. Derived from the Latin noun *curage*, the French term *courage* originally referred to any activity of the heart (*coeur*) and to any ardent desire. It later denoted any virtuous disposition of the soul. In the seventeenth century the term referred more narrowly to the specific virtue of steadfastness in the face of serious danger.

3. The one (*celle*) lecturing the pupils on courage is Madame de Maintenon.

EMILY: There is a great difference, Miss, between doing something and doing it well. Few soldiers are dispensed from the duty of going to war, but some plunge into it with passion, while others only go under the blows of a club.

SOPHIE: This comparison is perfectly illuminating. It helps me see that in fact the same sort of difference could be found among us.

EMILY: There are those who joyfully fulfill all their duties and who are first in everything. They wash themselves the moment they are awakened. They never complain that it's too hot or too cold. They find time for themselves and for service to others. They love work, they want to please their teachers, and they want to do even more than one asks of them. They count as nothing what they have done. They understand they will have many other problems in the world. I think these pupils clearly have courage.

VICTORIA: Describe for us the other kind of pupil.

EMILY: These are the ones who find it difficult to do anything. They can neither wake up nor go to sleep properly. They find the rule of the house intolerable. They would rather live like animals, getting up when they no longer feel like sleeping, going to bed when they feel the need to sleep, and eating whenever their fancy wants it. They never want to work, and they seek pleasure or at least a little rest in everything.

ELEANOR: You agree that these examples only concern the present moment and that, when we leave here, we will no longer be bound by these rules.

EMILY: Perhaps we won't have to suffer the same situations, but apparently we will have even greater challenges. What I've just been discussing are only trifles if we compare them with the poverty we may find in the future and with the foul mood of those with whom we shall have to deal. They might well criticize us without the moderation they maintain here.

FAUSTINE: So you want some courage in the soul as well as in external actions.

SOPHIE: I feel myself strong enough to overcome myself in all that only produces suffering in the body, but when it comes to contradictions, reprimands, and disdain, I cannot endure them without anger or without discouragement.

FAUSTINE: Personally, I tolerate more easily what only bothers my mind, but I admit that I am very sensitive to any external inconvenience.

EMILY: You see, Miss, that courage extends quite far and that it's necessary to have some in everything. What can we hope for in the rest of our lives if we don't want to suffer anything? How can we make our bodies and souls firm if the least difficulty discourages us or makes us surrender? A body can never make itself stronger than others unless it accustoms itself to tolerating fatigue. The soul can never become robust and courageous unless it accustoms itself to overcoming obstacles.

VICTORIA: It is the same with virtue. We can only acquire it through trials and through practices that do some violence to ourselves.

ELEANOR: What do we know about what God has in store for us? Perhaps we won't have to suffer anything.

EMILY: God has disposed things otherwise. We are only saved by following the narrow road,[4] and we can only arrive at happiness through suffering.

FAUSTINE: But does everyone suffer equally? Isn't there anything that could diminish our afflictions?

EMILY: If anything can diminish them, it's our expecting them, our preparing for them, and our accustoming ourselves to them. It's finding those that currently preoccupy us small and always imagining some that are greater. I think that a pupil of Saint-Cyr who courageously endures the inconveniences, the subjection, the restrictions, the humiliations, and the corrections that are inseparable from a good education will be far more capable of successfully confronting those she will find in the world than will a girl who is cowardly, overly sensitive, rebellious, and who, rather than fortifying herself by suffering, is further weakened by her complaints, her murmuring, and the voicing of her afflictions. These things are only good for adding the weaknesses of others to our own particular weaknesses.

FAUSTINE: I am beginning to understand that the pupils of Saint-Cyr need courage because of the misfortune of their financial state. This situation excites a little my envy of the rich and powerful who suffer from very few things.

EMILY: I wanted to explain everything that I said about courage to make it useful for you. But there is no state in life where there is nothing to endure and where there is no need of courage. The great of this world suffer great afflictions. We complain about the restrictions on us, but the powerful must endure even greater ones. They sustain major contradictions, while we must sustain minor ones.

FAUSTINE: At least their bodies are free and tranquil.

EMILY: The sufferings of the mind would lead us far astray, if we wanted to discuss them in any detail. As for their bodies, although they have the resources to relax, they are always on the brink of exhaustion. Whatever advantages of birth, wealth, or some other factor they might have, they are driven to have enough courage to distinguish themselves from others.

ELEANOR: What sort of suffering are they exposed to?

4. See Matthew 7:14.

EMILY: Miss, don't you see very well that our princes often go on foot on their journeys or on their walks? They don't do this for pleasure but they walk until the point of fatigue.

VICTORIA: Some time ago they found the king of Spain[5] on the path from Versailles to Saint-Cyr. He had removed his overcoat to walk more freely. He was hunting during a biting cold spell. He was on foot with a rifle on his shoulder.

ELEANOR: Now what good did that do?

EMILY: It strengthened his body and his health. It accustomed him to the type of fatigue inseparable from war. It made his mind freer and more courageous than it would have been had it been dowsed in conveniences and delicacies.

VICTORIA: Personally, I am content with our understanding of courage. Now let's say something about this good faith that they are also asking us to cultivate.

SOPHIE: That subject requires a discussion all its own.

ON TRUE GLORY[6]

ADELAIDE: I would very much like to have you judge a dispute I just had. Miss Sophie and I were passing through a square where there weren't many people. Everyone greeted us, and I returned the greeting. But Sophie made fun of me. She said that we only owed a bow to certain people of quality.

IRENE: I would have criticized Miss Sophie rather than you. I can never understand how someone could receive a greeting without returning it.

SOPHIE: Even to paupers? You would treat them as if they were aristocrats?

IRENE: I try to alter my bows according to the qualities of the persons whom I greet. But I must confess that I prefer to err on the side of showing too much recognition than too little.

SOPHIE: That doesn't seem to make you very glorious.

---

5. The king of Spain is Phillip V.

6. This translation is based on Madame de Maintenon, *Sur la bonne gloire*, in LC, BMV, Ms. F.729, 221–28. Derived from the Latin noun *gloria*, the term *gloire* (glory) originally had a religious meaning: the state of the blessed in eternity. By the seventeenth century the term often denoted a prominent individual's distinguishing traits, such as brilliance, magnificence, or renown. *Gloire* had also acquired complex moral connotations. Positively it indicated an individual's personal honor. Negatively it indicated an individual's vanity: *vaine gloire*. Maintenon elaborates on the morally opposed senses of the term.

IRENE: I do try to pursue my own kind of glory. But I consider rudeness a false version of glory.

EUPHRASIA: Could a good Christian woman know some true glory?

IRENE: Christian humility is not opposed to honor, to integrity, to disinterestedness, to courage, and that's what I call true glory.

SOPHIE: Do you really think that disinterestedness and true glory are the same thing?

IRENE: No, Miss, true glory is the incapacity to do anything base. Now, since it's ordinarily self-interest that pushes us to do base things, I included disinterestedness within true glory.

ADELAIDE: How do you relate courage to true glory?

IRENE: It's simple. You have to have great courage in certain circumstances to avoid doing base things.

ADELAIDE: Give us some examples to help us understand what your theory is.

IRENE: I knew some impoverished people who were offered considerable sums to do something against their honor. Didn't they need some courage and some true glory to refuse such temptations and to remain in their misery?

ADELAIDE: I know that a chambermaid once refused a good bit of money to give someone else an important letter. The money would have freed her from the necessity of working. She not only refused the offer, she denounced the very fact that someone had dared to make it to her.

EUPHRASIA: What a fine example!

IRENE: Now that's what we call true glory.

EUPHRASIA: Well-born people aren't exposed to such base propositions.

IRENE: They receive more delicate offers, but they are no less dangerous. Don't you think it requires great courage for a young person to prefer to be poorly clothed rather than receive attractive dresses? To prefer boredom rather than amusement, because she fears risking her reputation? To prefer serving her mother and her father, the poor and the sick, rather than going in search of diversion? To prefer not marrying at all rather than marrying a man without good family and without merit?

EUPHRASIA: You're giving a very broad definition to true glory. But I would like to know more clearly just what false glory is.

IRENE: I think it is to consider shameful what is not shameful and to consider meritorious what has no merit.

ADELAIDE: Like what?

IRENE: To be ashamed of being poorly dressed, of being poorly housed, of having to wait on yourself when you were born to another manner.

EUPHRASIA: But don't you find everything you just cited rather shameful?

IRENE: Of course not. Not at all.

DOROTHY: But where then do you place shame?

IRENE: In doing something evil.

DOROTHY: What kind of evil?

IRENE: Anything opposed to integrity, to honor, to courage, to fidelity, to gratitude . . . in a word, to true glory.

EUPHRASIA: But how do you relate this true glory to humility?

IRENE: The virtues don't contradict each other, Miss. They complement each other.

EUPHRASIA: But doesn't humility want us to place little value on ourselves. Doesn't it want us to be serene when others treat us with contempt?

IRENE: Yes, Miss, but it doesn't want us to earn this contempt by our cowardice or by our base actions.

EUPHRASIA: But how could I have a low opinion of myself, if I had all the virtues you were talking about?

IRENE: We always have enough faults to find a good foundation for some humility. Our virtues are never perfect. Furthermore, since our virtues don't come from ourselves, we have nothing to exalt ourselves about.

DOROTHY: I'd like some more information on false glory. You haven't explained it as clearly as you have the true.

IRENE: False glory is a vanity about what we are or what we think ourselves to be. This vanity concerns our birth and our talents. It is self-absorbed. It makes us always talk about ourselves, try to be the first one through the door, and try to grab the best seat. It gives us the desire to be handsomely dressed. It causes us to be mortified when someone sees us in poverty and to try to hide this poverty from others. Because of this, it makes us do ridiculous and dangerous things.

EUPHRASIA: Are you suggesting that you could place yourself beneath a person who is your inferior and let her pass through the door first?

IRENE: I would accept it without a word of protest.

DOROTHY: That would be difficult for someone with real courage.

IRENE: We already said that courage clearly concerns issues beyond these minor things. This is not where courage shows its mettle.

EUPHRASIA: Do you seriously think that we should live with paupers just as we live with those who are our superiors?

IRENE: I want you to respect those who, by birth or by fortune, or by position, or by age, are above us. I want you to treat with great delicacy those who are our social equals. But I also want you to show great goodness and politeness in your dealings with those who are our social inferiors.

DOROTHY: What! Do you think I would practice politeness with some peasant in my village or with some servant!

IRENE: Yes, undoubtedly. We should say hello to a peasant, ask him for the latest news, patiently listen to him, and, when possible, grant his requests. We should treat our servants more or less the same way.

EUPHRASIA: But then with whom do we get to pull rank?

IRENE: But we have no rank to pull. Our meager resources and our youth place us beneath everyone else.

DOROTHY: Are we somehow inferior just because we are young?

IRENE: No, but we do owe a certain respect to older people. The role of youth is to obey and to cede to the desires of others. We can only gain love by our gentleness, by our sense of service, by our generosity. No one will be impressed by our noble birth except when in our actions we seem to have forgotten it.

ON TRUE WIT[7]

AGATHA: Ladies, I've been trying for a long time to find someone who could explain to me the difference between wit and true wit.[8]

MARIE: I understand it, but I don't know how to define the difference as clearly as I would like.

ELISHA: I think that wit is a rather great light. It gives a certain taste for everything brilliant, it heats up the imagination, it makes conversation pleasant, and it adds to one's own pleasure and to that of others.

FLORIDA: Oh, Miss! You're already speaking about someone who is already far above everyone else. Undoubtedly you're already defining what true wit is.

ELISHA: I will tell you simply what I think. I think that true wit is to have a supple mind. It should adjust itself to everything, serve the pleasure

---

7. This translation is based on Madame de Maintenon, *Sur le bon esprit*, LC, BMV, Ms. F.729, 281–88. Derived from the Latin noun *spiritus*, the term *esprit* (wit) possesses a broad range of meanings. Since the Middle Ages, it has referred to spirit, mind, soul, and principle. In the sixteenth century the term acquired a new positive connotation: the vivacity and the finesse with which a particular mind makes judgments. This modern sense of *esprit* as wit enjoyed a particular vogue in seventeenth-century salons.

8. Following the literary procedure of the *précieuses*, Maintenon opens her exploration of a moral quality by a *distinguo*, in this case between *esprit* (wit) and *bon esprit* (true wit).

of others, love solid things, adapt its tastes to its state in life, enjoy pleasures with those who have some, and know how to do without pleasures with those who don't. It should avoid feeling superior because our wit gives us certain advantages over those who have little of it.

FLORIDA: What you say about true wit is exactly what I would say about wisdom and reason, if I wanted to define them.

MARIE: As a matter of fact, I find it difficult to see any difference.

HORTENSE: Still, Miss, there are people who don't seem very witty, yet who are wise, orderly, and reasonable.

VICTORIA: That's true. But I think we all still agree that wit is this light that makes us see further than others do.

AUGUSTINA: We belong to the sex with a greater obligation to have our mind well-disciplined rather than to have it broadly cultivated. We shall always see far enough, if we see that there is nothing so solid as to work on our salvation and to choose the state in life that will make this salvation easier and more certain.

CELESTINE: So, you share the beliefs of those who want to take away from our sex the benefits of being a scholar. I just don't understand what pleasure there can be in spending your time with people who know neither history nor novels. Why should we waste our time with women who are so preoccupied with housework that they can't tell the differences among an elegy, an ode, or a lyric poem?

AUGUSTINA: But what possible purpose is there for a girl or a woman to know how to make such distinctions? I'm completely ignorant of them and I have no desire to learn them. I only want to contribute to the happiness of the people on whom I depend.

CELESTINE: Oh! How could you possibly be happy in working from dusk until dawn at some job where you are always doing the same thing? What? Keep poking at some cloth and dragging your needle along? That is base and completely unworthy of a lady. She is born for something better! I could never subject myself to that.

AGATHA: Miss, I am very happy when I am doing my sewing. I don't have all the agitation that comes from other people's business. I am proud when I see my work advance, and I am satisfied when it's finished. I feel that I really accomplished something. I'm protected from the gossip that might make me offend God. I avoid sloth, which so easily leads to boredom. At night, when I pass in review everything that I did that day, I'm happy to have neither laziness nor wasted words to reproach me. I go to bed peacefully, and I sleep without disturbance.

CELESTINE: Well, it seems to me that you must like housewives then?

AGATHA: Yes, it's quite true that I admire them.

CELESTINE: I just don't understand this taste for low life. As for my-self, I could never accept the grinding schedule that farm women follow. What? Get up in the morning like countrywomen, who have barely left their bed when they have to get their families off to work and start the endless chores of housekeeping!

AUGUSTINA: Someone who acts this way is truly wise. She imitates the strong woman whom Solomon praises.[9]

CELESTINE: Are you telling me that if you still lived at your mother's house, you'd really like to play the part of the housekeeper?

AUGUSTINA: Hey! Don't make a joke of it, Miss. I would, and I would think that I couldn't do anything better.

CELESTINE: Honestly, I wouldn't do that for anything in the world. I have an enlightened mind. I would never stoop to do these kinds of things. I can only be happy in the company of orators, of poets, of philosophers— in a word, with true wits.

AUGUSTINA: But I only find satisfaction in doing my duty.

CELESTINE: Then you're going to have a very unhappy life, and you will always be the slave of your duty.

AUGUSTINA: Miss, I am happier than you are, because I always do what I want. And I only want what I am bound to do. But you will not always have the blessed few to guarantee you pleasure.

CELESTINE: How so, Miss?

AUGUSTINA: Because you like witty people, and there are so few of them around who will suit your tastes.

CELESTINE: I'm currently seeing a number of people who speak to me of exalted things.

AUGUSTINA: Please tell me. Do these people have good judgment?

CELESTINE: At the moment I'm spending time with some astrologers.

AUGUSTINA: Do you honestly think that knowing some astrology has anything to do with good judgment? Those who think they know the stars and can predict their movements know nothing about conducting their own lives.

CELESTINE: I suppose that you're right. But you're pushing me too hard. If I listen to you any longer, I think that I'll end up surrendering to your argument.

AUGUSTINA: I would be delighted with such an outcome. You would be wiser and happier. But I don't think that we should limit ourselves to a purely human wisdom. Ours must be one that has God for its principle and its end.

9. See Proverbs 31:10–31.

CELESTINE: What? First you try to make me behave, and now you try to make me pious?

AUGUSTINE: The fact is that you can't have one without the other. How awkward it would be if we settled for a human wisdom that had no final reward!

ON EMINENCE [10]

EUPHROSINA: What are they trying to say when they say, "This person has eminence?" I never know if it's a criticism or some kind of praise.

MELANIE: Miss, I'm delighted that you brought up this subject, because I was confused by this same term quite a while ago. And I find that people use it today in ways that are not accurate.

AUGUSTINA: But what is eminence in fact?

SOPHIE: I think it's to have a heart greater than one's fortune and to want to rise above everything by the stint of one's merit.

AUGUSTINA: What? To want to be greater than one's father?

SOPHIE: Yes, and to place no limits on one's ambition.

AUGUSTINA: But in that case you have a useless desire, because you are always the son of your father, and nothing else.

SOPHIE: But people can achieve certain positions or honors that make them greater lords than their father was.

MELANIE: Your ideas make a strong match with the spirit of our age, where you can see servants riding in carriages and nobles walking on foot. So, Miss, do you think that these servants have some eminence?

SOPHIE: Absolutely. And I can't think of anything else more worthy of praise.

HORTENSE: I have a very different point of view on this. I've always considered that sort of climber with contempt. I find them nothing short of insolent.

MELANIE: Then I would ascribe insolence rather than eminence to them.

EUPHROSINA: In that case, just how do you understand eminence?

MELANIE: True eminence is respecting only virtue. It is knowing how to live without fortune when it passes us by and how to avoid being intoxi-

10. This translation is based on Madame de Maintenon, *Sur l'élévation*, LC, BMV, F.729, 301–6. Derived from the Latin noun *elevatio*, the term *élévation* (eminence) originally referred to the physical act of raising an object. In the seventeenth century the term acquired a new psychological meaning: the comparative nobility or eminence of a person's mind. Maintenon often employs the term in the latter sense.

cated by fortune when it is favorable to us. It is knowing how to bring consolation to the unfortunate and never to hold them in contempt. It is the
willingness to be of assistance to everyone without wanting anything disproportionate to what we are.

SOPHIE: You would refuse a position someone offered you if it was too
far above you?

MELANIE: No, but if I tried to grasp it, I wouldn't call it a matter of
eminence.

EUPHROSINA: Then just what do they mean by "eminence" today?

MELANIE: An ambition without limit, wanting to become richer and
more prominent than the greatest of lords. It uses huge sums to buy titles
from people most of us would not even dare to speak to. It marries their
children and creates a household where nearly everyone except the master
is a noble.

HORTENSE: I would call that true madness.

MELANIE: I've always felt the same way. Still that's what they call eminence these days. They consider with contempt anyone who wants to do
the trade of his father and remain within the limits of his state, who is happy
with little, who lives modestly, who sees himself clearly just as he is, and
who believes that there are many people above him.

HORTENSE: You just gave a picture of true wisdom.

SOPHIE: What? If it pleased fortune to make me rise socially and if my
master wanted to make me a great lord, do you think that wisdom would require me to refuse this elevation?

MELANIE: No, but you should always recognize that neither fortune
nor your master could ever give you a birth other than the one you have. You
could enjoy this good luck but should never abuse it, because even with this
advantage, there are still many miserable people who are still above you.

SOPHIE: You seem to think that it makes no difference whether I am
born to the nobility or among the dregs of the masses. You seem to think
that there is really no difference between these states.

MELANIE: There are degrees of nobility. We should see ourselves as we
truly are. We should only raise ourselves up by our merit. That's where true
eminence is found.

AUGUSTINA: Just what do you think this merit consists of?

HORTENSE: I think it involves seeing things as they are and not valu-
ing them more than they are worth. It means being above the grip of chance
and acting in such a way that good luck clearly has not made us lose our head.

SOPHIE: If you were a soldier, don't you think you would like to become a marshal of France?

HORTENSE: Perhaps I might like to do my job so well that I would gradually arrive at that goal.

SOPHIE: And you wouldn't criticize an intention so distant from your humble estate?

HORTENSE: It seems to me I already told you that true eminence consists in wanting to merit everything. Let me finish this discussion with a good story. A poor soldier managed by his merit and by all kinds of war experience to become a general. One day he got into an argument with a very powerful lord. The lord reproached him for having such a high rank, since he had been born in dire poverty. The man responded, "It's true that I am nothing, but I'm convinced that if you had been born as I was, you would never have arrived where I am now."

EUPHROSINA: Don't you find this reply far too bold?

HORTENSE: If something can permit us to become the equal of those who are above us, it surely must be being more courageous than they are.

ON REASON[11]

ADELAIDE: If I may say so, I think that chance has brought together a very fine group today.

ANASTASIA: I'd gladly say the same thing.

MARCELLE: As for me, I'm delighted to be here. I may not have earned a place here by merit. Still, I think that my taste for the company of reasonable people indicates that I have some claim to be with you.

ELEANOR: And reasonable people are so rare! It seems to me that it's easier to find wit than real reason these days.

EUPHROSINA: I think just as you do.

ODILE: But I find that wit is more pleasant than reason.

---

11. This translation is based on Madame de Maintenon, *Sur la raison,* in *LC, BMV,* F.729, 178–85. Derived from the Latin noun *rationem,* the term *raison* (reason) had acquired multiple meanings by the seventeenth century: the faculty to think, a rule of thought or action, an argument or proof, a power to restrain emotion. By the end of the Middle Ages *raison* had acquired a specific philosophical sense: discursive thought, which arrives at its conclusions by methodical and logical argument, characterized by particular care in its use of concepts and facts for proof. In the seventeenth century Descartes built on this specialized notion of *raison* to construct a series of "rationalist" theories whose truth relies neither on faith, nor on custom, nor on feeling. The derivative adjective *raisonnable* (reasonable) developed a somewhat different meaning. Although it denoted what is conformed to reason, it referred primarily to what is measured, balanced, and prudent in an individual's conduct. Maintenon uses the term primarily in its latter, practical sense.

ADELAIDE: Wit might provide some passing amusement, and reason might irritate us when it contradicts us. Still, in order to live together, reason is clearly preferable to wit.

ELEANOR: How can you love what contradicts us?

ADELAIDE: It's because the same power that contradicts us on one occasion encourages us on another. Nothing is more pleasant than the approval of a reasonable person.

ODILE: Reason has something quite serious and opposed to pleasure.

MARCELLE: But aren't you confusing reason there with severity?

ADELAIDE: Yes, this confusion is typical. We have such a grim concept of reason when nothing is really more likeable than reason.

EUPHROSINA: But don't you find that people who are always reasoning are just boring?

ADELAIDE: But if they're always reasoning, they're not being reasonable. Obviously, we shouldn't reason all the time.

ELEANOR: But why not? What could they do that would be a better use of their time?

ADELAIDE: Some affability, some joy, some amusement, some silence, some sympathy, some attention to the needs of others.

MARCELLE: You offer a very attractive idea of reason when you add such accessories.

ADELAIDE: I don't think that reason is always severe, bristling, critical. It gives everything its due measure. It wants children to play games, adolescents to pursue innocent amusements, older people to look for real relaxation.

ANASTASIA: You're making quite a case for its allure. Give us some evidence for its solid value.

ADELAIDE: It adapts itself to everything. It's sympathetic with the weaknesses of others; it reduces its own. It consoles in times of affliction, and it knows how to foresee them. It moderates the use of pleasure. Now it plunges into social life, now it withdraws. It respects health, but it doesn't go to pieces over illness. It uses twists of fate. If need be, it knows how to live in poverty. It's peaceful, and it tries to bring peace to every possible place. It makes the best out of the most unfortunate situations.

EUPHROSINA: What a handsome portrait! I don't think that anyone knows reason as well as you do.

ADELAIDE: I still haven't said everything I could say about it. And it's certain that I still don't know the entire extent of reason.

MARCELLE: Then do you esteem it above everything else?

ADELAIDE: Yes, of course. You can never have too much of it. You must cultivate it so that it grows, because there is nothing more important for yourself or for others.

ANASTASIA: But surely you can't favor it over piety.

ADELAIDE: True, because piety can save without reason, but piety would accomplish far more good if it were ruled by reason. Piety can easily be misled, but reason never. Piety can be too emotional. That's never the case with reason.

ELEANOR: Honestly, I think that you like reason too much. It seems to me you're placing it above all the virtues.

ADELAIDE: The virtues need reason to act wisely and to avoid all extremes of behavior.

EUPHROSINA: Just what would reason do against a case of bad luck?

ADELAIDE: It would make the victim endure it with greater firmness. It would make her so attractive and so admirable that she would find people to give her some relief in her troubles.

MARCELLE: Miss X has a good bit of reason. Is she happier in her state of retreat from the world?

ADELAIDE: Don't doubt it for a minute. She finds strength in her reflections. She understands that many face situations more tragic than her own. Every evening she counts the days spent by those who are happier than herself—and she recognizes that nothing will remain from their fleeting pleasures. She is loved by the people with whom she lives, because she only thinks of pleasing them. She adapts to their tastes, to their customs, to their rules. In return these people do what they can to ease her situation.

ANASTASIA: So you think that the others are also reasonable?

ADELAIDE: It is possible for reason to soften and even to win over even the coarsest people.

MARCELLE: What you claim for reason is what others usually claim for wisdom, for righteousness, and for presence of mind.

ADELAIDE: I hardly think it's a catastrophe if we mix up all the fine things you just cited.

EUPHROSINA: But where does this reason come from?

ADELAIDE: It comes from God, who deigns to be called sovereign reason.

ELEANOR: This was certainly a useful conversation. You've given us a great desire to be reasonable.

ADELAIDE: Let's make sure to be reasonable in deed as in word. Those who only learn how to reason in their conversations don't really have true reason at all.

ODILE: I must admit that you've reconciled me to the demands of reason. Your explanation of reason is very different from what I previously thought about it. I think that each of us should start to obtain a better knowledge of reason through our personal reflections.

MARCELLE: Remember that Miss Adelaide said that it's nothing to reason only in our thoughts or in our speech. Reason must rule our entire conduct.

ODILE: But, Miss, we don't always have the power to govern our actions by reason. Sometimes we're forced to do things that don't seem to follow reason. We're dependent on the will of others. A husband wants to spend money when he doesn't have it—and he doesn't want you interfering in his business. A mother brings you into the world when reason seems to indicate that you should be taken out of it.

MARCELLE: We were just told that reason makes the best of everything. In the first case you cited, reason would try to adjust itself to the will of the one on whom you depend and try to limit these unwise expenses as much as possible. Reason would try to prevent the complete loss of an unreasonable person.

ADELAIDE: This is an inexhaustible topic for conversation. Whatever examples you may come up with, you'll see that reason always finds its place and manages to do good everywhere.

ON PIETY [12]

HORTENSE: Miss, I'm delighted to find you here today, because I've tried to see you so many times. They always tell me at your home that you're over at Madame X's.

SOPHIE: It's true that I often go there.

HORTENSE: She must be delighted to have the company of someone like yourself.

MELANIE: I never thought I would be jealous of Mme X. But that's just how I feel now.

HORTENSE: I don't think you're really jealous of her.

MELANIE: However that may be, I still envy her happiness.

---

12. This translation is based on Madame de Maintenon, *Sur la dévotion,* in *Conseils et instructions,* 1:192–98. Derived from the Latin noun *devotio,* the term *dévotion* (piety) originally designated any profound attachment, especially one characterized by love. By the sixteenth century the term had narrowed to refer to one type of affective attachment: religious devotion. In Maintenon's dialogues *dévotion* often refers to the virtue of piety or to a life of prayer.

SOPHIE: Miss, I think it would be better for me to go to see her than to remain much longer with you.

HORTENSE: If I were alone, Miss, I wouldn't dare to say that your taste seems very odd to me, but since I have such good company with me, I must admit that I don't understand why you would want to leave us to go over to Mme X's.

SOPHIE: You must always seek out what is disagreeable, Miss, and leave what you find pleasant.

AGLAIA: What a strange moral view!

HENRIETTA: I don't think it will please many people.

SOPHIE: That doesn't make it less true or less necessary.

HORTENSE: What? Do you think then that it's a good thing to search out what displeases you?

SOPHIE: Why otherwise, Miss, do you think I would seek out Mme X?

MELANIE: And you would avoid us out of the same principle?

SOPHIE: Of course. In fact, at the moment, I'm saddened to lose the pleasure of hearing you all talk.

HORTENSE: Do you think then that piety must involve no pleasure?

SOPHIE: Yes, Miss, I do. I'm not aware of any other sort of piety.

AGLAIA: What a grim view of religious devotion!

HENRIETTA: It's worse than that! It's positively dreadful!

MELANIE: But, Miss, do you find something in our conversation that might be offensive to God?

SOPHIE: No, Miss. On the contrary, I find it full of joy and of pleasure.

HORTENSE: If you found some pleasure in hearing someone speak about God, would you try to deprive yourself of that conversation?

SOPHIE: I would at least be suspicious about it.

MELANIE: What if your feelings inclined you to help your neighbor?

SOPHIE: In that case, my charity would count for very little.

AGLAIA: And if you felt a certain attraction for work among the heretics?

SOPHIE: I wouldn't expect a great reward.

MELANIE: If you felt a certain delight in consecrating your life to God and becoming a nun?

SOPHIE: What would such an easy vocation be worth?

AGLAIA: Honestly, Miss, you haven't thought this through. Do you think that having emotional inclinations toward the good is some kind of misfortune?

SOPHIE: Virtue only exists in combat.

HORTENSE: But we always have enough or even too many occasions for moral combat, since all of our inclinations do not lean toward the acquisition of the good. I think that, rather than trying to distance ourselves from our good affections, we should try to follow them in order to serve God.

SOPHIE: Just what are you saying, Miss? Follow our feelings? On the contrary, we must never cease to oppose them.

AGLAIA: Well, I look to please my teachers. So now I am going to try to enrage them.

MELANIE: I like to live calmly. So now I am going to try to make myself angry.

SOPHIE: Miss, you're making this into a joke. But it's still true that we have to mortify ourselves morning, noon, and night.

HORTENSE: Of course, Miss, in what might offend God and when we are trying to do penance for sin. But we shouldn't use mortification simply to avoid all pleasure.

SOPHIE: But every upsurge of pleasure should give us pause.

HORTENSE: Do you mean that you find no pleasure in serving God?

AGLAIA: Don't you eat at all? After all, there's pleasure in it.

MELANIE: I don't think there's any greater pleasure than to do one's duty and to have nothing to reproach oneself for.

HORTENSE: The yoke of God is easy. One day spent in His house is worth more than a thousand spent elsewhere. When we love God, love makes everything pleasant. Not only do pleasures then seem even more delectable to us, but we are then able to find some pleasure even in the crosses that He deigns to send us.

MELANIE: How blessed are those born with emotions that guide them toward God!

AGLAIA: How sweet it is to approach the pleasures one will share with God!

HENRIETTA: You can't serve God without experiencing that it is wonderful to be with Him!

SOPHIE: Everything that pleases us is bad. We should never let ourselves succumb to it. We have to keep rowing all our lives. We should tremble when something delights us and be grateful when everything seems to oppose us.

HORTENSE: You offer an idea of piety that would be quite dangerous for young people. As for me, I would give them a very different idea, because I believe that there is nothing so delightful as loving God. I do agree that we can't be saved without doing some violence to ourselves, but when we do it for God's sake, we experience rewards for it even in this life.

MELANIE: We have to oppose violently whatever leads us to evil, but we should follow our inclination when it leads us to doing God's law. We should bless Him for having enlightened us so early in our lives, and we should pray for those who were deprived of an education comparable to ours.

AGLAIA: I'm committed to serving God all my life. Still, I hope to delight in everything that is innocent.

ON PRIVILEGE [13]

CLAIRE: I've often come here without having had the honor of seeing you. And I must tell you, Madame, that several of your friends have made the same complaint.

THE LADY: It's true that more and more I prefer solitude.

AURORA: But how can you tolerate it, given how accustomed you were to high society?

THE LADY: Perhaps that's the reason why. I think that nothing so fosters disgust for social life as knowing it well.

LUCY: But you cut such a fine figure in it. That must have helped you to love it.

AURORA: I'd give half my life to be able to live the life I saw you pursuing.

CLEMENCE: You enjoyed a life of complete privilege. It was as if you enjoyed an endless holiday in a Spanish castle.

AURORA: The friendship with the powerful, the grand receptions in your honor—who could desire anything more?

LUCY: In fact, Madame managed to have the best of both worlds. She had the use and the luxury of wealth, but since she wasn't rich herself, she never became the object of envy.

CLEMENTINA: She was loved and admired. She developed a reputation for moderation in the midst of the greatest wealth and prestige.

THE LADY: I agree partially with what you're saying. But I can tell you without any exaggeration that I was one of the most unhappy people in the world.

CLAIRE: Is that because by temperament you tend to be melancholic and difficult to please?

THE LADY: No, by temperament I'm rather happy, joyous, and serene. As a matter of fact, it doesn't take much for me to be happy.

---

13. This translation is based on Madame de Maintenon, *Sur la faveur*, in *LC*, BMV, Ms. F.729, 91–97. Derived from the Latin noun *favor*, the term *faveur* (privilege) originally possessed a religious meaning: the approbation of the gods. Its meaning later expanded to indicate approval and support by any individual or group. In the seventeenth century the term also referred to the privileges granted to the person enjoying this approval. It is in this latter sense that Maintenon employs the term in this dialogue.

AURORA: But you were able to take whatever position you wanted. You were the mistress of everything.

THE LADY: I was the mistress of everything that wasn't important to me. But not for a moment could I command what I really wanted.

CLAIRE: What could you possibly want that you didn't already have?

THE LADY: To do good and at least sometimes to be really free.

LUCY: It seems to me that being necessary to the powerful of the world is a rather delightful form of slavery.

THE LADY: There is no such thing as delightful slavery. Furthermore, the friendship of the powerful is only present at the beginning of the relationship.

AURORA: You agree then that you had some happy times.

THE LADY: Vanity swells and inebriates you for a few moments, but these moments are quite brief. Then you start to feel the weight of your chains.

CLAIRE: But if you enjoy pleasures, you surely had your share of them.

THE LADY: You have them according to the tastes of the powerful, practically never according to your own.

CLEMENTINA: But if you wanted to have creature comforts, you could have had them.

THE LADY: It is more common to be refused than to receive what you ask for. Soon enough you have to steel yourself to desire nothing.

CLAIRE: I never thought you would learn how to become a philosopher at court!

THE LADY: Philosophy is not enough to deal with these problems. You must have a stronger source of assistance.

CLAIRE: Is it possible that your experience at court led you to cultivate piety?

THE LADY: I think it is as necessary for surviving a life of privilege as it is for surviving disgrace.

LUCY: But you would then be abandoning everything.

AURORA: But as long as you are in favor, you could still maintain some private pleasures. For example, you could still maintain the company of your close friends.

THE LADY: But when you're in favor at court, you no longer have any true friends. The position you hold becomes an object of jealousy and everyone wants to profit from it. There's no more real sociability, no more freedom, no more candor. Everything turns into manipulation, plots, feigned agreement. Bitter and limitless flattery carries all before it.

CLEMENTINA: But at least you still have family. You can't play games of rank with those who are close relations.

THE LADY: You become a stranger to your own family. Your brother becomes a spy and joins a cabal with others who are seeking some favor from you.

CLEMENTINA: But don't you think it's proper to want to advance your family interests?

THE LADY: Of course, but it's impossible to keep them happy. Their desires always transgress the bounds of the reasonable and even the possible. As a result, you suffer both from the effort expended to obtain certain concessions for them and by the fact that they are never satisfied.

CLAIRE: But what about this prince who so loves you that he has given you honors far greater than those given to his other subjects? Isn't he delighted to give you any pleasure you want?

THE LADY: This prince thinks that my only pleasure lies in seeing him and being loved by him.

CLEMENTINA: What? Without giving you any other sign of his friendship?

THE LADY: Princes are spoiled from their childhood. As soon as they begin to hear, they are told that the greatest possible happiness is just to see them. They build their ideas on this principle. And that's how they then form their philosophy and their conduct.

AURORA: I'm beginning to understand that the quickest way to happiness is to abandon everything in order to attach oneself to these princes. Then one can acquire happiness by having a share in their greatness.

THE LADY: But you must add that you must then share all their evils. You will suffer from their defects and their changing moods. You must be interested only in what interests them.

LUCY: In that case perhaps they're not so likeable after all.

THE LADY: There is nothing so cruel as to sacrifice your life, your work, and your time for someone whom you don't really love.

CLAIRE: Actually, Madame, you've succeeded in convincing me that there is nothing more dangerous than privilege and popularity. It's better to renounce them in order to live alone.

THE LADY: It's not as simple as that. When you have had such an exalted position, the transition can only come as a shock. It's as if you've been disgraced. Everyone mocks you. The privilege you once enjoyed never satisfied you, but you discover that it has spoiled you. Now you only seem to run into opposition and even persecutions. These are all the more painful because you've been so accustomed to compliments and flattery. Being deprived of them makes the sting all the sharper.

CLEMENTINA: But why would there be persecutions?

THE LADY: It's because you provoked jealousy when you rose above the others. Now that they have nothing to gain from you, they only want revenge.

CLAIRE: What's the remedy for such a grim situation?

THE LADY: The unique and universal remedy is devout piety.

ON CONSTRAINT [14]

MELANIE: At last, we have time for a chat. I thought of asking all of you what you thought constitutes happiness.

ATHENA: Being rich.

AUGUSTINA: For me, it would be being exalted over everything else I know.

SOPHIE: For me, it would be constant amusement.

FLORIDA: For me, it would be freedom from all constraints.

MELANIE: I don't think any of those conditions would produce real happiness. There's only one way that makes happiness possible.

ATHENA: Which one?

MELANIE: That of accepting some constraint. I think that everywhere you go, only the mad refuse all constraint.

FLORIDA: But then you're saying that we can never be happy.

HORTENSE: It's true that we are never perfectly happy, but there are many people who think they aren't unhappy because they have to accept a number of constraints.

FLORIDA: But I don't know a greater source of unhappiness.

MELANIE: That's because you don't yet know other causes of unhappiness. When you've come to experience greater causes, you won't be so critical of every constraint.

FLORIDA: But, Miss, isn't there some state where we don't have to accept constraints?

AUGUSTINA: If I were superior to all others in rank, what could possibly limit me?

HORTENSE: I think that there are very great constraints reserved for the most privileged positions.

ATHENA: Do you think that the king has to accept any restraints?

MELANIE: From morning 'til night.

FLORIDA: Oh, Miss! May I say that you're clearly exaggerating? After

14. This translation is based on Madame de Maintenon, *Sur la contrainte*, in LC, BMV, Ms. F.729, 260–64.

all, at least in his free time, he accepts no constraints, because if there were constraints, he couldn't enjoy any real pleasures.

MELANIE: If I'm exaggerating, you must agree that you are just as extreme, if you think that the least limitation somehow destroys all pleasure.

FLORDIA: Let's return to the king. Just what constraints do you think he endures?

HORTENSE: He wakes up every day at an assigned hour for the convenience of his attendants. It's impossible for him to have days when he rises earlier or later. He has to dress in public in order to please the grand lords of the realm, even though on many occasions he would prefer to be alone. In the same way he must dine in public and according to the strictest rules of etiquette.

MELANIE: He must work with his ministers, and this isn't always a pleasant affair. He must receive foreign ambassadors and hold public audiences. He must listen to things that secretly irritate or enrage him. Can all of this possibly be done without accepting some constraints?

HORTENSE: When he goes hunting or pursues other pleasures, he must often drag along certain people he personally doesn't like. He can't afford to offend or slight certain people with powerful positions. He must often leave behind those people who really do let him relax, because he must always guard against the possibility of jealousy within the court. In other words, there is constraint wherever you look.

ATHENA: After listening to your description, I'd rather be a peasant than a king.

MELANIE: You have to accept constraints in order to keep working when you would rather rest. You have to accept obstacles in your family, which isn't always going to go along with you. You have to live in peace with your neighbors. You have to learn how to deal with your superiors and even with your inferiors. Everything is ruled by constraint.

FLORIDA: And what would happen to me if I just decided not to accept all these limitations?

HORTENSE: You would end up being hated, despised, and judged as insufferable. Everyone would avoid you.

FLORDIA: Miss, you've overwhelmed me with your arguments. So, if it's impossible to avoid constraint, teach me how to bear it.

MELANIE: I think that the best way to endure it is to expect it and to adapt yourself to it.

HORTENSE: In fact, when you are accustomed from a young age to be concerned about others, to forget yourself, and to take responsibilities upon yourself, it quickly becomes a habit.

FLORIDA: But what could ever repay us for such a martyrdom?

MELANIE: This martyrdom becomes sweeter with the passage of each day, as Miss just explained to you. A real happiness repays us when we become loved and respected for our service. Doesn't that count for something?

HORTENSE: Constraint is a necessity you can't avoid. There's no substitute for it. You'd have to go into a desert to avoid it.

SOPHIE: Actually you're giving me the desire to do just that, because you're saying that it's impossible for me to live in freedom.

MELANIE: It's up to you to choose either disordered afflictions or constraint, because I don't think that you could ever survive in a desert.

AUGUSTINA: But I always thought that constraint was something only for our childhood or for the convent.

MELANIE: One day you will see that your days here were the happiest and freest of your entire life.

ON THE NECESSITY OF DEPENDENCE [15]

ODILE: Let's amuse ourselves today by imagining what we would do if we left here and were out in society.

HORTENSE: I refuse to even entertain the thought. I fear nothing more than the day I leave here.

AURELIA: Miss Odile doesn't want to speak about what she will do but what she would do if she only dreamed about it.

VICTORIA: But why rely on your imagination when you'll be more unhappy afterward?

MELANIE: Because if we only limit ourselves to what we can expect, we'd always be glum and we'd never be entertained.

ADELAIDE: And you think that you can make a pastime out of something that will never happen?

ODILE: Yes, Miss. Isn't it just common sense to try to have as much fun as you can?

VICTORIA: I'd prefer that we really look closely at what will happen to me once I leave Saint-Cyr.

AURELIA: Now what possible purpose can be served by dredging up some anxiety prematurely?

ODILE: It's not a question of inflicting some anxiety. If we prepare ourselves for our future, we'll be less thrown by it.

---

15. This translation is based on Madame de Maintenon, *Sur la nécessité de la dépendance,* in LC, BMV, Ms. F.729, 236–42.

MELANIE: Even if we have some tears to wipe away, at least we would be free. It seems to me that this freedom makes everything else tolerable.

HORTENSE: Describe this state of freedom to me. I must admit that I don't understand it.

MELANIE: I call freedom doing whatever I have a mind to.

HORTENSE: Let's get down to specifics. When you leave Saint-Cyr, where will you go?

MELANIE: I will go with my father. He won't bother me. He's often out. I will be the mistress of the house.

HORTENSE: That's all very general. What will you do in the morning?

MELANIE: I'd get up late, put myself together, then go to Mass.

VICTORIA: With whom? All alone?

MELANIE: A servant will follow me.

HORTENSE: So you think you'll have a maid, who just has to follow you and adapt to your every whim. But you have to give her direction. So here you are back from Mass.

ODILE: She'll sit down to dinner, if her father has returned.

ADELAIDE: And if he hasn't.

AURELIA: She'll wait for him.

HORTENSE: There she is—dependent on someone.

ADELAIDE: And if it's a bad dinner, poorly served, who will be blamed?

VICTORIA: The mistress of the house, of course. And what would you then say?

HORTENSE: Let's get beyond the dinner. Your father has gone out. Now what becomes of you?

MELANIE: I would make or receive visits.

VICTORIA: But you don't know anyone. You're only twenty years old and you think you'll be making and receiving visits? Who will accompany you?

AURELIA: Some friend of her mother.

HORTENSE: So you really can't do anything by yourself. You're now dependent on the mood, the desires, the health, and the will of this friend.

ODILE: I don't like this particular scenario. Let's imagine another one. Pretend that I have neither father nor mother.

ADELAIDE: All right! Let's go back to the morning. Where are you going?

ODILE: I'm going to see a princess. She gives me what I need to be really well dressed. I follow her to the balls, to the theater, to meet high society. I enjoy fine foods.

VICTORIA: Do you get along with her well?

ODILE: I am her favorite.

ADELAIDE: Does she permit you to leave her? Can you take a rest? Can you look at whatever takes your fancy? In other words, do you have a moment of freedom left?

AURELIA: You don't leave any place for religion in your projects. I want to have some. I want to retire somewhere with someone who thinks like me. We could put our goods together, do the same works, and enjoy the same pastimes. We could serve each other and achieve our salvation together.

HORTENSE: For the sake of appearances, she should be older.

AURELIA: Aren't there some older people who are quite reasonable?

HORTENSE: Undoubtedly. Usually they're more reasonable than others. But, as we already pointed out, you'll have to submit to this woman's mood, will, and state of health. In fact, you would be more dependent than you've ever been at Saint-Cyr. You'd be committed to a much more austere life. I only see a small room and the church. I only see poor clothing and a strict distance from every worldly pleasure. A convent would be less austere.

ODILE: You drive me to despair, Miss. I no longer know which side of the argument to support. For a bit of consolation, let me imagine that I'm living in what they call a castle in Spain.

HORTENSE: Your request is granted.

ODILE: I am now a widow. I'm rich, without children, without close relatives. I'm mistress of my own life, with enough maturity to determine my own course in life. I have a townhouse for the winter and a country manor for the summer. I only live to be entertained. Now you can't deny that I'm happy.

HORTENSE: Unless something happens to disturb you.

AURELIA: But what could happen?

ADELAIDE: The injustice of a neighbor who starts a legal case against you, the insolence of a peasant who doesn't respect women.

VICTORIA: A poacher who kills the game on your estate.

ADELAIDE: Some lord who argues with you over places in church.

ODILE: Well, justice is for everyone.

HORTENSE: So there you are at trial and dependent on the decision of your judges.

AURELIA: I'd like to add an amendment to Miss's idea. In addition to all this, I would be protected by the court, which always supports my cause.

HORTENSE: Really? Without your giving the court any services in return? Without your lending the court some clear token of approval? Without your being assiduous in being present at court?

ADELAIDE: These ideas are simply impractical.

ODILE: Well, then! What do you want to conclude from all this?

HORTENSE: That men very much depend on each other; women even more so; that we are actually weak and timid; that we need to be helped and protected. This is so obvious that we wouldn't dare to remain in a house without men.

VICTORIA: We wouldn't dare take a long trip without having a man accompany us, because we would the run the risk of all kinds of attack.

ODILE: But convents don't have men.

HORTENSE: They have some outside to protect them.

AURELIA: But how many homes in Paris are occupied by women alone?

ADELAIDE: Their neighbors protect them, if they know how to merit this protection.

ODILE: Well, the conclusion of all this seems to be that we are in a pretty miserable state.

HORTENSE: Yes, when we aren't reasonable, when we want impossible things. We have nothing but misery when we refuse to accept our state in life. We must live in a state of dependence, which we just saw is impossible to avoid.

ON THE DRAWBACKS OF MARRIAGE [16]

CLOTILDA: Ladies, I'm delighted to have the honor of your company. Personally I couldn't have made a better choice of companions than the choice made for us by chance.

ATHENA: You've seemed so melancholy these past few days that we decided to try to cheer you up. That's why we came here.

CECILIA: Right now, though, your mood seems to have changed.

CLOTILDA: I couldn't be sad around you. But I must admit that the closer I come to leaving here, the more concerned I become about my fate.

MELANIE: Each day brings suffering enough. Why worry about the future?

CLOTILDA: It may be true that each day brings its own sorrows, but it's still a good thing to think about what we want to do later.

ROSALIE: There's no destiny that doesn't have its drawbacks.

ALEXANDRINA: Still, we should try to weigh them. It's always good to be forearmed.

CLOTILDA: That's just what I've been trying to do.

---

16. This translation is based on Madame de Maintenon, *Sur les inconvénients du mariage,* in *LMM,* 196–206.

MELANIE: A vocation to be a nun is obviously the most difficult. I just don't understand how anyone can stay locked up in a cloister for the rest of her days.

ALEXANDRINA: But don't you think that marriage is also a kind of imprisonment? Does it take less endurance for this destiny rather than the other?

CLOTILDA: I tremble when I think that you have to give yourself over to a master you don't even know.

MELANIE: But would you have any better knowledge of the Mother Superior whom you would have to obey?

CECILIA: She might turn out to be very unreasonable.

ALEXANDRINA: Your husband might turn out to be even worse. He doesn't have to obey any particular rule. You are subject to his every whim.

CLOTILDA: In a convent you know what they expect from you. If there are certain people you must obey, there are also many in the same position as you. They're not going to put up with someone who orders you to do something other than what the rule of the order requires.

ROSALIE: Don't even talk to me about a rule and about sacrificing your freedom.

ALEXANDRINA: But don't you sacrifice it with a husband?

MELANIE: But there are any number of kindly husbands, doting husbands who love you and whom you love in return.

CLOTILDA: Undoubtedly, but there's no guarantee that you'll end up with a happy choice. Further, even the best husbands tend to act like tyrants.

ROSALIE: Why do you insist that all men are tyrants?

ALEXANDRINA: It's because duty is tyrannical. No matter how sweet a husband may be, he wants you to be a completely devoted wife. He wants you to live only for him and for your family.

ATHENA: According to you, just what are the duties of a devoted wife?

CLOTILDA: To forget herself and to think only about her family.

CECILIA: Forget herself? Now there's a convent phrase you rarely hear in the world.

ALEXANDRINA: It may be a convent phrase, but it's a social fact. If you glance at the typical day of a devoted wife, you'll see that she scarcely has any time for herself.

CECILIA: A woman awakens, washes herself, dresses herself, receives visitors, takes a walk, plays—that doesn't seem so austere.

MELANIE: She goes to shows, she makes friends, and she has a good time.

ALEXANDRINA: And you think her husband would be happy with all that? You imagine one who is unusually tolerant.

CLOTILDA: And aren't you supposing that this wife was willing to risk her reputation?

ROSALIE: I don't think all these activities are incompatible with maintaining a good reputation.

ATHENA: I wanted to speak about a devoted wife who never risked her good name. I just don't understand how anyone could even risk her reputation.

ALEXANDRINA: A devoted wife arises early in the morning to have more time. She starts with prayer. She gives her orders to the servants. She takes care of her children and is involved in their education. She hosts guests whom her husband brings occasionally to dinner, even if these guests are not always to her liking. She is the premier servant for making sure that everything is properly prepared. After the meal, she remains with her guests regardless of her own desires. After she is left alone, she works on her needlepoint or at her business. She writes to merchants. She rarely goes out. That is how the day ends. It starts the same way the next day.

MELANIE: If that's how a wife has to live, I'd rather become a hermit.

ATHENA: Yet, this wife is not an especially unhappy one.

ALEXANDRINA: True enough. I tried to make a portrait of a happy, serene, and relatively affluent wife.

CECILIA: Do you mean that it's possible to have a picture of one worse off?

ALEXANDRINA: Easily: that of a woman who loves her husband, but who is not loved by him, and who falls into jealousy.

MELANIE: That's terrible.

ATHENA: Or would you prefer one of a wife who hates her husband? He loves her, but she is irritated by all his attention, by his jealousy, by his tyrannical acts, and by the most terrible deeds imaginable.

ROSALIE: But those are exceptional cases. Describe for us a more common marital state.

ALEXANDRINA: Very well. A husband and wife live together honorably but their love is lukewarm. Thanks to the wife's demands, he brings the family to bankruptcy and the family members end up as paupers. This tragedy is not so rare.

ATHENA: Another couple lives together well enough, but the woman is overwhelmed by her numerous pregnancies. I knew one who lost control of her limbs with each new pregnancy and who ended up losing complete control of her arms and legs. I saw that they had to carry her everywhere. I don't have the time to give you all the cases of similar suffering. And I'm sure that there are many more we simply don't know about.

ALEXANDRINA: A woman commits herself to death and slavery when she marries. There are too many examples to argue the contrary.

CLOTILDA: Truly, Miss, you make me very afraid of marriage. Do you want then that all of these girls become nuns?

ALEXANDRINA: No, I'd be very disturbed by that, because an insincere nun is no happier than a married woman.

ROSALIE: So then what do you want us to do?

ALEXANDRINA: I want you to understand the problems in all states of life. Don't imagine that there are any which are happiness itself.

ATHENA: What would you counsel a good friend to do?

ALEXANDRINA: To pray to God very carefully before choosing a particular state.

CECILIA: So you're sending us back to piety.

ALEXANDRINA: It's the only thing that can help us endure the burdens of life.

ON THE DIFFERENT STATES IN LIFE [17]

LUCILLE: I often hear it said that the different social states are confused with each other these days. I don't clearly understand what people are trying to say by this.

CONSTANCE: I'll gladly explain it to you. No one is more disturbed than I am by this social upheaval.

LUCILLE: Thank you very kindly.

CONSTANCE: People are perfectly right when they say that the difference between the social states has been lost these days, because you never see anyone who is happy to remain in his or her social position. Everyone wants to be more important than someone else. The gentleman wants to be a lord. The lord wants to be a prince. The prince wants to be as great a prince as those who are above him, and so on.

EUGENIA: But just why do we have these social differences in the first place? When you are born a gentleman, why do you have to defer to some-

---

17. This translation is based on Madame de Maintenon, *Sur les différents états*, in *LMM*, 293–304. In archaic English the term *état* is often translated as "estate." Hence, the "three estates" of ancient France: the clergy, the nobility, and the commons. However, since the term is used more loosely in this dialogue to designate a variety of social conditions, *état* has been translated as "social state" or as "state in life."

one else who thinks he belongs to a better family because he has more wealth or a better office than the other one has?

CONSTANCE: This protocol isn't just a matter of personal opinion. It's a question of truth. There's even a certain public consensus one must respect.

ALPHONSINA: I don't know what you mean by the term, "public consensus."

LUCILLE: I think it's what everyone believes and says, and what passes for true, although you cannot prove it.

PLACIDA: But anyway, Miss, please explain more about this confusion of social states, where you would like to place a little more order.

CONSTANCE: It is certain that God has placed human beings in different social states. If they were wise, they would remain within their proper state of life, because there is not one of them that is not honorable.

LUCILLE: Do you find the condition of a peasant something honorable?

CONSTANCE: Very much so. We couldn't live without them. How would we live, if someone didn't work the earth and harvest the wheat?

LUCILLE: I agree that it's necessary, but I still find it a base condition.

EUGENIA: All the different kinds of work are necessary. In this state as in the others, it's individual merit that distinguishes one person from another.

PLACIDA: What merit could a peasant have other than working well?

CONSTANCE: The same as in other kinds of work: to live as a good and honorable person. There is a scarcely a single village where you do not find some peasant whose probity of life is known to all and who becomes a confidant for the others. They have good sense and a good soul.

PLACIDA: Have you actually spoken with them?

CONSTANCE: Often.

PLACIDA: Frankly, I'd be embarrassed if someone saw me talking to a peasant.

ALPHONSINA: These are the ideas of a child who knows nothing of life. The king himself would happily speak to them. I'm sure he has done so on many occasions.

LUCILLE: Do you think they would be comfortable with our style of conversation?

CONSTANCE: No, you must speak to them about their own concerns: their work, their families, the goods of the land. On these subjects, you will find them bright, well-informed, and most reasonable.

LUCILLE: Please indicate the various degrees of the different social conditions.

CONSTANCE: Next, you have the artisans in the towns and the cities. These states are also necessary and honorable. You'll find much of the good sense I just talked about in them. Next, you have the merchants, who are useful to the public and to trade. Among them you have what we call "the bourgeois." These are the aldermen, the elected officials, and the dignitaries who govern the cities and maintain civic order. For the security of material goods, you have notaries who are preoccupied with the placement and the value of money.

ALPHONSINA: Then there are the public prosecutors who draw up the necessary papers to let judges know the reasons for various trials.

CONSTANCE: There are the lawyers who plead the cases.

ALPHONSINA: There are the counselors and the presiding judges.

EUGENIA: And all those you just named are separated by degrees of social distinction?

CONSTANCE: Yes, the prosecutor is less eminent than the lawyer, the lawyer less than the counselor, the counselor less than the judge, and so on.

EUGENIA: I didn't think there were so many social degrees in the nobility. Personally, I think that once you can prove you were born a gentleman, greater or lesser really doesn't mean anything.

ALPHONSINA: The nobility has several degrees. There are the more ancient noble families. There are other noble families made so by great wealth, or by marriage, or by some kind of illustrious service. These are basically the different ranks.

EUGENIA: But all these distinctions don't change the fact that the most ancient nobility is still the most noble of all.

ALPHONSINA: That may be literally true, but it is also true that you must defer to rank. For example, this gentleman who can prove that his family has been noble for five hundred years must yield in precedence to a Marshal of France,[18] even if the latter came from a less ancient house.

LUCILLE: I would find it very difficult to yield to anything obtained through wealth.

CONSTANCE: Wealth often has a great role in these elevations to the nobility, but the will of kings is also central here. They want to reward merit, encourage others to emulation, give a token of friendship. When we're truly wise, we defer to these various conventions and customs.

EUGENIA: We have to yield to force, but surely you'll admit that this is not easy to endure.

18. *Maréchal* designates the highest rank in the French military.

ALPHONSINA: Everyone loses when there is social disorder. If you don't want to submit to those above you, those below you will feel likewise toward you. Your social inferior will rebel, will fight you over who goes first through the doorway or who takes what seat in church. This disorder will reach right down to the peasants.

CONSTANCE: If you were the only one who had to defer to someone else, this would be more difficult to bear. But let's say that you must defer to a great lord in your province. He in turn must defer to someone with a title, the titled person to a prince, this prince to an even greater prince, this last prince to the king. But the king must also defer: to reason, to the laws, to custom, and especially to the will of God.

EUGENIA: What difference is there among princes?

ALPHONSINA: As in the nobility, the oldest houses are not necessarily those that hold the greatest rank. But since it is so difficult to find the right rule of precedence here, they try to avoid appearing together as much as is possible.

PLACIDA: Now if kings found themselves together, what would they do?

CONSTANCE: In the kings and in the princes, there are different degrees. These derive from the relative greatness, power, and extent of the kingdoms.

ALPHONSINA: The king of Portugal certainly has no claim against the king of Spain.

CONSTANCE: Neither would the king of Denmark against the king of France.

PLACIDA: What are the greatest kings or kingdoms?

ALPHONSINA: France, Spain, and England.

PLACIDA: And of these three, who is the most eminent?

CONSTANCE: That is a contested point. But we saw our king give his hand to the king of Spain,[19] and we see him everyday treating the king of England[20] as if this king were above him.

PLACIDA: Does he do this because he recognizes that they are greater than he is?

ALPHONSINA: No, it's just that in his own home he shows them the same honor and courtesy old friends would show each other.

PLACIDA: But, really now, who is the greatest?

19. King Phillip V of Spain.
20. King James II of England.

ALPHONSINA: Without contest, it's obvious that the greatest house we know is that of the Bourbons, who presently govern us.

ON CURRENT DISCUSSIONS [21]

VICTORIA: Ladies, have you heard about the new law they just passed against printed fabrics? [22]

CLOTILDE: I just heard about it. I am astonished that the king and his ministers bother about such trifles when there are so many serious issues to deal with.

MELANIE: Truly, it just makes no difference whether you're wearing some printed fabric or taffeta.

ROSALIE: It must be some special interest that managed to launch this attack against the poor people who sell this kind of merchandise.

VICTORIA: We only see injustice these days. A few days ago I heard people condemning an injustice done to a man who only wanted to sell shoes at a discount. He just wanted the freedom to sell these shoes at low cost, but the authorities turned him down.

ROSALIE: Well, that's not the way to encourage competition. You should be giving rewards to those who come up with innovations.

CLOTILDE: Is there any injustice comparable to these property taxes? [23] When you think what a poor worker has to pay to the king!

MELANIE: And the poor man has only his work to feed himself and his entire family!

VICTORIA: We'll never finish this discussion if we try to list all the kinds of violence that the authorities do these days. But I wonder if

---

21. This translation is based on Madame de Maintenon, *Sur les discours populaires,* in LC, BMV, Ms. F.729, 162–71.

22. The law (*arrêt*) discussed here confirmed the trade decrees of Colbert, Louis XIV's finance minister, issued in 1664, 1667, and 1671. The law mandated high tariffs to protect the French textile industry against cheaper imports, especially from the Netherlands, then the center of the textile trade. While popular with the owners and workers in the domestic textile industry, the protective tariffs were widely unpopular with French consumers, especially aristocratic and bourgeois women. The entire dialogue defends the protectionist economic policies of Louis XIV's government against its free-trade critics.

23. The tax criticized here is the *taille,* a tax placed on commoners and calculated according to the extent (*taille*) of one's holdings. Implemented by the financial administration of Colbert (1661–83) to combat the chronic French deficit, the *taille* fell with particular harshness on land-owning peasants. The exemption of the clergy and the nobility from this tax increased popular resentment toward it.

Pauline and Celestine think as we do about this. They've been quite silent so far.

PAULINE: It's true, ladies, that I have a very different view on this. I think it will be easy to convince you that there's really no injustice behind everything you've just discussed.

CELESTINE: As a matter of fact, I can prove that there's a great deal of justice, of reason, and of goodness behind all these things.

MELANIE: What? How can you possibly find all these virtues in the law forbidding us to use these printed fabrics?

PAULINE: One of the great problems in the kingdom is that money moves out of it. It leaves to buy the merchandise you can't find in France.

CELESTINE: One of the great achievements of a kingdom is the establishment of various kinds of manufacturing. But these factories fail when people don't buy their products. And people don't buy them when they have the freedom to buy products coming from abroad.

PAULINE: Women, who determine society's taste in fashion, always prefer things that come from a distance.

VICTORIA: Well, I feel a little more enlightened about the issue of fabrics. But what would you ladies say about this poor shoemaker?

PAULINE: I would say that his initiative is admirable. He should be able to sell his shoes, but he shouldn't be able to set the price on his own, because this concession to him could easily ruin all the other shoemakers.

VICTORIA: But couldn't the others use his innovations?

PAULINE: An innovation that enriches one person, but that leads many to the poorhouse, would be a bad innovation indeed.

CELESTINE: Miss, I think that your shoemaker should be able to sell and profit from the new way of making shoes he has invented. Undoubtedly his project will be profitable. Then the others can imitate him. They would earn a little less than he, but everyone would be better off than before.

PAULINE: Nothing is so unjust as granting privileges concerning the necessities of life.

CLOTILDE: I'm not too sure what a privilege is.

PAULINE: It happens when one individual, exclusive of all others, receives permission to make or to sell a particular item.

CLOTILDE: Would you also like to prove that it's right to impose taxes on a man who relies only on his work to feed his entire family?

CELESTINE: He couldn't even feed his family in peace if the prince didn't provide for the family's security. He would be the object of pillage by his enemies if the soldiers didn't protect him.

MELANIE: True enough, but why does this impoverished man have to be the one who pays the solider?

PAULINE: Who else will pay him? The king has no private wealth. He takes money from his subjects in order to give it back to them.

CLOTILDE: Who started these rights?

CELESTINE: Whoever established kings and sovereigns. As soon as Caesar existed, we paid a tribute to Caesar.

CLOTILDE: What is a tribute?

PAULINE: A token of subjection, a recognition of the rights of one's sovereign.

ROSALIE: But wouldn't it be better for a prince to leave his subjects in abundance, peacefully living from their work?

CELESTINE: We already said that you need armies to protect you against your neighbors. Moreover, even without this reason, people would scarcely have a motive to work if they just lived in abundance.

ROSALIE: They could just rest then. What would be wrong with that?

PAULINE: What would happen to us if no one wanted to serve us and do what is necessary to provide our food, our clothing, our housing? What would happen to the earth if it were not cultivated? Everything that is harvested requires work. People must need to work.

CELESTINE: How many evils would attend this sloth! How many vices, debaucheries, feuds, quarrels! If it's important for educated people to keep busy, how much more important it is for all these rough and uneducated people!

PAULINE: These pupils have a good character and are clearly influenced by a pious faith. Experience will teach them that pious intentions can easily be misplaced.

MELANIE: So, are you trying to convince us that there is no injustice, that everything is as it should be, and that the unfortunate are rightly so?

PAULINE: No, Miss, there is nothing perfect in this world. Although the laws and the orders of the prince may be just, the execution of them is often faulty. Their authority serves as the cover for a thousand injustices. But that's an evil we have always had and we always will. There's no solution for it.

VICTORIA: But why is there no solution?

CELESTINE: Because human beings are very imperfect. The best government is the one that does the least amount of harm. But it's simply not possible to avoid all imperfections.

VICTORIA: So we should pay attention to complaints of injustice, since you yourself agree that people are suffering and will always be suffering.

PAULINE: No, we can't tolerate complaints and criticisms coming from people as well-educated and as enlightened as you are here.

CELESTINE: Not only should we ourselves avoid such behavior, we should oppose such behavior in others. We should try to console them when they complain and try to let them see reason in their situation.

MELANIE: But what reason can you give to console someone in an unfortunate state? What about someone whose meager wealth is found only in his hard work, while others lounge about in ease and comfort?

CELESTINE: A good worker and a good artisan are usually happier than we are. They earn their bread and lead a more tranquil life than the powerful do.

PAULINE: God has created different states in life. If people would just remain peacefully in their own state, everything would go better.

VICTORIA: I never thought that discussing printed fabrics would lead us to such serious issues.

CELESTINE: We should examine everything as seriously as we are doing now. Otherwise, we will end up being carried away by the flood of bad arguments people make without having really studied the issues in depth.

VICTORIA: People will say that we treat these issues this way because we were raised in a place totally committed to the king and to his approval.

PAULINE: Rather, they will see that we know what our duties are. We fear God, honor the king, and submit ourselves to all authority.

MELANIE: What! Do you really want me to submit to the will of some village judge?

CELESTINE: Absolutely. All authority comes from the prince. You must know that.

VICTORIA: That seems tyrannical to me.

CELESTINE: That's because you don't want to see the reason behind it. This tyranny is actually to your advantage when it places your life and your possessions in security. When this security is threatened, you are only too happy to use the police, the judges, and everything else that helps to repair the harm someone did to you.

PAULINE: Ladies, don't you see that all these criticisms are made without any real reflection? Is there anything more violent, more tyrannical, and more unjust than the power that men give themselves to kill other men just like them? Ladies, how could we even live if we didn't punish such crimes?

VICTORIA: Ladies, you are so convincing that it's impossible to resist your arguments. I hereby resolve to profit from everything you just told us.

ON EDUCATION AT SAINT-CYR [24]

ELEANOR: Ladies, I'm delighted with the dialogues they give us to entertain ourselves. It's impossible to find something so entertaining, yet so useful.

FLORIDA: It's true, Miss, that all the games they might permit us to play would give us less pleasure.

OLYMPIADE: Speak for yourself, Miss. Personally I could never understand how something educational could also be entertaining.

DOROTHY: Now, Miss, it's not possible that you really believe what you're saying.

CLEMENTINE: Miss, you're most unfortunate if you think that something educational must always be boring.

OLYMPIADE: Well, Miss, do you think it's right to laugh during the sermon or during catechism class?

ELEANOR: No, Miss, but I think it's possible to experience pleasure without laughing.

OLYMPIADE: It seems to me that laughing is the best part of pleasure.

EUPHROSINA: But Miss, wouldn't you find pleasure in seeing the happiness of someone you love? Still, you wouldn't laugh about it, would you?

DOROTHY: And if this person owes this happiness to you, wouldn't you have a heart full of joy? Still, you wouldn't laugh about it, would you?

OLYMPIADE: I don't see too clearly just what I think about these issues. What you just said made me rethink my position. I know very well that I wouldn't laugh in a situation like that. Still, I must confess that I'm never so relaxed as when I laugh.

EUPHROSINA: Laughter arises from something that surprises us and that seems pleasant or ridiculous to us. But there are things that give us much greater pleasure.

OLYMPIADE: But if I agree with what you say, just where are these great pleasures that you claim to find in the dialogues that they've made us perform for a good while?

FLORIDA: How could you find greater pleasures? We perform, others listen to us, we say things full of wit and truth.

EUPRHOSINA: Our mind is enlightened on certain things that we might never have known. At the very least, it would have required us to have had some lengthy experience.

24. This translation is based on Madame de Maintenon, *Sur l'éducation de Saint-Cyr*, in *LMM*, 177–84.

ELEANOR: It's not just our mind that is enlightened. Our heart is formed in all kinds of virtue.

OLYMPIADE: Ladies, your pleasures seem very serious indeed.

EUPHROSINA: They are still no less pleasures.

OLYMPIADE: But don't you think it's possible that you might find it much more amusing to jump, to dance, to play at different kinds of games, rather than to study what indiscretion is, to grasp the difference between intelligence and wit, to learn an infinity of the things they are urging us to learn?

DOROTHY: Miss, would you rather spend your time playing *La Belle Germaine*?[25]

CLEMENTINE: Or singing, "Who owns this cart that comes and goes?"[26]

OLYMPIADE: Don't make fun of me, ladies. I'm not the only one who likes this sort of thing. These games have existed since children have walked the earth. You don't have to force children to come up with definitions in order to enjoy these games.

ELEANOR: Honestly, Miss, at this very moment aren't you trying to support a losing cause with a great deal of argument?

OLYMPIADE: It's true that I'm having a good time in seeing all of you arguing against me. But I must confess that I'm disturbed by the relentless desire to instruct us that seems to reign around here.

DOROTHY: What you're saying, Miss, seems strangely opposed to something that is good.

OLYMPIADE: It's only natural, Miss.

DOROTHY: But this is a corruption of nature. Shouldn't we abandon it and try to profit from the extraordinary concern they show for our welfare here?

OLYMPIADE: Sorry, Miss, but the education at Saint-Cyr isn't exempt from criticism.

ELEANOR: How is that possible, Miss? It seems that everyone admires and rightly admires the education here.

OLYMPIADE: Critics argue that they try to make us too clever here and that we're less happy than we could be because of this.

EUPHROSINA: Personally, I never thought that by instructing us in our religion and by shaping our reason, they could make us unhappy.

---

25. A popular children's game of the period.
26. A popular children's folk song of the period.

OLYMPIADE: They say that we might have developed too much wit for the people with whom we will have to live.

ELEANOR: It seems to me that our teachers are trying to strengthen our reason rather than to flatter our wit.

EUPHROSINA: The more Christian and the more reasonable we become, the more we shall know how to adjust to the destiny that God deigns to send us. The reason they cultivate in us will help us to endure life with those who lack reason.

ADDRESSES TO STUDENTS

VOLUME EDITOR'S INTRODUCTION

Usually presented in the classrooms at Saint-Cyr, Maintenon's addresses to students are interviews in which Maintenon poses and fields questions on moral issues. Like her dramatic dialogues, the addresses often clarify a particular virtue which the pupils must pursue. Justice, courage, temperance, and glory pass in review. The intellectual virtues hold a comparatively minor place in the Maintenonian universe. Wisdom is more a type of prudence than of intellectual prowess.

Cognizant of the aristocratic background of her audience, Maintenon presents a number of addresses on the class-based issue of politeness. *Of Politeness* and *Of Civility* explain more than the etiquette of opening a door or of bowing to a dignitary. They celebrate the discreet, self-sacrificial charity that characterizes the soul of the authentically polite woman.

Many of the addresses detail the probable vocational paths to be taken by a Saint-Cyr alumna. *Of Religious Vocations* depicts the convent, while *Of the Single Life* examines the comparative merits of married and unmarried life. Each address presents a realistic portrait of the restrictions on freedom facing women in each state of life. *Of the World* and *How to Maintain a Good Reputation* provide a series of cautionary tales on the moral dangers awaiting provincial aristocratic women. In *Of Education and of the Advantages of a Demanding Upbringing*, Maintenon defends the need of a strict pedagogy to disabuse students of their illusions concerning their freedom and their future.

Sensitive to questions of social class, the addresses also clearly appeal to the gendered concerns of her exclusively female audience. *Of True Glory* redefines the virtue of glory in terms of the deportment and character proper to a prudent woman. *Against Religious Innovations* examines why women often find themselves attracted to dissident religious movements, such as Jansenism. Like many other addresses, *Of Avoiding the Occasions of Sin* unmasks the cynical strategies by which men seduce women into the destruction of their reputations. Capped by a harrowing depiction of an abortion, this address graphically describes the sexual exploitation of women.

In *Of Education and of the Advantages of a Demanding Upbringing*, Maintenon focuses on one particular source of the oppression of women: the neglect of their education. Not only does she denounce the slovenly education of royalty and nobility in general; she criticizes the specific injustice of contemporary education of women, which is often little more than a superficial apprenticeship in the social graces.

The structure of most of the addresses is dialogical. Maintenon and several of the pupils mutually question each other on a moral issue relevant to students of their age. Although there is little doubt about the moral truth to which Maintenon is leading the pupils, the addresses often manifest a surprising give-and-take. Maintenon both praises and criticizes the questions and responses offered by the students. On occasion the students criticize the positions taken by Maintenon. In *Of True Glory*, Mademoiselle de Mornay complains that Maintenon's warnings on the danger of communications with unknown men had digressed from the lecture's announced topic of glory.

As in her dramatic dialogues, Maintenon often employs edifying tales drawn from her experience at court to illustrate her moral counsels. Louis XIV is featured as the embodiment of justice in *Of the Cardinal Virtues* and as the harried worker in *Of the Utility of Reflection*. In a remarkably self-flattering portrait, Maintenon herself serves as the icon of piety and efficiency in the autobiographical *Portrait of a Reasonable Person*.

As an ensemble, the addresses sketch the moral character of the ideal aristocratic woman who is to emerge from the chrysalis of Saint-Cyr. Pious, considerate, temperate, patient, and polite, she exudes the inexhaustible desire to serve that is so characteristic of Maintenon's temperament. But in their more somber passages, the addresses warn the students that these steely virtues will be tested in Spartan convents and impoverished manor-houses ruled by unreasonable superiors and husbands.

On the surface the addresses appear to encourage women to accept their social subordination to men. As critics of Maintenon have argued, the addresses often underscore virtues, such as obedience and reverence, allied to submission. But many of the addresses also defend the legitimate freedom and authority of women. *Of the Cardinal Virtues* presents an elaborate typology of justice (simple justice, equity, disinterestedness) to show the right and the duty of women to use reason to resolve disputes in a variety of circumstances. *Of Politeness* and *Of Civility* explore how women should exercise their power in the governance of pupils and of servants. *Of the World* examines the skills for marriage and other states of life required for women to use their authority successfully in the tasks of domestic management. If many of the addresses defend the dependence of women on male authorities, *Of True Glory* praises the independence of women in its heroic portrait of the widow who is economically self-sufficient through hard work and through the refusal to rely on the resources of others. In their portrait of the ideal Saint-Cyr woman, the addresses balance the virtues of deference with the virtues of personal judiciousness and personal initiative.

In treating the legitimate power of women Maintenon frequently employs a double language. The strictures against women's authority are often contradicted by Maintenon's own exercise of that authority. *Against Religious Innovations* illustrates Maintenon's double-edged rhetoric in the religious sphere. On the surface Maintenon explicitly argues that women should not engage in theological controversy, a domain allegedly reserved to male clerics. But the entire address is nothing but Maintenon's own engagement in theological controversy. With scriptural citations in hand she defends the controversial Catholic doctrines of papal infallibility, of indulgences, and of sacramental confession. She defends the Jesuits against the Jansenists in the dispute over Jesuit casuistry occasioned by Blaise Pascal's *Provincial Letters*. In her discussion of spiritual reading, she praises several mainstream French and Spanish Catholic authors but condemns the Jansenist literature produced by the priest, nuns, and lay associates of Port-Royal.

This tension between Maintenon's theoretical subordination of women and her practical empowerment of them is not confined to the religious sector. In many addresses passages that appear to justify the social subordination of women coexist uneasily with other passages depicting the oppression present within that subordination and detailing educational and work-related practices that will mitigate this oppression.

OF THE CARDINAL VIRTUES [1]

When she was with the "blue" class, Mme de Maintenon spoke to the pupils on the cardinal virtues.

---

1. This translation is based on Madame de Maintenon, *Instruction de Madame de Maintenon aux demoiselles de la classe bleue: Des vertus cardinales*, in *LE*, BMV, Ms. P.66, 355–65. The audience for this address was the "blue" class, composed of pupils from seventeen to twenty years of age. The address was originally delivered in 1705.

First, she said that the word *cardinal* was taken from the Latin word for "hinge," because just as a door revolves on its hinges, so must our conduct revolve around these four virtues, which contain all the others. She exhorted them to love them. They should practice the virtues and not limit themselves simply to knowing how to define them. In that way they would begin to acquire merit as early as possible.

Mlle de Villeneuve[2] asked her in what merit consisted.

She answered, "Having a good collection of virtues and other good dispositions. Religion and reason hold pride of place."

Then she explained what justice was. She said that a just action consists in giving each person what is her due. It also involves accepting that people treat us as we deserve.

Mme de Maintenon then asked, "What do we merit when we've done something wrong? What is your answer, Mademoiselle de Landonie [*sic*]?"[3]

Mlle de Landonie replied, "We deserve punishment."

Mme de Maintenon said, "Yes, it's right for us to suffer when someone punishes us for having done something wrong. Moreover, it's one of the best ways to make reparation for our faults. No one else can do that for us. It's a sign of a good soul to be able to recognize her faults and accept punishment. On the contrary, it's a petty soul who is incapable of recognizing her faults and who searches for false excuses to justify them."

Next she said, "Beyond this sort of justice, which should exist in all our actions, there is another kind present in our judgments, which is called 'equity.' This equity frees us from being dominated by our likes and our dislikes. It permits us to form objective ideas about every situation. With it we can distinguish good from evil, even to the point of seeing faults in our friends without being blinded by our affection for them and of sincerely recognizing the good points in people whom we like the least or who are most opposed to us.

"Now I'm not saying that we have any obligation to reveal the faults of our friends, since friendship commits us to conceal them and easily excuse them, unless there is some grave evil we must stop. However, justice demands that we should judge good as good and evil as evil, regardless of our feelings concerning the persons in whom we find one or the other.

"The surest rule to avoid mistakes in judgments is to conform them as closely as possible to God's judgments, manifest in Holy Scripture, especially in the Gospel. The second rule, also taken from the Gospel, is to judge

2. Mlle de Villeneuve de Gramont was born in 1689 (*MRSC,* 430).
3. Apparently Mlle Couradin de Laudonie, who was born in 1685 (*MRSC,* 427).

others as we want to be judged, to think and to speak about them as we would like them to speak and to think about us, and to treat them in every way as we ourselves would like to be treated.[4]

"But there is another degree of justice even more excellent than this and which requires yet another virtue: that of disinterestedness. It makes us capable of judging against ourselves in favor of those who have right on their side. There are many people with sufficient sense of equity to judge the cases of others. However, once they have a personal interest in the outcome, they are incapable of seeing beyond their interest. This is opposed to justice, which insists that we should decide in favor of the stronger case, wherever it may be found.

"On this question the king performed an action which aroused widespread praise and admiration. Some time ago there was legal action pending against several inhabitants of Paris. They had thought that in an area of Paris where the ramparts were falling down, they were free to construct their homes. Some years later, the fiscal agents of the king came to the following conclusion: since this land legally belonged to the king, the houses constructed there must also belong to the crown. At the very least, those who built these houses without permission should pay for the value of the land on which the houses stand. The defendants insisted that the long time during which they had occupied these houses had given them sufficient title to them.

"The controversy was appealed to the king and judged in his presence. Half of the judges sided with the crown. The other half sided with the defendants. This show of conscientious judgment was praiseworthy in itself, since the king was personally present. Now it's a law of the kingdom that in the trials judged before the king, when there is an even split among the judges, the king personally determines which side has won. It only took the king's will to give his own side the victory. Since the split was equal, he could have supported the side favorable to himself. But instead of doing so, he chose the side opposed to the crown. He said that since there were good arguments on both sides, he would rather relinquish some of his rights than push them in a way that might prejudice those of his subjects.

"Let's turn now to prudence. It's a virtue that regulates all our words and our actions according to reason and to religion. It helps us to determine what to do or to omit, to say or to be silent about, according to different circumstances. It is opposed to indiscretion, which involves speaking about the wrong things at the wrong times."

4. See Luke 6:31 and Matthew 7:12.

On this topic she asked Mlle de Saint-Maixent [*sic*]⁵ which of the following was a greater fault against charity: mocking someone for a physical defect or mocking someone for a moral defect?

This pupil responded that it would be criticizing someone for a moral defect.

Mme de Maintenon answered, "It's never proper to reveal anyone's faults. Charity urges us to excuse everything. But I find that it's cruel and reprehensible to mock someone for some physical defect which is not her fault and which cannot be corrected. Good hearts and good souls are incapable of laughing at these types of defects. They tolerate them and they charitably hide them out of kindness for those who have them. Personally I think it's more excusable to criticize a moral or intellectual flaw. After all, the person is capable of correcting or at least diminishing it. It's simply wrong to let this defect continue, although charity does forbid us from public reproaches, just as in the other cases.

"A good way to avoid indiscretion, which is so distasteful and intolerable in society, is to become prudent. We need to reflect on what we want to say, in order to make sure that there will be no evil consequences and that we will disturb no one.

"Temperance is a virtue that moderates us in everything. It makes us hold to a just middle between too much and too little. It is useful everywhere. It prevents us from being carried away by our emotions, either sad or joyful. If we laugh, it's in moderation and modesty. If we cry, we do so without abandoning ourselves completely to sorrow. We express our grief quietly and patiently. Temperance avoids all excess.

"I knew three people plunged into great grief by the death of their brother, equally beloved by them. One was so overwhelmed by grief that she banged her head against the wall, refused to eat, and gave every sign of being deranged. On the contrary, the other two wept so quietly, although bitterly, that they didn't surrender to the least gesture of excessive grief.

"Now which of these approaches to mourning do you consider the most reasonable? Undoubtedly the one which remained in the bounds of moderation and of patience.

"Temperance is necessary at any age. But it is especially important for you at your age. That's because the weakness of youth is its taste for pleasure and happiness. Everything tends to prevent this age from gaining temperance, although this age so clearly requires temperance to moderate its ardent appetite for play.

5. Apparently Mlle de la Roche-Aymon Saint-Maixent, who was born in 1700 and later married (*MRSC*, 434).

"Remember well what I'm going to tell you: every one who is not the mistress of herself will never acquire merit, either in the sight of God or in the sight of the world. You must be the mistress of yourself to prevent outbursts of laughter or other excessive demonstrations of emotion. Every corporal gesture showing your personal emotion violates moderation and, consequently, opposes temperance. You never hear a well-bred person laugh raucously. As you know, the Holy Spirit Himself says that the laughter of a fool is heard everywhere, because he laughs without control, but the laughter of a wise man is not heard, because even in laughter he is the master of all emotions and knows how to moderate them.[6]

"Fortitude is the virtue that makes us pursue our projects courageously and that makes us overcome obstacles we find in ourselves and in others. We achieve the good we are pursuing without surrendering to the difficulties that emerge. We withstand irritating events with firmness and without any weakening of resolve.

"Mlle de Beauvais,[7] who needs this virtue of fortitude the most?"

The pupil replied, "The person who has the greatest faults in this area, the person whose faults are the most difficult to destroy."

Mme de Maintenon said, "Yes, I think the way you do."

Then she added, "Now, do you think that those who have the greatest faults or who feel they didn't have a high birth should feel discouraged and imagine that they can never achieve the destruction of these faults?"

The pupil said, "No, Madame, because our merit depends on our work, aided by the grace of God."

Mme de Maintenon exclaimed, "Now there's an admirable answer! Never forget it, children. Our merit depends on our work.

"I'll leave you with this fine thought. When I return, we'll speak some more about this together."

OF POLITENESS [8]

Madame de Maintenon invited six of the most mature students of the "green" class to come to her apartment.

---

6. See Ecclesiastes 7:6.

7. Mlle de Beauvais de la Cossonière, born in 1697, later married (*MRSC*, 433).

8. This translation is based on Madame de Maintenon, *Instruction de Madame de Maintenon aux demoiselles de la classe verte: Sur la politesse*, in *LE, BMV*, Ms. P.68, 219–26. The original audience for this address was the "green" class, composed of students from eleven to fourteen years of age. The address was originally delivered in 1716. Derived from the Italian noun *politezza*, the term *politesse* (politeness) originally referred to a physical state of maximal cleanliness, such as resulted from the careful washing and polishing of wood. By the seventeenth century the term

She said to them, "My children, it's not to teach you catechism that I sent for you today. Rather, I wanted to talk to you about how to live politely and with proper manners. Since God has made you ladies by birth, have a lady's manners. May those of you who were properly raised by your parents conserve these manners. May the others try mightily to acquire them.

"This is more important than you imagine. Coarseness repels everyone, even the most virtuous people. Despite our best intentions, a lack of manners causes us to feel a certain disgust. It makes us avoid interacting with people who possess neither consideration, nor politeness, nor any knowledge of the proper way to live.

"I've often told you this in class, but the student body changes so quickly in your school that I must often repeat the same things. My children, I tell you once again that you can never start too early to begin to act politely with each other. This is the best way to become polite with everyone. Don't use slang with each other. Don't use your first names with each other. Get rid of those loud, common expressions that anyone would be astonished to find in the mouth of a lady.

"Let all your actions be graceful, sweet, and modest. Never use all your strength to open a door, a seat, or a book, as if you were a day laborer pushing a rock. Open the door gently. Do the same with a seat, a book, and other things. Don't pass in front of someone without making a bow. Do this with each other in order to develop the habit. Yield to others in front of a door or at least make some sign of polite recognition before you walk through it. Don't wait for someone else to be the first, as I've seen you do often enough.

"Never answer with a curt 'Yes' or 'No.' It is absolutely necessary to add, 'Yes, Sir,' 'No, Madame,' 'No, Mother,' 'No, Miss,' etc. Otherwise, you'll be acting like the most unlettered peasants. Never receive or present anything without making some preliminary gesture of politeness.

"Speak good French. Don't invent thousands of words which have no meaning and which are nowhere considered proper usage.

"Once again, my children, since God has given you noble birth, give yourselves noble manners and nobler sentiments. Realize once and for all that whatever virtue or merit or talent or other good traits you may have, you will be intolerable to well-bred people if you do not understand how to live properly.

---

had begun to denote the moral and intellectual culture of an individual. It often referred positively to the refinement of this culture. In salon society *politesse* often indicated the good taste and refined speech of an individual. By the end of the seventeenth century the term referred to conduct conforming to the conventions of cultivated society. It is in the latter sense that Maintenon often employs the term.

"Some time ago I realized the truth of this when a very virtuous young girl presented herself as a candidate for our novitiate. Her coarse manners, her poor posture, her voice tone, her uncouth expressions, and all her other traits displeased me so much that I had to force myself to act as if I didn't notice them.

"I no longer have enough strength to come up to your class as often as I did in the past. My children, I'm counting on you to tell your companions everything I told you. I trust that by your actions as well as by your words, you will inspire in them the desire to acquire the good manners we were just discussing. Although you've been given a small amount of authority over your companions, that doesn't mean that you have the right to speak to them in a haughty, or imperious, or dismissive way. On the contrary, you should try more than anyone else to do this with the utmost politeness, so that you may serve as a role model for the others.

"For example, you might say gently to one pupil, 'Would you have the kindness to move back so that you don't block the light for the other pupil?' To another, 'Please make a little space for the other pupil.' Another time you might say, 'You would make me very happy . . .' or to another pupil, '. . . If you would help her finish her needlepoint or help her go over something on which the schoolmistress is going to question her today.' And so on, through the thousands of things that present themselves for your consideration every day.

"Always maintain your external composure. Stand up straight. Carry your head well. Don't let your chin fall down. You have to show modesty by the way you carry your eyes, not your chin. Whatever you say or do, be careful not to anger or to inconvenience anyone. You must pay careful attention to this. Otherwise, you may find yourself constantly displeasing important members of society.

"If you are sitting down, be careful to bother no one, either by being too close or too far. Take the place that's right for you. Never take the place of someone else. Never become so close to someone that you would be able to push them. If by some unfortunate accident that happens, you must excuse yourself. Several days ago one of you pushed me rather rudely in trying to enter the classroom before me, without even seeming to notice it. I drew the conclusion that you must have the habit of treating each other this way. That's exactly what I would like to destroy forever. Your education is pointless unless you can rise to the level of this politeness which we are asking of you and which should become second nature to you.

"The small examples of consideration I just gave you should whet your desire to serve in all other situations. This politeness is applicable every-where. It must accompany all our external actions right down to the tone, the style, the method, and the manner with which we do them.

"Dear children, permit me to know that this interview has borne some fruit. Please work to make it useful to all your companions here. Please give them my greetings."

OF CIVILITY[9]

Mme de Maintenon had the goodness to ask the pupils on what subject they would like her to speak. Mlle de Bouloc[10] asked her to instruct them on civility.

She told them that civility had more to do with actions than with words and formulas of politeness. She said that there was only one sure rule for civility.

She said, "It's the Gospel that sheds such a clear light on the duties of civic life. You know that Our Lord said that we should do unto others what we want them to do unto us.[11] That's the great rule in this area. Still, it doesn't exclude certain conventions used in the countries in which we hap-pen to find ourselves.

"As for what concerns society, I would say that civility consists in for-getting yourself in order to devote yourself to the needs of others. It means paying attention to what can be a help or a hindrance, so that you can use one and avoid the other. It means not talking about yourself, not making others listen to you for too long, and listening attentively to others. It in-volves not letting the conversation focus on you and your own tastes. You should let it revolve naturally around the different concerns of others. It means moving away when you see people are trying to speak in confidence. It means thanking people for the least service and, *a fortiori*, for a great one.

"My children, you can do nothing better than to practice these good manners among yourselves and to make them so habitual for you that they

---

9. This translation is based on Madame de Maintenon, *Instruction de Madame de Maintenon aux demoiselles de la classe jaune: Sur la civilité,* in *LE,* BMV, Ms. P.65, 840–48. The audience for the ad-dress was the "yellow" class, composed of students from fourteen to seventeen years of age. The address was originally delivered in 1702. Derived from the Latin noun *civilitas,* the term *civilité* (civility) refers to courteous sociability. Starting in the sixteenth century, the term acquired a more specific meaning: the observation of the rules of conduct governing social life. In the sev-enteenth century many manuals of *civilité* employed the term in this restricted sense. Maintenon often uses the term in this rule-observant sense.

10. Mlle de Bouloc, born in 1684, later married (*MRSC,* 427).

11. See Matthew 7:12 and Luke 6:31.

become second nature. I assure you that this careful attention to the needs of others will help to make you beloved in social circles. For persons well born or well bred, this civility costs nothing. Most of you have both of these advantages, so use them to your benefit. The respect and affection that these considerate manners will bring you will more than compensate for the constraints you will experience at first.

"Believe me, my children, if you try to be polite, you will appear to be perfect, as you wait for true perfection to arrive. A polite person never shows anything except kindness. She knows how to control her mood so serenely that others can never guess any of the ambitions, or dreams, or even quirks that she might have.

"When you see society people who know how to live, even the most worldly and the least pious, you would think that they possessed a perfect virtue and humility. To see and to hear them, you would think that they have little concern for themselves and that they are completely devoted to the people with whom they speak—even when, as is often the case, they secretly hold these people in contempt.

"My children, I would like you to acquire these same fine external manners. Given how well educated you are, you can add to these the sentiments commanded by the Gospel: charity, respect of others, humble estimate of yourself. Don't you think it's shameful that uniquely worldly motives can inspire people to do by pride and vanity what our religion commands and, yet, we often fail to do? Our Christian faith adds an additional motive: this effort to avoid anything displeasing to our neighbor helps us to merit heaven."

Mlle de Rafiac[12] asked how one should thank a socially prominent person.

Mme de Maintenon replied, "As simply as possible. Just tell her, 'I humbly thank you, Madame. I'm very obliged to you.' Say other similar things.

"Personally, I don't ask for any compliments. But I certainly want to know if I'm making someone happy. I once knew a lady who received many fine presents. She even received substantial sums of money placed under her mattress. But she never thanked the donors, although she knew exactly who they were, since she saw them every day and even took her meals with them."

Mlle de Chaunac[13] said that she would be so appalled by this boorish behavior that she wouldn't give this lady any more gifts.

12. Mlle de Mealot de Rafiac, born in 1688, later married (*MRSC*, 429).
13. Mlle de Chaunac de Montglois, born in 1687, later married (*MRSC*, 428).

Mlle de Ragecourt [*sic*] [14] asked if one should thank a servant.

Mme de Maintenon replied, "Yes, but it's not necessary to get up. Just nod your head or say 'Thank you,' depending on the circumstances. You must be careful to avoid any affectation in this."

Mlle de La Gâtine [15] asked, "But what about a servant in our employ?"

Mme de Maintenon replied, "No, in that case it's not customary. However, I sometimes happen to do it. Still, it's usually not done."

"Should we thank someone else's chambermaid? And should we stand up to bow to her?"

She said, "It all depends on the circumstances. You should do it if you're not familiar with this person and if you don't have the run of the house. But if you're an habitual guest there, on familiar terms with everyone, a bow of the head or a word of acknowledgment is sufficient."

"Should we use the term 'Sir' in addressing servants?"

"Yes, when they're not yours. This honors both the master and the servant. I don't know anyone at the moment who wouldn't do this. However, the members of the king's entourage may call servants according to their royal function. For example, you should say, 'Coachman of the king, please stop,' and not 'Stop, coachman,' as you might say to your own coachman. In the same way you should say to the king's valet, 'Valet of the king, please give me a particular item.' This manner honors and pleases them. You know, of course, that the king has no servants as such. They carry the title of valet."

"Should we use the term 'Sir' with a craftsman who came to see us for family reasons?"

"It depends. Some of these people, who are accustomed to it, should be called 'Sir.' Others are rather poor people who would think that you're making fun of them by using this title. In this as in other cases, common sense is the only rule."

"If, when we enter a church, a man hands us holy water, should we take it from him?"

Madame de Maintenon answered, "Again, it depends. If this is someone we know well who's doing this out of courtesy, there's no harm in doing it once. But if this starts to become routine, we should appear not to notice it and should not take it."

"If, in crossing a ditch, a man gave us his hand to pass over, what should we do?"

"If you see that he's taking some pleasure in this and that the offer is af-

14. Mlle de Ragecour de Brémoncourt, born in 1687, later married (*MRSC*, 428).
15. Mlle Absolu de La Gatîne, born in 1686, later became a Bernardine nun (*MRSC*, 428).

fected, you should never give him your hand. However, if you were part of a group of women of good repute and a man of integrity gave everyone his hand out of courtesy, you should give yours to him, just as the others did."

"If a prominent person offered you some tobacco, could you refuse it?"

"I think it's a question of respect to take at least a little. If it bothers you, you could discreetly let the rest fall away."

Mlle de Saint-Bazile [16] asked why you don't bow to the king when you pass in front of him.

Mme de Maintenon said, "It's a matter of custom. Still, when the king bows to you, you must respond with a profound bow. He's the most courteous man in the world. He bows to the lowest subjects, even to chambermaids."

"Should we observe the same manners for the duchesse de Bourgogne?" [17]

Mme de Maintenon said, "Yes."

"Should we bow to a man we meet on our path?"

"Absolutely. You should acknowledge everyone you meet in passing. Only in great cities have they abandoned this custom. I knew a duke and peer who greeted everyone. He only lifted his hat. It was wonderful to see him in the court at Versailles, where we often had great crowds. He often greeted his own servant and lifted and removed his hat for him, just as for everyone else. Everyone talked about this and even made fun of him. But these actions only gained him greater respect."

"Should we bow when we are riding in a carriage?"

"No, unless you're dealing with people you know well or who are socially prominent. In that case you make the carriage stop, you roll down the windows, and you make a deep bow, especially if you're in the presence of the king or of some prince or princess. In all of this you should follow the customs of the country you are in. Some time ago I saw some ambassadors stand up in a carriage and make a deep bow. In France, you don't stand up, but you should make a profound bow.

"Good night, my beloved children. Remember everything we said at the beginning of this conversation concerning what the Gospel and I are asking

---

16. Mlle de Blanchard de St-Bazile was born in 1687 (*MRSC*, 428).

17. Marie-Adélaïde de Savoie, duchesse de Bourgogne (1685–1712), married Louis, duc de Bourgogne, son of the Grand Dauphin Louis and grandson of Louis XIV, in 1697. Mme de Maintenon personally supervised the education of the duchess, apparently destined to become a queen of France. Deeply attached to Maintenon, the duchess frequently visited Saint-Cyr and supported its various endeavors. The sudden death of this beloved in-law in 1712 deeply saddened Louis XIV and Maintenon in the closing years of Louis's reign.

of you in terms of Christian politeness. These two sources, of course, are of unequal authority. Still, everything is useful for good souls. I hope that both may prod you in the right direction."

OF TRUE GLORY [18]

The students of the "blue" class had asked Madame de Maintenon to speak to them about true glory.

She told them, "I think that true glory consists in loving one's honor and in never doing anything base."

Then she asked Mademoiselle des Bois [19] what "doing something base" meant. Mademoiselle des Bois answered that a base act would be, for example, divulging a secret or stealing.

Madame de Maintenon said, "It's true that all vice is base, and those acts that you just cited are great vices, but I'd like to discuss something closer to home. Receiving gifts could be a base action. It's better to refuse them from anyone except close relatives, like your father, your mother, a sister, or an aunt. Those people are safe. It is difficult to give absolute rules. They vary according to the family situation. Unfortunately, there's sometimes a libertine uncle or even brother that you should avoid, especially if they are without religion and hostile to your piety. They will mock you: 'What? Always in some church pew? Always saying your rosary? Always praying? You'd be better off keeping company with so and so.'

"If these proposed companions are dangerous, you should find some reason to excuse yourself or take so little part in the activities that they wouldn't dream about inviting you back a second time. If they are people who have lost their reputation, or even if they are the least bit suspect, you absolutely must refuse to go."

Mademoiselle de Partenay [20] asked if it was a base action to go to different people's homes for dinner.

Madame de Maintenon replied, "That could be, if you made a habit out of it. On occasion, you could go to visit someone and have dinner there, without having the intention of returning the favor. Ordinarily, however, it's better to live frugally at home rather than to try to find gourmet fare at somebody else's house.

18. The translation is based on Madame de Maintenon, *Instruction de Madame de Maintenon aux demoiselles de la classe bleue: Sur la bonne gloire,* in *LE,* BMV, Ms. P.66, 501–8. The audience for this address was the "blue" class, composed of students from seventeen to twenty years of age.

19. Mlle de Courtemanche des Bois, born in 1688, later married (*MRSC,* 429).

20. Mlle de Partenay d'Inval, born in 1693, later married (*MRSC,* 430).

"I always admired the mother of a Saint-Cyr student for the life she led. She started work early in the morning and kept at it the entire day. She lived from her savings in order to avoid being a burden to someone else."

Mademoiselle du Tot[21] asked, "Is it a base thing to work in order to buy something?"

Madame de Maintenon replied, "No, it's far more noble to live off one's work and one's savings than to live off one's friends. I made a skit for you out of the proverb, 'The worth of a man determines the worth of his land.' In it you see one man who loses everything because he neglected his possessions rather than working to make them worth something. You see another man who lives happily with his family, because he's conscientious in his business and he lives on little, only eating vegetables in order to guarantee some resources for his children. Which of these two manners of living would you prefer, Mademoiselle de Cugnac?"[22]

Mademoiselle de Cugnac said, "The second."

Madame de Maintenon said, "You're absolutely right. Still, that's easier said than done. You have to start saving at a young age. I wouldn't tell rich people, 'Go sell your embroidery.' But I would advise those who aren't so rich to do so. They couldn't do better."

Mademoiselle de Segonzague [*sic*][23] asked her how they should conduct themselves with men.

Madame de Maintenon said, "You must avoid them and never give them the least liberty with you. One day I was in the company of the king. In the room there were many women seated on chairs, because His Majesty grants many privileges to those who have the honor of seeing him often.[24] The king was still young and, as he chatted away, he pulled out the chairs of these ladies, letting them fall on the floor. They ended up in some very comical postures. However, he came to one lady—who wasn't from a more noble house than were the others—and he said, 'Ah! I wouldn't dare with this one.' In a few words he pronounced an entire eulogy about this lady. It's not by some affectation that you establish your reputation. It's by proper reserve in the presence of men. That in no way prevents you from being charming or natural, because true virtue is neither austere, nor pained, nor ferocious."

---

21. Mlle du Tot de Villefort, born in 1690, later married (*MRSC*, 430).

22. Mlle de Cugnac d'Immonville was born in 1685 (*MRSC*, 427).

23. Mlle de Bardon de Segonzac, born in 1690, later become a Capuchin nun (*MRSC*, 430).

24. An elaborate etiquette at Versailles governed the privilege of sitting in the king's presence during certain receptions and whether the privileged subject had the right to a stool or to a chair.

Mademoiselle des Miers [*sic*]²⁵ asked if a girl could write to someone without telling her mother about it.

Madame de Maintenon answered, "No. A girl must never do anything without the permission of her mother or of other persons on whom she depends. This is the proven method for avoiding serious mistakes. There is no reason to be furtive when you're not trying to do anything wrong."

A teacher asked what should be done if you receive a letter from someone unknown, especially if it's a man.

Mademoiselle d'Escoublant²⁶ answered that you should burn the letter after having read it.

Madame de Maintenon spoke up and said, "That's not sufficient. You shouldn't even read the letter. You should take it to your mother or to other people who act as your guardians. You should say to them, 'I recognize neither the seal nor the handwriting on this letter. Would you have the kindness to read it and to see what it's about? Personally, I don't want to know unless you judge that it's relevant.'

"It's dangerous for a girl to receive letters from men she doesn't know. These men only make advances to girls and to women whom they believe will be happy to entertain them. You must never write to any man, except to your immediate relatives, and even then only on family business or due to some real necessity."

Mademoiselle de Mornay²⁷ said that we were drifting away from true glory, which was supposed to be the subject of the conference. But Madame de Maintenon said that everything we had just discussed was tied to true glory. She said that there was nothing so glorious or so honorable as the establishment of a good reputation.

Then Madame de Maintenon asked Mademoiselle de Verdille²⁸ if it wasn't a good exercise in humility to accept the loss of our reputation. The student answered in the negative. Madame de Maintenon responded, "Your answer is absolutely correct. We must do everything to guard jealously our reputation."

A teacher said that she had always considered true glory, liberality, and generosity to be the same thing.

25. Mlle d'Esmier Chenon, born in 1691, later became a nun (*MRSC*, 430).

26. Mlle Anne-Françoise d'Escoublant de Fourneville, born in 1690, was professed as a Dame de Saint-Louis in 1711 and died at Saint-Cyr in 1765 (*MRSC*, 430).

27. Mlle de Mornay de Montchevreuil, born in 1687, later became a Benedictine nun (*MRSC*, 429).

28. Mlle de Livesnes de Verdille, born in 1698, later married (*MRSC*, 430).

Madame de Maintenon answered, "In effect, these virtues bear some resemblance, but generosity has something greater than liberality and is clearly superior. We naturally like to give something. Few people are simply against it. But there are few really generous people. Those who are generous always go beyond what you expect from them. They have a noble soul and a great heart, which makes them admired by everyone.

"Calling someone generous is one of the greatest praises we can give. Generosity is one of the finest qualities a person can possess. It abolishes self-interest. It makes you succeed in everything you endeavor, because it provides the courage to overcome the obstacles which prevent you from arriving at your ends. With generosity, you are simply incapable of base actions.

"False glory is the contrary of what I've just said about the true. It's really idiotic to be speaking always about our relatives, about their nobility, and about everything that concerns us. People subject to this defect quickly become insufferable, just like people who live without concern and without consideration for others. We usually can recognize nobility by its honesty, and even by its humility, by its concern to please others, to relieve pain, to avoid giving offense, to serve others.

"My children, clearly remember and understand that true nobles are inclined neither to brag about themselves nor to hold anyone in contempt. Haughty and disdainful airs always indicate a very petty person.

"Jeanne, this good vineyard worker who works for me—whom I so admire for her common sense and judgment—says sometimes, 'You know, poor people like us have certain virtues that other people just can't match.'"

"Goodbye, my children. Always cultivate true glory, not false glory, not pride."

PORTRAIT OF A REASONABLE PERSON [29]

Mme de Maintenon asked Mlle de Provieuse [*sic*] [30] if she knew what a reasonable girl was. The pupil didn't know how to answer this question.

Mme de Maintenon told her, "A reasonable person is someone who always does what she has a duty to do. She does it at every hour of the day.

---

29. This translation is based on Madame de Maintenon, *Instruction de Madame de Maintenon aux demoiselles de la classe rouge: Portrait d'une personne raisonnable,* in *LE,* BMV, Ms. P.65, 745–52. The audience for this address was the "red" class, composed of pupils from seven to eleven years of age. The address was originally delivered in 1701.

30. Mlle de Sacconin de Pravieux was born in 1693 (*MRSC,* 431).

She begins the day by wholeheartedly adoring God, not only because someone told her to do it or because the others do it, but because she knows it's proper to offer herself and everything that will happen to her that day to God.

"She arises promptly, dresses carefully, modestly, and as quickly as possible. She makes her bed well. She carefully puts away her clothes. Then she helps the younger pupils if she has some time remaining.

"She goes down to the classroom. She prays to God with reverence and devotion. She avoids any chatter or laughter, because nothing is more serious than prayer. After that she eats heartily. If it's permitted to speak, she does so; if not, she maintains her silence and focuses on God. She goes to the church choir to assist at Mass. She tries to take a good seat. She makes sure that her companions have enough room, and she seats herself accordingly. She doesn't look around to glance at those entering or leaving the church. She diligently follows each part of the Mass with the greatest reverence and devotion. Of all the things of religion, this is the holiest.

"She returns to her class, where she busies herself with the assignments. She tries hard to read and to write well. If she is capable of helping others to achieve this, she does so zealously, as if her entire life depended on it. She listens attentively and respectfully to what the teacher is saying. She tries to understand what is being said and to apply it to her interior and exterior conduct, if the subject matter permits.

"Before going to dinner, she makes her examination of conscience. She tries to see what she did to displease God that morning in order to ask His pardon and to make a resolution to do better the rest of the day. She especially focuses on whether she in any way fell into the principal fault she had committed herself to combat.

"Now we see our reasonable person in the refectory. What is she doing now? She is eating with a good appetite. She does not act like a glutton, with her head plunked down over her plate. She eats correctly and with good manners, because God wants us to find a certain pleasure in eating. Without any scrupulosity, she simply enjoys her meal. She listens to the reading at table with even greater pleasure. This is the principal object of her attention.

"She pursues recreation after dinner with the same wholeheartedness. She gladly jumps, dances, and plays whatever games the others desire. And she does all this joyfully. She always tries to cheer them up, because this reasonable person always does well whatever she has to do. It just would not be reasonable to be serious during recreation and to only want to talk about somber or pious things.

"Next she listens to the reading or the lecture. She tries to retain what she heard and to ask questions about what she didn't understand. She is as assiduous for the afternoon classes as she was for the morning ones. She works as hard as she can and never loses a minute. She sings with the others and is delighted to chant the praises of God. She listens to the catechism without any sign of boredom and tries to become knowledgeable about it. She goes to supper as she went to dinner. Next, during evening recreation, she once again walks, jumps, plays, and laughs, because this is a very happy person. She then prays and makes her examination of conscience. Then she goes to sleep, perfectly happy with her entire day."

Addressing herself to these young pupils, Mme de Maintenon said to them, "Don't you find all this perfectly reasonable? Isn't this all about adoring God, loving Him, and learning to serve Him? That is why we were placed on the earth. It is the first thing they teach us in the catechism, because it is the most important and the most necessary truth. You must learn to do this all the days of your life.

"Isn't it just as reasonable that young people learn to read, to work, and all the other things that you're shown here? When you return to the world, you'll be very happy to know how to do something useful either for your family, or for your relatives, or for yourself, according to the circumstances.

"It's also quite reasonable to be proud of certain of the advantages you have, my children. You are Christians. What a source of happiness that should be! So many people aren't and never will be! Here you are in a fine school, sheltered from all kinds of physical and spiritual evils. You are young and happy. So be proud of all this. My children, I pray God that all your life you will have as many reasons for legitimate pride as you have now."

Mlle de Saint-Bazile[31] said, "Our headmistress is always telling us about the importance of reason. She often says that if it were a piece of merchandise you could buy, she would surely buy some for each one of us."

Mme de Maintenon said, "In fact, it's an excellent piece of merchandise. Reason teaches us to adapt ourselves to everything, to live with different types of people, and to know how to survive without those who are personally more pleasing to us."

Mme de Gruel[32] said that a recent alumna of Saint-Cyr couldn't bear it with the people with whom she had to live, because they didn't lead lives of serious religious devotion.

Mme de Maintenon replied, "It's her devotion that wasn't serious

---

31. Mlle de Blanchard de St-Bazile was born in 1687 (*MRSC*, 428).

32. Mme Louise-Renée de Gruel, a teacher at Saint-Cyr, was professed as a Dame de Saint-Louis in 1699. She died at Saint-Cyr in 1730 at the age of fifty-two (*MRSC*, 412).

enough. She knew the definition of devotion, but she didn't practice it, because it consists in adapting yourself to your state in life and to the people with whom you have to live. A truly reasonable person knows just how to tolerate patiently people who aren't, without even letting them perceive that she is tolerating them. She makes a personal decision to be cordial with everyone she meets, so that nothing can really shock or disturb her.

"Perhaps you think that when you are adults you won't have to follow any more rules. Now I can assure you that if you are really as reasonable as I hope you to be, you will be wise enough to draw up a daily order for yourself which you will follow faithfully, if there's no such order imposed on you where you live. Usually, when we have nothing but our freedom to follow, we have no idea what to do.

"That's why some time ago, when several ladies and I were making a long journey that lasted about six weeks, the first thing that we did was to draw up a common daily order. Being with the Richelieu family for a good part of this time,[33] we organized our days in a most pleasant manner. We got up at the time we wanted, then went to the room of Mme de Richelieu to wish her a good morning, then went to Mass together, then returned to chat with her until dinner time. During dinner we listened to a pious reading, after which we conversed with each other as we worked on our needlework. It was during these weeks that I made the ornamental tapestry which I gave to the Dames de Saint-Louis. After our afternoon get-together, each of us retired to her room and did what she wanted. At half past three, we gathered back at Mme de Richelieu's room either for silent meditation or for song. At four o'clock, we took a walk until supper time. After supper, we chatted for about half an hour. After a time of prayer, made in common, each of us retired to her room.

"During these six weeks we never missed one detail of this daily order. This time has always seemed to me the happiest time in my life. I must confess that, since my arrival at court, I have never had a time as wonderful.

"My children, this should help you to see that you are not the only people who have to follow rules and regulations. Every reasonable person needs to have a rule of life. She or her spiritual director should draw one up. She should follow it faithfully, when nothing prevents it. We customarily have a negative opinion of a person who leads a disordered life, who gets up at all different hours, who has dinner at different hours, who does everything in such a chaotic way.

---

33. One of the close friends of Maintenon was Anne Poussart de Fors du Vigean, duchesse de Richelieu. Named a maid-of-honor to the Dauphine de Bavière (wife of the Grand Dauphin Louis, son of Louis XIV), Duchesse de Richelieu died in 1684.

"Goodbye, my children. If you truly become reasonable, you will become the most attractive women possible."

OF THE UTILITY OF REFLECTION [34]

"My dear children, I'm delighted to have found in you the same docility and simplicity which I found among the younger pupils. I intend this as a great compliment.

"If the Dames de Saint-Louis didn't love you so ardently and if they just sought their own comfort, they would relax their expectations of you. They would only concern themselves with how things are going on the exterior. However, since we love you for your own sake and since we are looking for your greatest good, we are going to work on forming your interior.

"I want to begin by teaching you how to profit from the moments of silence we have designated in the daily order. We did this for excellent reasons. I want to explain them to you. I think that you are wise enough to understand them.

"The first reason is to teach you how to maintain silence. Nothing is so disturbing in a girl as a tendency to speak all the time. Even if she is the wittiest person in the world and if she says wonderful things, it's still a grave fault.

"Another reason for these obligatory periods of silence is to give you the time to engage in serious reflection. We're convinced that if you know how to use this silence well, it will be more valuable than anything else to make you wise.

"In order to do this, however, you must understand what reflection is. Reflection is thinking attentively several times about the same thing. I'm afraid that you might be wasting the time you're supposed to be using for different reflections.

"For example, the appropriate reflections you should be making at the moment concern the state in life you will choose. You should be thinking about what you will become once you leave Saint-Cyr. You should be thinking about how you can apply yourself to the good states of life you hear about. You should be trying to imitate the conduct of wise people in this regard.

"The more pious should use this time to think about God and to enter

---

34. This translation is based on Madame de Maintenon, *Instruction de Madame de Maintenon aux demoiselles de la classe bleue: Sur l'utilité des réflexions, et qu'il ne faut point éviter la peine*, LE, BMV, Ms. P.66, 65–73. The audience for this address was the "blue" class, composed of students from seventeen to twenty years of age.

into dialogue with Him. Others could use the time to count from memory, to repeat a lesson in order to better understand it, to go over what they have learned by heart, to learn something, to narrate a story they would like to remember, or retell, or write down. In other words, always use your time usefully.

"I'm really curious to know just what happens in your minds when you are obliged to follow these periods of silence. I really would like to know. In any event, learn to keep this silence as you should and to make this time useful.

"I also want to discuss with you the various methods you are using to avoid any hard work or other difficulties. It seems that some of you believe that you are exempt from the common law and refuse to accept the least inconvenience. However, what you must tolerate now is nothing compared with what you are going to find in the world.

"There is no one who is exempt from suffering. For a long time I've had the honor to see the king close up. If anyone exists who should be able to shake off the yoke and have no problems, surely he's the one. However, he is always running into difficulties. Sometimes he must spend the entire day in his office, tallying up his accounts. I've often seen him working hard, looking for something, starting over again, and working until he has finished his business. He doesn't delegate this to his ministers. He doesn't rely on some official in the army. He has a detailed knowledge of his troops and of his regiments, just as I have a detailed class list for all of you. He holds several councils every day. These councils usually discuss the most disturbing questions: war, famine, losses, and other afflictions.

"At the moment he's actually responsible for the government of two great kingdoms, because nothing happens in Spain today without his order. The king of Spain has no money, so this has created new worries for our king. Business takes all of his time. He practically has no leisure left. Still, is there any social position that on the surface appears to be as free from worry as does the monarchy?

"The king's ministers—whose positions are so senselessly coveted and fought for—more than deserve anything they gain from their post, because of the burdens and exhaustion they must face. Monsieur de Chamillart,[35] for example, is in a perpetual state of work. He no longer has any time to relax, let alone to really entertain himself. He can't even find sufficient time to spend with his family. From dawn to dusk he does nothing but listen to bit-

35. Michel Chamillart (1652–1721), a member of the cabinet of Louis XIV, served as finance minister starting in 1699 and as war minister starting in 1701.

ter disputes: for example, does Pierre or Jacques have the right in this case? We are afraid that he might fall very ill. The burdens of office have changed him. He had his daughter come up nearer to him so that he could see her marriage. He couldn't go down to see her. Yet, this is a man many believe to be so fortunate.

"Judges must also face many difficulties. They spend their entire lives in studying disputes in which they have no personal interest. They must decide where the side of justice is. They must often defend the rights of the poor, who can never really reward these judges for the good they do for them.

"Bishops also have very great problems they must surmount when they do their duty. They are often hated when they must correct those who are not acting properly. They are always refusing dispensations demanded by people who don't really need them. Their pastoral visits in their dioceses often lead to dangerous exhaustion. Some time ago Monsieur de Noyon [36] told me that he had administered the sacrament of Confirmation to four thousand people in the same day. He thus had to repeat the words which are the form of this sacrament four thousand times. By the end of this ceremony he had become completely hoarse.

"I don't have the time to go through all the other states of life to help you see that there is not a single one where there isn't some kind of difficulty and some kind of hard work, either mental or physical. In war or in marriage, everyone experiences some kind of difficulty. I don't know any pupil at Saint-Cyr who would have it any other way. At least, that's true for most of you.

"We even see this problem in the games you play. You often don't want to work to find the right answer in a game. At times it seems that the greatest pleasure we could give you would be whispering the right answer immediately.

"I've always loved children. I think God has given me this special affection for you and other children. I've raised several of them myself. Just like you, they played various games where they had to think and search out the answer. Rather than trying to avoid difficulties, however, they actually increased them. They reduced their freedom to use anything they could to resolve their problem. For example, they strictly limited the material they could use to make some item of clothing, to decorate a kitchen, to furnish a room, or to make a meal.

"Your inclinations are very different from theirs. The first thing you say when we propose to do something is, 'That's too hard. That's impossible.

---

36. Claude-Maur d'Aubigny served as the bishop of Noyon (1701–7) and as archbishop of Rouen (1707–19).

I don't know how to do that.' When you do arithmetic, you don't try to find the sum. You want someone else to tell you the right answer so that you can avoid all the hard work. You're delighted to hear someone else tell you a story, but you don't want to accept the obligation of telling a story to other pupils.

"I remember that, after living for three years with my mother, she forbade my brother and me to talk about anything else when we were together than what we had just read in Plutarch.[37] His book contains the actions of the great men and women who distinguished themselves by their virtue or by some other memorable deed. We never could finish our discussions about this book. After we had done our reading, we always compared the relative merits of the deeds of each person. I would tell him that this woman was more distinguished than this man, because she did this or that action. My brother would prove that his hero was the more wonderful one. He would say that his hero performed a particular noble deed. I would run quickly to see if there wasn't something more striking done by someone else in the book.

"Both of us pressed our cases as passionately as we could. This amused us a great deal. Since our mother had forbidden us to speak about anything else, we found every conceivable pleasure in it rather than finding her command difficult or irritating. I'm afraid that many of you would have found such an order too constraining. You would have found it too difficult to endure.

"My children, all the examples I've just cited are of little consequence. Still, they should make you see that you project this fear of hard work onto everything, even your recreation. The only reason for this evasion would seem to be that you consider yourself better than everyone else, since you consider yourself exempt from what everyone in general must endure.

"My children, I'm telling you all this in order to encourage you to imitate these good examples. I want to push you to be more courageous, to accept hard work, to confront difficulties gladly whenever they arise. Learn to accept difficulties, whether they are necessary or just useful. On such occasions, isn't it infinitely better to do these things courageously and wholeheartedly rather than surrender to your own repugnance and distaste?

37. Writing in Greek, Plutarch (45–125 CE) was a philosopher who achieved his greatest literary success in the genre of edifying biography. His *Parallel Lives*, recounting the virtues of the legendary heroes of Greek and Roman antiquity, quickly acquired an enthusiastic readership throughout the Roman Empire. A favorite of Renaissance classicists, *Parallel Lives* was translated into French in 1559 by Jacques Amyot. Mme de Maintenon undoubtedly studied Plutarch in the popular Amyot edition.

"I've been speaking to you in a rather adult manner, because I am speaking to you pious girls, as I am convinced most of you are. I only need to appeal to religious motives to persuade you that every good Christian must carefully deal with every difficulty and every restriction that appears on her path, especially those involving her state in life. It makes no difference what kind of difficulty this may be, whether it is great or small. She knows how to make a holy use of it. And this, my children, is what I desire you all to be."

OF RELIGIOUS VOCATIONS [38]

Madame de Maintenon visited the "blue" class shortly after the ceremony for the profession of religious vows by Madame de la Noüe. [39]

She asked the pupils if they had been moved by the ceremony. Everyone said yes, but since very few pupils at the moment were considering the possibility of becoming a nun, she told them, "My children, I must confess that your attitude baffles me. You've witnessed so many of these religious professions, yet they seem to make little impression on you. In the past mothers didn't dare to take their daughters to witness these ceremonies because they feared that their daughters would want to enter the convent. If you took ten girls to these professions, nine would ask to enter a religious order.

"My children, I'm not telling you this in order to pressure you to become nuns. As I've told you often enough—and I'm sure you believe me—I could never use force on such an issue. I know only too well that God must give you a particular call to enter this way of life. When I was coming up to your classroom, Mme de Fontaines [40] told me that when she was young, she used to burst into tears whenever she went to a clothing ceremony or to a profession of vows and she then had an ardent desire to enter the convent. I told her that I felt the same things at the same age.

38. This translation is based on Madame de Maintenon, *Instruction de Madame de Maintenon aux demoiselles de la classe bleue: Sur la vocation religieuse*, in *LE*, BMV, Ms. P.66, 303–17. The audience for this address was the "blue" class, composed of students from seventeen to twenty years of age. The address was originally delivered in 1703.

39. Mme Françoise-Jacqueline de Vasconcelles de la Noüe Piéfontaines, a teacher at Saint-Cyr, was professed as a Dame de Saint-Louis in 1703 and died at Saint-Cyr in 1705 at the age of twenty-three (*MRSC*, 412).

40. This refers to one of two sisters, both teachers at Saint-Cyr: Mme Marie de Gautier de Fontaines, professed as a Dame de Saint-Louis in 1693 and deceased in 1718, or Mme Anne-Françoise de Gautier de Fontaines, professed as a Dame de Saint-Louis in 1693 and deceased in 1743 (*MRSC*, 410).

Mlle de Merbouton[41] replied, "Madame, it's not that we don't want to follow a religious vocation. It's just that we've heard so often that if you're not in the state of life to which God has called you, it's almost certain that you can't be saved. That's because God usually withdraws the graces which He had designated for the state of life He desired for you. That makes us very fearful."

Mme de Maintenon said, "Are you counting on God to give you some visible declaration of His will on this subject? That's usually not His way of doing things. He doesn't give you personal directions. He doesn't come down from heaven, nor does He send some of His angels to tell you with a trumpet blast whether you should become a nun or not. These days, we rarely witness those extraordinary graces that beat down your heart and push you immediately to the convent door. He uses methods that are less dramatic but just as effective, if you are faithful to responding to them.

"You say that you're afraid of being pushed toward the choice of becoming a nun because of your lack of wealth. That doesn't seem to you a good motive? It's true that this could be a bad motive. But it's also possible that this could be quite a respectable motive. It's possible that from all eternity God has determined to use this motive to draw you to the religious way of life and to save you there.

"Let's see if I can help you to determine whether this motive is good or bad in each one of you. Make an examination of your own conscience and study your real motives as I speak to you. Now, let's suppose that some of you argue like this: 'I have no worldly goods, so I can't expect to make a great impression on society. Obviously I can't look forward to any kind of economic comfort. So, it would be better for me to go into the cloister, where at least I will be guaranteed the necessities of life. I'll look for a lax convent, not too demanding in observation of the rule. I want to be able to meet visitors in the parlor often and to avoid any real restraints on my freedom. In a way I'd be able to have some compensation for the worldly pleasures I'd be missing. I would pass the time as pleasantly as possible.'

"Now if you have feelings like that, be assured that you don't have a vocation to be a nun! Stay in the world. Better for you to be a mediocre Christian laywoman than to be a bad nun.

"On the contrary, however, you might be thinking something like this: 'I'm poor, I don't really belong in high society, because there is little good I can do and I will have to face so many evils. Apparently God had some plan in letting me be so poor. I want to respond to this by entering religious life

41. Mlle de Girard de Merbouton, born in 1690, later became a Clairette nun (*MRSC*, 430).

in order to serve God with all my strength. I want to do freely and virtuously what necessity seems to require. I want to choose a convent that is austere or at least faithful in its observance of the rule, in order to assure my salvation. I want to do the greatest good there possible.'

"Now if these words express your feelings, you can be sure that you have a very solid vocation.

"My children, you know quite well that when God sends affliction our way, He is trying to make us return to Him and to urge us to be more strongly attached to Him because we lack everything else. It is certain that He does nothing without a purpose. The Gospel teaches us that our hairs are counted and that not a single one of them falls without the express command of our heavenly Father.[42] Now, if such a little thing can't happen by chance, how much truer must it be that adversities come directly from God to guide us to our ends.

"Consider the following example. A man was a libertine and didn't even know the basic duties of Christianity. God took away a son he loved passionately, and on whom he had based all his hopes for the future of his family, in order to make him reflect more deeply on himself. This man was overwhelmed by the depth of his loss. This led him to start reflections which brought him finally to return to God. He underwent a conversion and changed his way of life.

"A woman or a girl was intoxicated by her physical beauty. This can be the cause of a great deal of evil. This can even cause someone's downfall through vanity. God sent her a deformity through smallpox or through some other accident. The loss of her beauty became the occasion of her conversion and sometimes even of her withdrawal from the world.

"He permitted another woman to fall from the heights of great fortune to the depths of poverty. This opened her eyes to her real situation. She grasped God's plan for her life, changed her manner of living and even her state in life.

"Such repentant vocations are good ones. These kinds of women make excellent Christians and nuns.

"Do any of you share the fashionable opinion of those who argue that there's a greater danger of committing sin in the convent than in the world? They argue this because they say that the nuns have contracted the obligation to observe the vows and the rules of the order.

"This view is obviously mistaken. The vows and the religious rules are privileged means to avoid sins. When you follow the path of sanctification,

42. See Luke 12:8.

it's clear that you sin less. All the occasions of sin are placed at a distance. Everything is firmly marked out, from dawn until dusk. You only have to follow the rule, which doesn't even bind under pain of sin, unless this failure is accompanied by some other fault, such as disobedience or contempt. As Saint Francis de Sales points out, these are already sins anyway.[43] But these things happen rarely, almost never in well-regulated convents. In the world, on the other hand, we are always exposed to dangerous occasions of sin. We have great duties to fulfill. And it's quite easy to commit great faults in fulfilling them.

"My children, you can never imagine just how demanding are the basic duties of a simple Christian. Just look at what the First Commandment requires: 'You will love the Lord your God with your whole heart, with your whole mind, and with your whole strength.'[44]

"Do you think that it's so easy to do this in this world: to give your undivided heart to God? Yet, it's exactly what we're supposed to do in whatever state we find ourselves. Many people delude themselves, because they don't understand the scope of this precept, which demands high perfection. It's much easier to achieve this in the religious life than in any other way of life.

"Please don't think that you are too young to think about your choice of vocation. Start by asking God ardently to make this known to you. Make yourself worthy of it by your piety and by your faithful execution of your present duties. Speak about it with your confessors. They're very experienced men. Discuss it with your teachers. Make a mature choice. Let your only purpose be obeying God, doing something for Him in order to witness your love and to assure your salvation.

"May those to whom He grants this grace beg Him everyday to preserve it, because this is the greatest happiness you could ever possess. They could attempt to show greater courage through mortification of the body. Still, they should avoid anything too austere. You're still young and you have a duty to let your body grow stronger so that you will be able to support the religious rule that you might embrace. I encourage you right now to avoid having any fastidiousness in your eating. Never show any dislike for any type of food someone might serve you. Learn to eat everything on your plate. Learn to do everything on time, without the slightest concession to sloth. Work hard. Learn how to maintain silence, as they do in the convent. Only use heat in the winter when it's necessary. Accept the summer heat

---

43. See Saint François de Sales, *Introduction à la vie dévote*, ed. Étienne-Marie Lajeunie (Paris: Éditions du Seuil, 1995), bk. 3, chap. 11, 151–54.

44. See Matthew 22:37, Mark 12:30, and Luke 10:27.

without complaining about it. Endure with peace and tranquility all the mortifications Providence sends you. All these actions would be clear signs that you truly have the desire to become nuns and they will give you a marvelous preparation to be a solid nun, without in any way threatening your health.

"The decision to become a nun is surely one of the greatest effects of grace. It requires a great courage, because it requires you to renounce everything that is natural. Now, if you don't accustom yourself to these sacrifices early in life, you will only find life in the novitiate all the more difficult. You might think that you'll be able to do this well enough whenever you want to, but you would be seriously mistaken. God has no obligation to send you His grace when you've decided to receive it, if you neglected it when He presented it to you.

"This reminds me of two men who had both decided to enter the Trappist monastery. One of them said that they should eat sparely as they walked toward the monastery. He argued that this would help accustom them to the strict rules of abstinence they would meet in this monastery. The other said that he wanted to enjoy the world's pleasures until the very last moment. As a consequence, in whatever inn they stayed, he would indulge himself while his companion practiced the strictest abstinence. They both entered the novitiate. The one who practiced abstemiousness remained there and became a great saint. The other had to leave. This illustrates what I was telling you: God has absolutely no obligation to send us His graces when we have made ourselves unworthy of them."

Then she added, "I've always noticed that people who sincerely begin to live a pious life tend to start practicing the types of austerities you read about in the lives of saints. You often need to put a brake on their fervor. Otherwise, they would end up doing dangerous austerities.

"When Mlle de la Vallière was touched by God and was on the verge of entering the Carmelite convent,[45] I warned her, as others did, that she could not pass smoothly from the indulgent life of the court to the austere life of Carmel. I encouraged her to first take a time of retreat from the court. She could live as the lay benefactress of a convent, seeing up close just what the religious rules would demand of her. I also added, 'Now, you realize what a

---

45. Louise de La Vallière (1644–1710) became the mistress of Louis XIV in 1661. Having borne the king four children, La Vallière underwent a religious conversion, recounted in her book *Reflections on God's Mercy*, first published in 1680. In 1674 she left the court and entered the Carmelite convent, where she led a secluded life of prayer and penance. La Vallière's dramatic life history was widely discussed in the religious literature of the period and became the subject of subsequent novels and plays.

taste for fashion you have! Can you really imagine yourself covered in burlap from head to toe in a few days?' She was in fact one of the court's most elegant dressers.

"She then confided to me that under these high-society externals she had long worn a hairshirt, slept on a plank, and pursued all the other austerities of the Carmelite order. As for the advice I had given her about retiring as a benefactress in a convent to serve God peacefully as a pious laywoman, she responded, 'Would that be a penance? This path would be far too easy. That's not what I'm looking for.'

"See, my children, what grace does in a heart that corresponds to its movements.

"Do you think that only nuns engage in meditation and mortification? Several ladies of the household of the duchesse de Bourgogne withdraw at certain times of the day for prayer.[46] They know how to take their leave of company in order to devote themselves to meditation. I know one of them who has slept on a plank for more than twenty-five years. She discreetly dismisses her entourage, who believe that she is going to sleep after her final prayers. However, as soon as they leave, she removes the mattress from her bed so that she can sleep on the planks. She puts everything back in its place in the morning before anyone else enters the bedroom.

"I know another person at the court who just underwent a conversion. This is a delightful young person, who used to give herself to every kind of pleasure. She had the fine habit of reading a chapter from the New Testament every evening. She tried to let the passage sink in. She thought about it as she went off to sleep. This reading was very helpful to her because in the midst of the whirl of shows and other pastimes in which she indulged, she told herself, 'My current life is very different from that of Jesus Christ, whom I am supposed to be imitating.' Constantly repeated, this conclusion made her reflect on herself and resolve to change her way of life.

"She started by excusing herself from a ball to which she had been invited. This action astonished the court, because there didn't seem to be any obstacle to her attendance. I personally found this refusal so extraordinary that I asked her why she had done this. She simply told me that she had her reasons. I didn't press her any further.

"A short time later we saw her break openly with her former social life and pursue an openly devout life. Afterward she told me that the reading of a chapter from the New Testament, combined with the reflections I just told you about, were the cause of this change.

46. See above in this section, note 17.

"Please note, dear children, that it wasn't reading alone, excellent as it was, which lead to this conversion; it was her serious reflection on what she had read. She carefully compared her worldly life with the humble and mortified life of Jesus Christ. This is how you should apply what you hear and read to your own lives. You should conduct a serious examination of conscience on your manner of life and reform what you notice needs reforming, according to the light that is given to you.

"Goodbye, my children."

OF THE SINGLE LIFE [47]

After she entered the classroom, Mme de Maintenon said, "My children, your teacher would like me to speak to you about the single life. Apparently most of you are enthusiastic about this state in life because you could then avoid the restrictions of marriage and the vowed commitments of the cloister.

"This view is just not reasonable. There is no state in life where you can avoid the state of dependence to which God wants to restrict persons of our sex. This neutral state, which you call the single life, is actually one of the most dangerous states. You must take the greatest precautions to avoid losing your reputation in it.

"If I had to speak to girls who were thinking about establishing themselves in this state, I would tell them what I yesterday told one of your companions who came to bid me farewell, 'Take this advice from this old mother of yours. When you leave here, get married or become a nun. Don't remain in a state without commitment. Apparently it's only a love of freedom that makes you feel that remaining in this uncertain state is some kind of happiness. If you want to find a state where you won't depend on anyone, where you can do your own will morning and night, and where there is neither constraint nor subordination, you are looking for the impossible.

"'If you marry, you will depend on the will of your husband. If you are a nun, you must obey your rule and your superior. If you become neither, you will still depend on your father, or your mother, or some other relative. If you have none of those, you will have to find someone of good reputation to act as a chaperone, because a woman cannot live alone. If you live with a devout laywoman, you will have to accept her customs and her desires,

---

47. This translation is based on Madame de Maintenon, *Instruction de Madame de Maintenon aux demoiselles de la classe bleue: Du célibat*, in *LE*, BMV, Ms. P.67, 432–40. The audience for this address was the "blue" class, composed of students from seventeen to twenty years of age.

which will not always match yours. You must accompany her on her hospital visitations and other good works. You will not be able to leave her for a moment. This is the type of behavior one expects from a woman who does not want to lose her reputation.

"'You could still retire to some convent or another. But then you would have to submit yourself to the rules and regulations of the convent. There is nothing sadder or more tedious to endure for someone who does not have the vocation to this way of life. Few women have the courage to remain in the convent for more than two or three years. Everyone admires Mlle de La Mothe,[48] who had been lady-in-waiting to Queen Anne d'Autriche,[49] because she has remained at the Chaillot convent for thirty years. Now I can't honestly say whether she has ever wanted to leave or whether she has found this life tedious. I can only say that she knew how to overcome the taste for diversion so natural to our sex. Her example is so rare that everyone is astonished by it.

"'I've known people who strongly feared the commitment demanded in religious life and hesitated right up to the day of their religious profession. However, once they had overcome their repugnance and made their vowed commitment, their problems vanished and they found themselves perfectly happy. It's true that there is the grace of vocation, which doesn't always remove a natural repugnance to the restrictions of this life, but it's also true that once the will has been firmly fixed by the very commitment you had once so feared, you are no longer concerned about anything else.'"

Mme de Vandam[50] said, "Madame, I often recall to them the example of Mme de Loubert,[51] our former superior. When the time came to pronounce solemn vows, she said that she didn't want to make them because she con-

---

48. A lady-in-waiting to Queen Anne d'Autriche, Mlle de la Mothe d'Argencourt caused a scandal by her affair with the young Louis XIV. After a religious conversion, she retired as a lay associate to the convent of the Filles de Sainte-Marie in Chaillot. Devout circles of the period frequently invoked her narrative of conversion and repentance as that of a modern *Madeleine*.

49. Widow of Louis XIII and mother of Louis XIV, Queen Anne d'Autriche (1601–66) served as regent of France (1643–61) during the minority of Louis XIV. With her controversial prime minister, Cardinal Mazarin, she continued the absolutist policies of Richelieu and successfully resisted the attacks of the *Fronde*, a loose coalition of aristocrats and parliamentarians opposed to these centralizing policies.

50. Mme Marie-Henriette Vandam d'Audegny, a teacher at Saint-Cyr, was professed as a Dame de Saint-Louis in 1698. She died at Saint-Cyr in 1768 at the age of ninety (*MRSC*, 412).

51. Mme Marie-Anne de Loubert professed simple vows as a Dame de Saint-Louis in 1688. She succeeded Mme de Brinon as superior in 1689, but transferred to the Ursuline convent at Poissy in 1692 (*MRSC*, 410). Her disagreement with Mme de Maintenon over the Quietist controversy contributed to her departure.

sidered her simple vows just as binding. She was just as determined to spend her whole life here as if she had actually contracted the obligations of solemn vows. However, scarcely six months passed before she wanted to transfer to another convent. The fact that she was the only one not to have pronounced solemn vows made her feel isolated."

Madame de Maintenon responded, "Believe me, if she hadn't died shortly thereafter, she would have changed her mind yet again, although I don't think that she was a particularly inconstant person. Experience teaches us that as long as someone is not firmly committed to a particular state of life, she always runs the risk of having a thousand thoughts urging her to change her residence or her lifestyle. Beloved children, how can you keep these ideas of false freedom after everything I've so often told you to convince you that some sort of necessity and dependence is inevitable?

"You have many other things to do beside following your own will. The meager financial resources of most of you will make it impossible for you to keep up with the social externals of others. Some of you in the future, as already in the present, will have to work terribly hard just to have the basics of existence. That is the issue many of you need to face. Rather than going to your confessors on trivial matters, it would be better to ask them, 'What should I do, given my precarious resources? What means should I use to endure the inevitable humiliations tied to my lack of fortune?'

"The wealthier among you shouldn't think themselves exempt from these concerns. Among the many ladies who graduated from this school, Mlle de X., for example, is certainly one of the wealthier. Nonetheless, she still has to care for her parents, do the shopping, and do many other menial chores. Her parents love her deeply. She loves them just as much, and she rightly says that if she were certain that they would live for a long time, she would be the happiest person in the world. She does not have a real social life. She spends her day hard at work in her room. Her greatest pleasure is to come here to visit us every three months. Mlle de Y., another of your companions, must provide food for her mother on a scant fifty crowns a month and must take care of her by unending work."

The mother superior then told Mme de Maintenon that the Marquise d'Havrincourt[52] had written to Mlle de Y., who was an old friend of hers. She had invited her to spend the summer vacation with her. In fact, she had

52. An alumna of Saint-Cyr, Anne-Gabrielle d'Osmond, marquise d'Havrincourt (1680–1761), became a close friend of Mme de Maintenon and of the duchesse de Bourgogne, a frequent visitor at Saint-Cyr. Their patronage facilitated the impoverished pupil's advantageous marriage to a distinguished aristocrat, the Marquis d'Havrincourt.

made the offer several times. However, Mlle de Y. answered that although she was very grateful for this kindness, she was unable to accept this offer. She preferred serving and taking care of her mother over any other pleasure.

Mme de Maintenon said, "Now, there is a fine and praiseworthy heart."

She next addressed the pupils. She told them, "I hope I've convinced you of the importance of embracing a particular state in life. Still, I must tell you that you will not always be able to determine on your own just which state it will be. Those who do not have a vocation to the convent will usually not be able to contract an advantageous marriage. I would never advise you to enter into a bad marriage or to marry someone as impoverished as you are. Your lack of resources might force you to remain in the single state which we just described in such somber colors. It's a state especially dangerous for your reputation.

"I've often cited the example of the Misses Z., who were once your companions. They remained with their mother because they didn't have a religious vocation and because they couldn't marry according to their noble rank. In fact, few French families had the same degree of nobility. Yet, even with their noble birth, they didn't dare to show themselves often in public. Their mother told me that she had taken them only once to the Tuileries and that she had carefully chosen a time when no one would be around.[53]

"Now, some of you might be counting on some relatives who have a little wealth, but you are sadly mistaken in this hope. Beside the fact that one person rarely decides to give a fortune to another, you should not forget that your relatives have their own children and that they will do little to help you instead.

"Some time ago the little Master de la Maisonfort[54] went to see Monsieur de Beauvillier,[55] who is his relative. He is certainly wealthy and pious, even charitable. Nonetheless, when the boy saw Monsieur de Beauvillier, Beauvillier told him, 'May you become a wealthy man one day!' He gave him nothing, not even some clothing, although he practically had no clothes. But as I just said, this is quite a virtuous man whom many people consider a saint.

---

53. The Tuileries are the public gardens adjacent to the royal palace of the Louvre. During this period they were a famous site for aristocratic promenades and for amorous intrigue.

54. Brother of Mlle de la Maisonfort, a Saint-Cyr pupil.

55. Paul de Saint-Aignan, duc de Beauvillier (1648–1714), pious tutor to the grandchildren of Louis XIV, was considered a lay saint in the devout circles of Versailles. A prominent courtier, Beauvillier also served in the king's council of finance and in the king's cabinet.

"Maisonfort then went to visit one of his aunts. She greeted him graciously, but when it was time for dinner, she said to him, 'Farewell, nephew. Come back to see me when you're properly dressed.' You can see clearly that this aunt did something more than refuse to invite him to dinner. This is a case of the humiliations which so often accompany indigence."

Mme de Maintenon gave them another example. This was the case of Mlle de Breuillac.[56] She said that this woman had once been wealthy and had once been quite prominent in high society.

Mme de Maintenon said, "Despite her past, you now see that she is reduced to living at Madame d'Heudicourt's.[57] Despite the kindness of this lady for her, Mlle de Breuillac has suffered through a number of unpleasant experiences. The other day she told me that Mme d'Heudicourt had gone to Paris and had left her at home. When it was dinner time, she saw that nothing had been prepared for her, and she asked to have an omelet. The cook told her that she had other things to do than to serve her and that if she really wanted an omelet, she had only to make it herself. She knew where the eggs were. She told me that if she had been alone in her own home, she would have done so without difficulty. But she found it very difficult to use a frying pan when she was standing right next to this cook. This she found impossible to bear.

"My dear children, when you live with a stranger or even with a relative, it is difficult to get along with the servants. They always resent you. They think you are being given something that is being taken away from them. This belief always inflames their jealousy.

"As for myself, I wish I could give you every happiness, but many of you know how difficult it is for me to have any available time when I am at Versailles. I gladly prefer your company to an infinite number of people whose rank and position demand that I spend time with them. In the times in which we live, money determines everything.

"Goodbye, my dear children. My hope is that real merit, a wise and prudent spirit, courage, and especially piety will compensate you for any material resources you lack."

56. Mlle de Breuillac appears to have been an unofficial ward of Mme de Maintenon. Maintenon arranged for housing her at the home of her friend, the Marquise d'Heudicourt, and discussed her difficulties in several of her letters. The will and testament of Maintenon provided Mlle de Breuillac with a modest inheritance.

57. Bonne de Pons, marquise d'Heudicourt (1644–1709), was a close friend of Mme de Maintenon.

OF FRIENDSHIP [58]

Mme de Maintenon said to the pupils, "My children, my intention today is to speak to you about friendship. There are two kinds of friendship, one good and the other bad. A good friendship mutually leads both friends to the good. On the contrary, a bad friendship does just the opposite.

"My children, you can never have enough unity and enough affection among you. However, as long as you remain here, this friendship must be universal. None of your companions should ever feel excluded. You must avoid particular friendships. Particular friendships are quite proper in the world, where it is acceptable, indeed desirable, to build a little society of select and meritorious people. However, particular friendships are not acceptable in a community, because they always create factions that wound the feelings of those who feel less loved, even abandoned, by the others.

"Your regulations have been made in such a way that you can never group yourselves together in a little clique. You must adjust to those pupils with whom you happen to find yourselves. You must treat each one properly, without any prejudice, although it's acceptable to feel a greater attraction, respect, or affection for some rather than others. Nonetheless, I strongly urge you to develop the fine habit of not letting these particular feelings manifest themselves. In that way, you can avoiding disturbing the perfect charity, unity, and equality that should reign among you.

"This lesson is given to all members of a religious community. In fact, people often say that particular friendships are the plague of a religious order. Friendship, such a sweet and pleasant virtue, is not really a virtue for the nun. Rather, it is a virtue specifically for lay people. Now, although you are laywomen, it's not central to you yet, because you still live in a community. When you leave here, you will be free to develop particular friendships. Just be careful then to use prudence and discretion, because you risk the loss of your reputation by a single relationship with a woman or a girl who herself lacks a good reputation.

"I'm told that you really love your schoolmistresses. I admire your affection. It shows the good quality of your heart. I only urge you to show them affection more by your docility and by your eagerness to profit from everything in which they counsel you than by hugs and embraces, although the latter are quite proper up to a certain point.

58. This translation is based on Madame de Maintenon, *Instruction aux demoiselles de Saint-Cyr: Sur les amitiés*, in *LE*, BMV, Ms. P.67, 564–72. Delivered to the entire student body, this address was originally given in 1714.

"I remember that when I was a boarding student at a convent,[59] I so loved a certain teacher that words could not describe the feeling. My greatest pleasure was to sacrifice myself for her service. I was so far ahead in the school lessons that whenever she left the classroom I could lead the entire class in reading, writing, arithmetic, penmanship, and recreation. I delighted in finishing her needlepoint for her. Just knowing that I pleased her was reward enough.

"I spent entire nights working on the fine linen of the boarding students, so that it was always clean and so that they would honor the schoolmistress, who didn't have to worry about it. I had the pupils go to bed promptly. I pressed them if they were tardy, but they usually went to bed happily enough because they respected me and held me in great affection.

"I collected many little stumps of candle. I collected so many that we didn't need to burn anything else in the classroom for a week. I placed them on small sticks of metal. This went so well that I had the honor from time to time of being able to give an entire candle to my schoolmistress for the reading and other projects she pursued during the night.

"I thought I would die from grief when I left this convent school. During two or three months, I naively asked God to let me die. I begged this every day, morning and night. I didn't think that I could live without seeing her. And this was during a time of religious fervor, when I was wearing a hairshirt and a chain. This desire was due to lack of proper instruction. If I had known that we shouldn't seek death for such motives, I would never have done this. I fell into this desire quite simply and quite naturally, because I was speaking to God. Neither bitterness nor resentment colored my prayer. I think that, seeing my innocence, God treated me gently enough.

"I prayed for her everyday. I never forgot her once I entered society, even the whirl of high society. I wrote to her twice a week. I couldn't do it more frequently, since the mail for Poitou didn't leave more frequently than that.[60] No matter how busy I was, I never failed to write to her on Wednesday and on Sunday.

"Everyone praised me for my fidelity and for the goodness of my heart. My friendship with her ended only when her life did. When I was established in the world, I asked to make a trip to Poitou to see my relatives, but in fact I wanted to see my dear Mother Celeste—this was the name of the

---

59. This is the Ursuline convent school in Niort.
60. Poitou is a region of southwest France surrounding the city of Poitiers.

teacher. I traveled fifty leagues expressly to see her, although I used another pretext.

"I've always loved those who took care of me. Mme de Delisle, my current *maître d'hôtel*, was my governess. She was the chambermaid of my aunt, with whom I was staying. I loved her with a great tenderness. I taught her how to read and write. Whenever I did something wrong, she would say to me, 'You've done something wrong. So you can't show me how to read and write today.' I would then be upset and cry bitterly.

I would also comb her hair. She had these thick, rather greasy hairs. But that didn't bother me at all. When I did something wrong, she would say to me, 'No combing for you tomorrow.' I would be upset, even inconsolable.

"I always maintained a great affection for this woman. That is why thirty years later I had her come to court to work near me.

"I also love her son, Delisle, not only because he's a fine man in his own right, but also because he's the son of this woman who was my governess. This is an example of a strong friendship, but one free of anything that could be criticized.

"I will always praise the affection which you show for your teachers and the respect which you show them. I only ask that your external marks of affection be given equally to everyone, although, as I said before, it's only natural that you prefer the company of one person over another. Still, I repeat once again, every external manifestation of these preferences has a bad effect on the life of the community.

"As for your peers, I repeat that you should avoid showing, at least in too dramatic a way, greater affection for some than for others. The only exception should be if you show greater admiration for those pupils who are really wiser, more virtuous, and more pious than the others. In this case, anyone should be able to discern your motive. Such a preference would actually be the visible sign of a good soul and of a heart truly attached to the good."

OF THE WORLD [61]

"Having neither sufficient strength nor sufficient health to give you as many conferences as I had hoped, I thought it would be good to speak to all of you

---

61. This translation is based on Madame de Maintenon, *Instruction aux demoiselles des deux grandes classes: Sur le monde,* in *LE,* BMV, Ms. P.66, 655–61. The audience for this address included students from both the "yellow" (ages fourteen to seventeen) and the "blue" (ages seventeen to twenty) classes. The address was originally given in 1707.

assembled here together on a subject I want to warn you about as soon as possible. That subject is the world.

"My children, I fear that, since you came here young and without any real knowledge of it, you might have some ideas about the world that are just the opposite of what the world really is. My fear is that you might judge the world only by its seductive appearances, which, I must admit, have everything to attract a young mind. Just look at the dress and the adornments of the duchesse de Bourgogne and the ladies of her entourage![62]

"Beyond the fact that you do not have the resources to dress that way and that most of you could not do so without becoming an object of ridicule, I must recall the fact that you have been raised and instructed in a pure Christian spirit. Unlike most people in the world, you don't ignore the fact that Jesus Christ denounced the world and that He did not pray for it even when He prayed for His executioners.[63] You renounced the world by the baptismal promises you made to shun the world's pomps, pleasures, counsels, and scandals.

"Saints Peter and Paul advise members of our sex to dress modestly, to wear neither gold nor silver, to avoid curling our hair.[64] In the early years of this school I was delighted to see the first pupils, to whom we granted the freedom to use curls and other adornments, do away with them voluntarily. They did this out of piety after a retreat with Abbé Tiberge.[65]

"It is my duty to welcome here the Duchesse de Bourgogne and the other ladies of the court on a daily basis. I would be driven to despair, however, if I thought that the presence of these ladies, who must assume certain social refinements because of their state in life, introduced a certain worldliness among you at the very moment that your school is making such progress in every area.

"My children, remember that you can't love the world without displeasing Our Lord, Jesus Christ. Be aware that when you leave here, you might have very little because of the precarious situation of most of your families. Even if some of you manage to achieve what people call a fortune, you

62. See above in this section, note 17.

63. Jesus' negative comments about the world are spread throughout the gospels, but it is not clear that Maintenon has any particular passage in mind here. On Jesus praying for his executioners, see Luke 23:34.

64. See 1 Timothy 2:9; 1 Peter 3:3.

65. Abbé Louis Tiberge was part of the community of Lazarist priests and brothers who assumed the spiritual direction of the academy at Saint-Cyr in 1691 as part of Mme de Maintenon's project of pedagogical and moral reform.

shouldn't hate the world any less. You should adopt ideas, principles, and ways of conduct completely opposed to it. Everything emanating from the world of high society is corrupt. I know that there are some very fine Christians, even saints, who live in this world. I fervently pray God that those of you who will be obliged to return to the world may be among this happy number.

"Abandon the taste of youth for shows. In order to avoid ever going to plays, it's enough to know that usually there's something offensive to God in them and that you run serious moral risks in the places of performance. Moreover, it should be obvious that this taste for plays would simply be in vain in your case. You would make yourself a criminal before God without reason, since you will hardly hear a word about opera or drama in the provinces where you will live. These things only exist in a few great cities of the kingdom.

"Have they told you what happened to your companion, Mlle de Loras,[66] when she left here? Her mother wanted to take her to the theater and took her to Versailles, because theatrical performances are free at court. She was still wearing her Saint-Cyr uniform. Many people recognized her. Still, she didn't get a better seat because of that. The duchesse de Bourgogne who, as you know, very much loved her, said to her attendants when she spotted her, 'There's Loras.' That's all she said. On leaving, the duchess didn't say a word to her and didn't even give the impression of seeing her.

"This is just a small sample of what the world is. Everyday you see thousands of these bitter disappointments. You see them especially with those who don't have enough money to cut a figure comparable to the others. At present nothing is so easily dismissed as is the impoverished nobility.

"If you don't have a vocation to the convent, most of you, after you leave here, will return to live with your mother or father. They might be ill or widowed or senile. You must be ready for everything, including caring for children, whose number you will probably increase. Often enough you'll spend the day at work in your mother's room or in your own. You certainly won't be thinking about spending ten francs to go to the opera. You won't even hear anyone talking about it. If you're honorable, you would think even less about being escorted to the opera by a man who would pay for your seat. That would destroy your reputation.

"Others among you—these will be the happiest—will find themselves buried in the countryside in a household. They will supervise the domestic servants, seeing if they do their job well, if the work is done properly, if they

66. Mlle de Loras, born in 1681, later became a Bernardine nun (*MRSC*, 425).

take proper care of the cattle, the turkeys, and the poultry. They will have to oversee all the details of the household. Often enough they will have to pitch in to do some manual work themselves.

"My children, if anyone needs a supplement of piety and virtue, it will certainly be these homemakers. Your objective situation will expose you to many difficult things. You must make a wholehearted sacrifice to God, who wants it this way. Of course, we're not obliged to offer up what we're suffering when we can't avoid it. Still, God's goodness is so great that He always accepts these sacrifices. They count a great deal in His sight when we do them voluntarily.

"My dear children, humble yourselves. God has permitted the great decline of the nobility only to humble it and perhaps to punish some of your ancestors who abused their authority and wealth. So humble yourselves in order to respond to God's plan. I would never ask you to let your heart grow despondent. On the contrary, your heart should be filled with true glory and hold firm to the commitment never to do anything base. I am simply asking you to adopt ideas about the world which are closer to the truth and which are closer to the demands of Christian piety."

HOW TO MAINTAIN A GOOD REPUTATION [67]

When they had finished the reading of the chapter,[68] Mme de Maintenon said, "My dear children, I am convinced that every single one of you wants to have a good reputation. After all, it would be absurd not to be concerned about this.

"I am sure that when you hear about certain women whom everyone admires, you immediately say to yourself, 'How much I would like to be like her!' This is a good and understandable reaction. However, it's not enough simply to want this if you are not also ready to do everything necessary to establish the kind of reputation which Saint Francis de Sales calls true renown."[69]

She then asked Mlle de Maulne [*sic*][70] what reputation was. The pupil

---

67. This translation is based on Madame de Maintenon, *Instruction aux demoiselles de la classe jaune: Comment il faut conserver la bonne renommée, pratiquant néanmoins l'humilité,* in *LE,* BMV, Ms. P.65, 851–57. The audience for this address was the "yellow" class, composed of students from fourteen to seventeen years of age. The address was originally given in 1702.

68. The reading was probably taken from the Bible or from Saint Francis de Sales's *Introduction to the Devout Life.*

69. See Saint François de Sales, *Introduction,* bk. 3, chap. 7, 137–41.

70. Mlle de Maune d'Hunon, born in 1685, later became a Visitation nun (*MRSC,* 427).

replied that reputation was the positive opinion which the public held regarding a particular person.

Mme de Maintenon added, "What must we do to merit a good reputation?" The pupil replied that we must conduct ourselves well in every circumstance.

Mlle de Saint-Laurent,[71] to whom Mme de Maintenon had posed the same question, added, "And in front of everyone."

Mme de Maintenon pressed her, "Do you think it's enough to be respected by a select group of people without being concerned about other people?"

The pupil replied, "I don't think that this would be enough. It's essential that everyone who knows us say the same thing."

Mme de Maintenon replied, "You're quite right. This consensus is in fact what makes a reputation. Let's begin with the most important people. Your father must say, 'I am so happy to have a daughter such as mine!' Your mother must say, 'My God, how well-behaved my daughter is!' Your other relatives, whom you might be living with, must say, 'It's such a delight to have such a girl with us!' Your chambermaid must say, 'Mademoiselle is so easy to serve! She is so sweet!' It should be the same with your shoemaker, your tailor, your other domestic servants. Don't forget that when they are alone, the servants have nothing else to discuss except their masters and their mistresses. If there is the smallest evil thing to reveal, they will immediately divulge it. They reveal everything they notice. One's reputation often depends more on these people than on the more elevated people who don't see us so closely.

"I will always remember what I heard from a shoemaker who made shoes for me when I was young. When these people come to your house, they bring some large display cases full of shoes for different kinds of people. Among all these shoes, there was a small pair which I really wanted. I asked him who these shoes were for. He answered, 'They're for Mademoiselle X.' I said to him, 'What? You actually make shoes for her? She's so sweet and pleasant!' He replied to me, 'She's a real little devil. When I go to her house for a shoe fitting and she doesn't find something exactly as she wants it, she becomes angry and starts to throw the shoes at my head.'

"This shoemaker may well have recited this same story to over a hundred people in just the same way. This should help you to understand that your reputation often depends on people about whom you have the least apprehension. This is why you must always be careful with everyone."

71. Mlle de Bedorède de Saint-Laurent was born in 1686 (*MRSC*, 428).

She next asked Mlle de Boulainvilliers[72] if this is especially difficult. The pupil answered yes, because not all of our inclinations equally guide us toward what is good. It's especially difficult to have the restraint necessary to show only what is good.

Mme de Maintenon replied, "This is true, but you are more than compensated for this restraint by the respect you acquire and by the attraction which virtuous people will usually have for your company. As for the libertines, we shouldn't care a bit about their criticisms. Despite their mockery, just keep walking carefully in the path of honor and virtue.

"You should start working as young as possible to establish your reputations. Even at the present moment, you shouldn't neglect cultivating the respect of your companions. First impressions are always strong and can rarely be erased. Quite simply, if they spot in you some bad habit, some poor behavior, or some major fault which you neglect to correct, they will keep this negative impression for the rest of their lives.

"There is already universal respect for those among you, for example, who are accommodating, who rarely interrupt, who happily listen to others, who sacrifice to serve others, who show moderation, wisdom, and piety in all you do. Now, how do you explain that all of you aren't like this?

"Once again, I realize that this is not as easy to do for everyone. It is more difficult for some of you than for others. But you must realize that there's not a single one among you who couldn't achieve this, because, happily for us, our entire merit depends on our work, aided by the grace of God, as a pupil in the "blue" class said so well the other day. Further, this divine grace will never be lacking for us when we faithfully, constantly, and humbly ask Him to bestow it.

"Reflect on what I've just told you, my dear children. From now on, take active measures to acquire a good reputation. Remember the excellent advice of Saint Francis de Sales: to make a Christian virtue agreeable to God and meritorious for yourself, don't forget to mix it with humility.[73]

"Mlle d'Ardenne,[74] you've been listening to this so attentively. How can we accomplish this?"

The pupil said, "We can do this by keeping a low opinion of ourselves. We shouldn't desire to have this good reputation simply for our own benefit.

---

72. Mlle de Boulainvilliers de Chepoix was born in 1687 (*MRSC*, 429).

73. See Saint François de Sales, *Introduction*, bk. 3, chap. 5, 128–33.

74. The school registry presented by Lavallée (*MRSC*) lists no student named d'Ardenne. The name may have been distorted in the process of transcribing the address.

We should pursue it in the same spirit as Our Lord told us to. We should do our good works before humanity, not in order to receive praise, but in order that God may be glorified."[75]

Mme de Maintenon replied, "Now that is a perfect answer. My children, put into practice everything good you know. Then you will never waste your time. Please pray for me."

OF AVOIDING THE OCCASIONS OF SIN [76]

"My dear children, I know that adding a lecture to the sermon you just heard might seem to you a great burden. Nonetheless, I can't help but say that I've heard many preachers in my life, but I've never heard any of them speak as well as Monsieur Briderey just did.[77] On the subject he treated, he said many wonderful things. He spoke as someone who knows the world and the recesses of the human heart.

"He is absolutely right to tell you that you don't fall suddenly into great evils. You usually only arrive there by a gradual descent. The Holy Spirit teaches us the same truth when He says that whoever neglects the small things will fall bit by bit.

"My children, you can't protect yourself enough from the contagion of the world. You can't fear it or hate it enough. I tremble for those among you who will enter the world without these safeguards. The world is so full of traps and perils, not only for faith, but also for reputation and honor. Members of our sex should guard these jealously, because, after the grace of God, these are the greatest goods we could possibly have.

"My children, you may be surprised that I spoke so candidly to you. I certainly understand that each of you is probably saying something like this, 'This doesn't concern me. I would rather die a thousand deaths than ever do anything that could tarnish my reputation in the least.'

"Please let me convince you that I've learned through long experience that many young, well-educated people, even those who appeared the most

---

75. See Matthew 5:16.

76. This translation is based on Madame de Maintenon, *Instruction de Madame de Maintenon aux demoiselles de la classe bleue: Qu'il faut éviter les occasions, et que, faute de cette attention, l'on tombe peu à peu dans le plus grands maux*, in *LE*, BMV, Ms. P.67, 289–98. The audience for this address was the "blue" class, composed of students from seventeen to twenty years of age. The address was originally given in 1710.

77. Abbé Briderey became the superior of the Lazarists in 1704. Given the Lazarists' responsibility for the chaplaincy of the school at Saint-Cyr, Briderey personally delivered occasional sermons to the faculty and the student body.

virtuous, have had terrible falls that scandalized the world and that destroyed them in the eyes of God and humanity. They suffered from too great a confidence in themselves and too small a sense of their own weakness. They exposed themselves to occasions of sin. They didn't avoid bad companions. They didn't take all the necessary precautions to maintain their reputation. I'd be willing to bet that there is not a single woman bereft of reputation who wanted to give herself to evil all at once and who coldly said one day, 'I want to dishonor myself.' No, you arrive at such excesses only step by step.

"Do you think, for example, that Mme X., who has been imprisoned three times, would ever have made such a resolution? Of course not. The decline begins gently by pretentious manners, by a love of adornment, by wanting popularity, by listening to flattery, and by believing it. Little by little the heart is tainted, and we surrender.

"On this subject I should tell you a story known by thousands of people. I won't be violating any confidence by telling it to you.

"It concerns a lady-in-waiting of the Queen Mother.[78] She came from a distinguished family and was both pretty and witty. She loved to dress up. This was the cause of her downfall. There was a man who noticed her. He started by telling her how lovely she was.

"You should realize that men usually set their sights on women they do not respect and in whom they spot some weakness. They don't always pursue the most beautiful women. On the contrary, they sometimes pursue rather dreadful-looking women. It's the conduct of the woman that makes the difference. They respect women who are wise and restrained. These women clearly send a signal that they do not want to be approached.

"Let's return to the fall of the pathetic girl I was telling you about. At first, she thought it was wonderful to hear that she was lovely and a thousand other compliments of this sort. This was how this man conquered his women. This isn't so difficult, because you only need to give a bit of money to these women. In a short time other men of the household were acting just like him. Everyone began to flatter her and to give her presents. She was stupid enough to receive them. She finally arrived at the ultimate degradation, living a scandalous life during an entire decade. She finished by dying a violent death in trying to obtain an abortion in order to hide the tragedy that had befallen her.

"I remember that when I heard this frightful news, my hairs literally stood on end in horror. The woman who had helped her to commit this

---

78. Queen Anne d'Autriche. See above in this section, note 49.

crime and the man who had encouraged her to procure it were burned at the stake. She herself would have died on the scaffold if she had survived it. What a combination of crimes! She lost three souls: her child's, the other woman's, her own!

"Now it's obvious that when she was young, she would never have believed herself capable of such actions. Her birth doesn't seem to have been worse than that of many others. However, her excessive taste for adornment, for her own beauty, for her pleasures, and for flattery led little by little to her own downfall.

"You must realize how swiftly men notice the particular weakness of members of our sex and just how we may be conquered. They give ribbons and other ornaments to those who like to dress up. They give candies, fruits, and other similar things to those who like to eat. They give other commodities to those who are clearly looking for them.

"My children, when you leave here, your main concern must be to ask God night and day to keep you from the occasions of sin. You must be very careful to avoid them. Otherwise, I would only give you a year to lose yourself and all the fruits of your education here, because the Holy Spirit teaches us that whoever loves taking risks will perish. But when He places us in a particular state of life, He is in a certain way obliged—if we can say it this way—to give us the necessary graces to deliver us from the dangers attached to this state."

She added, "What I find so consoling in the state where I am is that God has placed me here. I never wanted for a single moment to be in it. I've even desired to leave it. At first, I just couldn't understand why God would give me such a desire to flee the court and yet summon me to spend my entire life there. My confessors explained that one was precisely the reason for the other. This aversion to the court would act as protection against all the temptations I would find there.

"When I arrived at the court, I thought that when I had accumulated a little wealth—because I had none on arrival—I would retire to a private house somewhere. It was with this intention that I purchased site unseen the territory of Maintenon. I sent all sorts of furnishings down there. As soon as I had entered its courtyard, I was delighted to see the window of what I thought was the principal room. I thought to myself, 'That's where I'll spend the rest of my days.' I had no other plan than living peacefully with the peasants on my estate. However, as I was planning for this, God was disposing things quite differently.

"My dear children, I've always told you that those who become nuns will be the happiest among us. I certainly don't want you all to do that. I don't

love one who becomes a nun more than one who does not. But I must tell
you the truth. It's easier to achieve your salvation in the most obscure convent than it is in the most brilliant society, on condition that you have a true
vocation and that you sincerely want to save yourself. Even in the less austere convents, there are practically always some holy nuns whom you can
join as a support for the pursuit of good. Now it's possible that there could
be some lax nuns, even some libertine nuns, who destroy the reputation of
a convent. Still, in any convent, you will avoid many occasions of sin which
are routine in the world, where you are always exposed to the loss of your
soul and your reputation."

Mme de Saint-Périer[79] said, "Madame, the other day Mme d'Havrincourt[80] told us the story of a girl whose misplaced laughter apparently led
to her fall. This story plainly makes your point."

Mme de Maintenon replied, "It doesn't take anything more than that.
On this subject I should tell you what happened to me when I was in Paris.
I didn't know the customs of the region. One day I went to Mass at the church
of the Jacobins. It was no further than going from my room to the door of
the cloister here. I only had a single servant with me. Some men passed by
me and laughingly said hello to me. Completely the innocent, I started to
laugh back at them.

"After Mass, someone came to tell me that I had risked some serious
danger that day. Astonished, I replied to her, 'What are you talking about?'
She said, 'You laughed at the men who passed in front of you.' She let me see
that they could have done something quite untoward with me. I was completely naive about this. I wasn't older than the youngest of you pupils. Still,
I was wrong."

Addressing Mlle de Segonzague, [sic][81] Mme de Maintenon asked her,
"Would you tell me just where I went wrong?"

The pupil replied, "It's when you laughed."

Mme de Maintenon, "That's true enough, but I also erred in going out
alone. It's just not enough to have a male servant walking behind you. If I had
been accompanied by an older woman, she would have been able to tell me
what to do. You should always have an older, more mature woman with
you, even if she is just an elderly scullery maid. That's worth more than fifty

79. Mme Gabrielle-Françoise de Baudeville de Saint-Périer, a teacher at Saint-Cyr, was professed as a Dame de Saint-Louis in 1697. She died at Saint-Cyr in 1712 at the age of thirty-
seven (*MRSC,* 412).

80. See above in this section, note 52.

81. Mlle de Bardon de Segonzac, born in 1690, later become a Capuchin nun (*MRSC,* 430).

servants behind. You must learn to flee men if you want to be secure. You must know how to resist their speeches and how to beat a good retreat, as they say.

"Goodbye, my dear children. Profit from what I've just said. Be filled with God. Don't rely on your own strength, because you will inevitably fall if you do. If these girls who fell into such great crimes had turned to God, they would have been saved from this destruction.

"While I am still on this subject and before I finish, I want to counsel you never to put anything in writing that you would not wish everyone else to see. Sooner or later, it will be discovered. A short time ago, we were obliged to use a *lettre de cachet*[82] to enclose in a convent a young person who had pursued a correspondence with several men. I previously discussed the dangers of writing with you. I just want to remind you that the safest path is to use writing only when it is an absolute necessity.

"Farewell, my children. Please receive the counsels of your mother with as good a heart as she gives them."

AGAINST RELIGIOUS INNOVATIONS [83]

The schoolmistress of the "blue" class asked Mme de Maintenon to warn her pupils against the religious innovations that have swept the world.

Mme de Maintenon responded, "Fortunately they are not obliged to know all these different theories, since it's not their job to judge them. For this reason I've often thanked God for being a woman. It is our lot to avoid speaking about these controversies and even to ignore them. That's one less peril we have to worry about.

"My beloved daughters, this is the best advice I can give you to avoid falling into religious error: 'Flee all religious innovations and avoid all contact with those who are infected with these false opinions, even when it's obvious that they have other good qualities.' Hold firm to the simple, frank beliefs of our religion. Don't support any of the groups opposed to the Catholic faith and to the obedience which every good Christian owes to the decisions of the Roman Church.

---

82. Personally signed and sealed by the king, the *lettre de cachet* permitted the monarch to imprison or exile subjects independently of the usual judiciary procedures. During the Quietist controversy Mme de Maintenon used her husband's *lettres de cachet* to remove faculty considered too sympathetic to the censured movement.

83. This translation is based on Madame de Maintenon, *Instruction de Madame de Maintenon aux demoiselles de la classe bleue: Pour les précautionner contre les nouveautés en matière de religion*, in *LE, BMV*, Ms. P.67, 707–19. The audience for this address was the "blue" class, composed of students from seventeen to twenty years of age. The address was given in 1715.

"If someone asks you just where you stand religiously, tell them that you belong to no particular party in the controversies unresolved by Church authority, that you believe everything the Church teaches and condemn everything she condemns. Say that you suspend your judgment on every theory on which the Church has not clearly passed judgment and that you have no intention of entering into the details of the various controversies which are in vogue at the moment. Nor do you want to cultivate a religious faith that would somehow appear more sophisticated.

"This is the position I adopted in my youth when I spent time with ponderous thinkers who debated these sorts of issues night and day. I never became involved in the disputes. When I saw the bitterness and the animosity that usually arose from these disputes, I said to myself, 'I may not be really devout, but at least I'm not like these people. What is the point of embracing a devout life if you damn yourself by the hatred and the arrogance that is inspired by this sectarian spirit?'

"Presumption is so clearly the mark of these party-line activities that sect members commonly describe someone who is a member of the party as follows: 'This is a woman exalted beyond others.' They talk as if the Gospel somewhere commanded us to have a devotional life more exalted than others and that let us stand out from others.[84] But doesn't the Gospel counsel just the opposite? Aren't we supposed to have a humble and simple devotional life? Doesn't our religion always teach us to take the last place? Doesn't Saint Paul tell all Christians to consider others superior to them?[85] However, the result of these sectarian devotions is a clear disdain for those who don't belong to the group.

"Two types of people are easily attracted to Jansenism. The first are propelled by vanity. Trying to share in the grandeur of the souls who first started this cabal, these women hope to be considered women of wit and cultivation as well. They make it a point of pride to declare their allegiance to the Jansenist party. The second type is blinded by the austerity which the Jansenists glorify in their writings. These women think that they can serve God more perfectly by being a member of this movement. Usually, however, God does not permit these latter women to enter the movement too deeply before they are enlightened as to its errors. God protects their good faith.

"An excellent method to avoid being entrapped by this movement is to limit yourself to spiritual reading by ancient and approved authors. Gre-

84. This is a clear criticism of the Quietists, who frequently used *exaltation* as a term of praise in their literature.
85. See Philippians 3:13.

nada,[86] Rodriguez,[87] and Saint Francis de Sales are excellent choices. The books written by the Port-Royal authors[88] are all the more dangerous because they wrap their venom in a style that flatters our taste and cultivates the mind."

Mme de Maintenon added, "Be especially suspicious of books that are given to you secretly. If they are good books, why make a mystery of them? If these books are suspect, why read them at all?"

Another day, Mme de Maintenon was listening to the *Life of Saint Charles Borromeo*[89] as it was being read aloud to the older pupils. She commented on the passage that said that we must respect everything done by people in authority, especially by the Sovereign Pontiffs.

"My dear children, I'm sure you understand that we're speaking here of our Holy Father, the pope. My hope is that the greatest fruit you take away from your years at Saint-Cyr is a spirit of submission to the Church and of profound respect for the pope.

"When you leave here, you will find people who will try to turn you away from this spirit by telling you that the pope is a man just like anyone else. Now, it's true that he's just a man; however, he is a man who stands in the place of Jesus Christ, who promised us special assistance, and who doesn't refuse that special assistance, especially in the decisions which the pope makes as visible head of the Church. That is why these decisions must always be respected, even when a particular pope is not as irreproachable in his morals and conduct as his office requires. We owe him no less respect and we owe his decisions no less submission. We must see the clear difference between the person and his office. There may be popes who are disordered in

---

86. Venerable Louis of Grenada (1505–1588) was a Spanish Dominican theologian. His major works concerned the types of meditation and mortification proper for the Christian pursuit of spiritual perfection. His *The Sinner's Guide*, praised by Saint Teresa of Avila and Saint Francis de Sales, remains a popular devotional work.

87. Alphonsus Rodriguez (1526–1616) was a Spanish Jesuit theologian specializing in issues of ascetical and mystical theology. His work *The Practice of Christian Perfection*, first published in 1619, detailed the various virtues necessary in the Christian pursuit of holiness. The work quickly became a standard manual of asceticism in the Jesuit order and in other religious orders and lay confraternities of the Counter-Reformation.

88. The convent of Port-Royal became the Parisian center of the Jansenist movement. A group of male Jansenist scholars, known as *les Messieurs de Port-Royal*, settled in the environs of the convent and produced an abundant theological literature, widely praised for its excellent French style. Blaise Pascal's *Pensées* proved the most enduring of this Port-Royal literature.

89. Saint Charles Borromeo (1538–84) became the model of the reformed bishop during his tenure as archbishop of Milan (1560–84). His preaching, parish visitation, care of the poor, catechetical instruction, and development of a diocesan seminary embodied the reforming decrees of the Council of Trent. Canonized a saint in 1610, Borromeo was widely invoked as an ideal for a reformed episcopate and clergy in France.

their moral life, but they are always infallible when, as head of the Church, they make decisions concerning doctrine and when they act in union with the body of bishops.[90] The pope is the successor of Saint Peter, to whom Jesus Christ said, 'You are Peter, and upon this rock I will build my Church, and the gates of hell will not prevail against it.[91] I prayed for you, Peter, so that your faith does not fail.[92] Be assured that I will be with you until the end of time.'"[93]

Mme de Maintenon continued, "Throughout the centuries, errors have arisen against true religious doctrine. They have always been condemned by the Church of Rome, which is the center of catholicity. That is why bishops are not content to examine and condemn the errors of their time only in their local synods. They send their decisions to our Holy Father, the pope, because they are convinced that his decision as head of the Church will confirm theirs and will serve as a rule for other churches.

"You can expect libertines and heretics to call you 'daughters of the pope.' What a praiseworthy title, my daughters! God willing, you will often receive this title. Now, it's true that your education here is simple. It's this very simplicity that makes it superior to the type of education preferred by your opponents. You only need to try to become good Christians, reasonable people, and to base yourself on the Catholic religion. You can then carry it with you wherever you go."

The schoolmistress said, "But, Madame, how can our pupils recognize people who belong to the movements opposed to true Catholicism?"

Mme de Maintenon answered, "First, you will see that these people give them other counsels than those we teach here, which are in conformity with the universal faith of the Church. I gladly agree with Saint Paul on this: 'If anyone announces a Gospel to you that is different than the one I announced to you—even if it be an angel or I myself who do so—let that person be anathema.'[94]

"Don't let yourself be deceived by the appearances of virtue, of auster-

---

90. Maintenon's theory of papal infallibility shows both the influence of and the resistance to Gallicanism, a powerful theological movement in the French Catholicism of the period. Defending the alleged rights and privileges of the French Church, the Gallicans attempted to limit papal authority. They argued, for example, that an ecumenical council of bishops was superior to the pope in the governance of the church. Against the Gallicans Maintenon defends papal infallibility. With the Gallicans, however, Maintenon insists that the pope can make binding doctrinal declarations only when he acts in communion with the universal body of bishops.

91. See Matthew 16:18.

92. See Luke 22:32.

93. See Matthew 28:20.

94. See 2 Corinthians 11:4.

ity, of holiness, even of humility which you might notice in these people. Heretics have always appeared under a mask of feigned piety. To look at them, you would say they have a perfect humility and spirit of mortification, but at the bottom of their doctrines, there are only pride and contempt for the neighbor. Facing this edifying exterior, we must attack them and call them what they truly are! You will see soon enough what they are. You will also see how bitterly they condemn and criticize everyone who does not belong to their faction and who does not think as they do.

"The Jansenists have written defamatory letters, full of bitterness, and animosity, and falsehoods, against the Jesuits, because this order has always been the firmest in denouncing these religious innovations.[95] These letters are so odious that they were burned by the hand of the public executioner. No one can read them without danger of committing a mortal sin. Since there is danger of mortal sin in willingly listening to a falsehood against one person, there is even greater risk in avidly reading these libels, which denigrate an entire respectable order.

"My dear children, the entire purpose of this lecture is to encourage you to remain always attached to the simplicity of the Catholic faith and to avoid ostentation in your devotional life. Don't try to cultivate what they call a spirit out of the ordinary. Your soul will be expansive enough if you know how to save yourself. This exaltation is especially dangerous for our sex. This spiritual overcharge is usually destructive, because it is nearly always mixed with pride and vanity. You know very well that God severely punishes such sins, even in this world."

On another occasion, Madame de Maintenon told the pupils that they should respect indulgences[96] and that they should neglect none of them. "They are the treasures of the Church which our Holy Father, the pope, opens to the faithful at certain times and on certain conditions. We must be scrupulous in benefitting from the precious good of indulgences, because it is the very blood and merits of Jesus Christ which are applied to us through them. It would not be Christian to dismiss them."

She added, "But be careful, my children. Indulgences alone can never save you. Indulgences are pointless if you lead yourself to damnation. You

---

95. With research assistance from the Jansenist scholars Antoine Arnauld and Pierre Nicole, Blaise Pascal published *The Provincial Letters* (1656–57), a series of attacks on the Jesuits for their alleged laxism in moral matters and their alleged denial of the Augustinian doctrine of grace.

96. Indulgences are the remissions of temporal punishment due to sin. They are gained by certain pious practices (such as prayers, almsgiving, pilgrimages) approved by Church authority. The practice of indulgences became one of the disputed points between Catholics and Protestants during the Reformation.

must place yourself in a proper state to receive their fruit by a true conversion of the heart.

"The same goes for bad confessions. These improperly received absolutions will do nothing to prevent you from going to hell. Everything pivots around real conversion, a sincere return of the heart to God. This conversion and this transformation of life must be wholehearted. It must never be undercut. God has placed our salvation in persevering attachment to the good."

OF EDUCATION AND OF THE ADVANTAGES
OF A DEMANDING UPBRINGING [97]

Mme de Maintenon entered the classroom and told the schoolmistress Mme de La Haye[98] to have the pupils do their lesson as if she wasn't even present. Mme de La Haye had a pupil summarize a lecture which Mme de Maintenon had had the goodness to deliver some time ago.

Mme de Maintenon was delighted with the pupil's performance and told her, "My dear daughter, it would be a crime if you didn't profit from what you know. It's a pleasure to listen to you because you retain so well what you've been told. Now it's only a question of putting the theory into practice."

As the pupil continued, Mme de Maintenon said, "This is wonderful, but, Mlle Cateuil,[99] you seem to be embellishing what I said. You're adding your own words. It's just not possible that I would have said all these fine things."

Next, Mlle de La Barre[100] recited what she remembered from a lecture on right conduct. She offered several examples. For example, the Dames de Saint-Louis wouldn't be doing their duty if they neglected to teach us.

Mme de Maintenon replied, "Not only if they neglected to teach you, but even if, having taught you, they spent the rest of the day in prayer rather

97. This translation is based on Madame de Maintenon, *Instruction de Madame de Maintenon aux demoiselles de la classe verte: Sur l'éducation et sur l'avantage d'être élevé un peu durement*, in *LE*, BMV, Ms. P.66, 11–20. The audience for this address was the "green" class, composed of students from eleven to fourteen years of age.

98. Mme Marie-Anne-Marguerite Lemetayer de La Haye Le Comte, a teacher at Saint-Cyr, was professed as a Dame de Saint-Louis in 1695. She died at Saint-Cyr in 1706 at the age of thirty (*MRSC*, 412).

99. Mlle Marie-Madeleine de Vendretz de Cateuil, born in 1689, was professed as a Dame de Saint-Louis in 1711 and died at Saint-Cyr in 1758 (*MRSC*, 413, 430).

100. Mlle de La Barre de Martigny, born in 1694, later became a nun (*MRSC*, 431).

than supervising you and paying attention to all the other details of your education. Although prayer is an excellent work, they should not lose themselves in it, because their great duty is to teach you and to give you a good upbringing.

"Although as nuns they are obliged to say the divine office and to have other prayers in common, you will notice that they space out their departures so that there are always some present with you. You are never left alone, because your moral and religious education is the principal end of the Institute. That is what their founders expected of them before everything else.

"But my children, what account will you render to God for the advantages of this fine education? Imagine for a minute that you found yourself in the usual state of young ladies in your condition. Your mother would have at most two chambermaids, one of whom would be your governess. What sort of education do you think such a girl would give you? Usually they are peasant girls or, at best, members of the minor bourgeoisie. They only know how to stand up straight, how to lace a corset, and how to make a good curtsey. In their eyes, the greatest crime is getting your blouse dirty, for example, by dripping ink on it. This is a crime that will merit a severe punishment, because it's the governess who has to clean and iron the soiled clothing. You can lie about it as much as you want. The punishment will be the same, because the governess won't know how to iron or to sew well.

"This governess will carefully dress you up as if you're a little doll, so that you can make a good impression on company. The brightest among them might know a few lines of poetry, some of the stanzas of Pibrac that she insists on having her charge recite at every occasion.[101] And the child will recite them as if she were a little parrot! Everyone will say, 'What a pretty baby! How cute!' The governess will be carried away with joy and will go no further than that. Very few have anything reasonable to say.

"I remember that when I lived with my aunt, one of the chambermaids took care of me. She was always correcting me and always telling me to stand up straight. But for everything else, she just let me do what I wanted.

"We can even go up to the example of royalty. Just how do you think they are raised? They're given a governess who is some socially prominent woman, who has often been raised just as I've just said. Usually she's the

---

101. Guy du Faur de Pribac (1529–84) was the author of *Quatrains du Sieur de Pribac.* From their first publication in 1574, this collection of brief poems became a staple of early childhood education in France.

wife of a court favorite or the relative of some cabinet minister, who clearly doesn't have the qualities required for such a post.

"How do you think she talks to the little princess? Do you think that it's all piety and reason? That would be the ideal, but usually she only talks about what made her so prominent in high society. When the princess goes out, the governess takes great care in dressing and adorning her and tells her to be well-behaved. If the princess is a child, she pulls her by her skirt. If she is older, the governess follows her. The governess instructs her on how to receive company in her apartment. The rest of the day, the governess just lets the princess play with some peasant, who was formerly her wet nurse and who has become her chambermaid. This person can scarcely be expected to speak intelligently to the princess. Much less can she instruct the princess on matters of faith, righteousness, and probity.

"I'm always astonished when the king describes his education to me. He told me that his governesses played all day long and left him in the hands of the chambermaids, without showing the least concern for the young king. As you know, he started to reign at the age of three and a half. He ate everything he liked without any concern for what might be dangerous to his health. This is what made him so careful later in life. If somebody fried an omelet, he always grabbed a few pieces and ate it in the corner with Monsieur.[102]

"He told me that most often he was left in the care of a peasant woman. His usual play companion was the little daughter of a chambermaid who worked for the chambermaids of the queen. He called this girl "Queen Marie," because they used to play together the game called *À la Madame*. She always played the queen, and he played a page or a valet. He carried her train, pushed her in a chair, or carried a flag in front of her. Do you think that little Queen Marie could give him good advice? Do you think that she could have been useful to him in anything at all?

"My dear children, I warn you once again that you will be guilty before God if you do not profit from the unceasing care we take to make you as perfect as possible in the eyes of God and even in the eyes of the world. By 'the world' here, I mean those pious, reasonable, and polite people who remain in the world. As for the libertines and for all those who have neither honor nor religion, it should be your glory not to suit their tastes, because you so clearly think and act differently.

---

102. Philippe, duc d'Orléans (1640–1701), younger brother of Louis XIV, was officially referred to as "Monsieur."

"Since I'm already speaking to you, I'm going to tell you several things which I usually keep for older pupils, but which would be just as good for you to hear. My dear children, in God's name, don't be haughty or arrogant. Count your nobility for nothing. Never talk about it. What good is it, if you don't have virtue? Isn't it virtue that determines true nobility? Be polite to everyone. Show respect for persons of a certain age or in a certain state, even when they lack noble birth. The world is full of these sorts of people. You will see, when you are in the world, that one should use one's best manners with them.

"Once and for all, understand that nobility is nothing without merit. It is merit that lays the ground for honor, esteem, and respect, in whomever it may be found.

"Let's illustrate this by an example. Mlle d'Andrieux,[103] which would you prefer to be: a young noblewoman raised in her village, who is vulgar, uncouth, dirty, and ignorant, or a girl without noble birth who, having some goodness, was properly raised and turns out to be sweet, polite, gracious, well-tempered?

The pupil said, "I'd rather be the latter one."

Mme de Maintenon replied, "I completely share your opinion. This example should show you clearly what a supreme good a fine education is and with what care you should profit from it.

"I also implore you not to be too delicate. By your own free will, you should try to toughen up your upbringing. Be happy when you have the opportunity to do some work that's rather menial. This strengthens you. It's good for you. You know that the Holy Spirit praises the strong woman when she braces her arms for work.[104] That's because she has overcome her natural weakness and delicacy in order to take care of her household.

"Don't complain about anything. Our treatment of you is always as just as it can be. We have tried in everything that pertains to you to take a middle course. As a result, those of you who must return to material poverty will not experience too great a fall and those of you who will have material comfort will be all the better for having been raised a bit austerely.

"I see this trait every day in the marquise de Dangeau, who is a German princess.[105] Having twelve sisters and several brothers, she didn't have all the usual comforts of noble birth in her youth. Even with this charming and delicate air which she projects, nothing bothers her. I don't know anyone who

---

103. Mlle Seran d'Andrieux, born in 1694, later became a nun (*MRSC*, 431).

104. See Proverbs 14:1.

105. Sophie-Marie de Löwenstein, marquise de Dangeau (1664–1736).

finds it easier to be serene. She may have serious problems, but she always appears to be happy. When she is sick, she suffers patiently. She doesn't run after doctors and medicines. She just says, 'I would just as happily die from this illness as from fever. It's whatever God wants.' Doesn't real happiness consist in being so resigned to suffering from a young age?

"I was married at the age of fourteen. Ordinarily at this age, you're delighted to do just what you want. I naively thought that by doing this I could play the great lady and do a thousand other things that still attract me. But I was gravely disappointed in this.

"I knew an old woman, the duchesse de Richelieu,[106] who was more reasonable than I was about this issue. As a result, she was much happier. She had taken the resolution of always maintaining a firm and upright posture. She wouldn't permit herself the least indulgence in how she stood and sat. No matter how ill she was, she never leaned on anything. The most she would concede to herself was relaxing her hands a bit. People said about her, 'Duchess, you can't possibly endure this any more.'

"My children, why do you think that I am telling you all this? It's for your own good. It's to encourage you to develop the habit of voluntarily restraining yourself from seeking what is most comfortable. This is the best method to soften a little the material problems that might await you. And even if you end up with thirty thousand pounds of income, I would still tell you the same things. In whatever social state you find yourselves, it will always be beneficial to have had a demanding upbringing.

"Goodbye, my children. I apologize for having spoken to you at such length. Put in practice what I have told you and what you have so clearly retained."

---

106. One of the close friends of Maintenon was Anne Poussart de Fors du Vigean, duchesse de Richelieu. Named a maid-of-honor to the Dauphine de Bavière (wife of the Grand Dauphin Louis, son of Louis XIV), Duchesse de Richelieu died in 1684.

ADDRESSES TO FACULTY

VOLUME EDITOR'S INTRODUCTION

In her addresses to the Saint-Cyr faculty, the Dames de Saint-Louis, Maintenon details her philosophy of education. The primary objective of education is moral, with religious piety serving as the foundation of the virtues to be cultivated. Rather than focusing on the details of curriculum, Maintenon emphasizes the moral character of the teacher. It is the teacher's successful modeling of the virtues and her capacity to draw moral lessons from academic and nonacademic subjects that foster success in her students' ethical progress. The addresses' astringent critique of an educational emphasis on the classics, on rhetoric, or on history springs from the strict primacy accorded the formation of moral character.

The addresses to the faculty also focus on the dialogical method to be used at Saint-Cyr. The conscientious teacher must participate in several types of conversations with her pupils: regularly scheduled interviews; informal discussions before and after class; confidences shared during recreation. In the classroom itself, dialogue takes precedence over lecture. The effective teacher carefully calibrates her remarks to be easily understood by her pupils and to elicit their response. Rote memorization and displays of erudition only suffocate the teacher-student dialogue that constitutes the heart of Maintenon's pedagogical method.

The purpose of this educational dialogue is clearly moral. Only through multileveled interviews can the teacher accurately gauge the student's moral temperament, her distinctive blend of virtues and vices. Only with this psychological knowledge can the teacher properly encourage the student by counsel and by example. The trust generated by this interpersonal knowledge helps the teacher assist the student to discern her future state in life. The addresses to the faculty manifest two salient traits of Maintenon's educational philosophy: its rationalism and its moralism.

Maintenon repeatedly warns her faculty to act reasonably with their pupils. *Of the Education of Ladies* insists that the teachers must attempt to form the reason, not the memory or the eloquence, of their pupils. *Of Solid Education* emphasizes reasonable piety, focused on virtue rather than devotions. Only a faith freed from credulity and superstition can survive the acids of religious skepticism. The faculty are to provide students with a reasonable explanation of all school practices and classroom commands, even of punishments. Both faculty and students are to rely on reason in maintaining discipline over their emotions.

Maintenon's repeated emphasis on the centrality of reason bears a Cartesian echo. In fact, she had read and approved the early works of Descartes in her early years as a prominent *salonnière*.[1] Parallels with Cartesian rationalism can be found in Maintenon's suspicion of emotion and insistence that all major decisions must be accompanied by rational justification. As Descartes criticized Jesuit education for its book-centered humanism, Maintenon rejected bookish education, productive of vain erudition, in favor of an education fostering personal, rational reflection. Even in religion Maintenon's plea for reason bears Cartesian traces. For all her publicly avowed Catholic orthodoxy, Maintenon champions a type of personal meditation more akin to rational self-scrutiny than to biblical meditation open to the movement of grace. Her effort to subordinate piety to the dictates of reason is not foreign to the moral radical project of certain Cartesians to contain religion itself within the limits of reason. Maintenonian rationalism, however, carries its own distinctive moral stamp. For Maintenon the reasonable woman is the person who knows how to avoid moral peril, how to adjudicate domestic conflicts, and how to discern her personal vocation. It is the practical rather than the speculative power of reason that Maintenon prizes as an antidote to passion or illusion. Prudence rather than science is the preeminent ally of Maintenonian reason.

Focused on the cultivation of virtues, the addresses to the faculty also exhibit Maintenon's adamant moralism. Her effort to stress moral character over cultural sophistication involves more than the banning of novels. In *Of the Danger of Profane Books*, she limits the teaching of history to a schematic presentation of geography and dynasties that will permit the students to avoid gaffes in polite conversation. In *Of the Proper Choice of Theatrical Pieces for Pupils*, Maintenon is at her most censorious. Her insistence on the sur-

---

1. For a fuller study of the complex relationship between Cartesianism and female authors of the period, see Harth, *Cartesian Women*.

veillance of literature entering the school becomes so acute that she condemns even the acceptance of a gift wrapped in a page from a questionable book.

As many critics allege, the prim censoriousness of Maintenon reflects the narrowness of an education devoted uniquely to the formation of moral character. The humanities and sciences play only a minor role in such a pedagogical system. The moralism of the educational philosophy expounded in the addresses, however, represents more than a simple horror of sin. First, the strict emphasis on moral formation reflects Maintenon's disillusionment with the school's earlier—and in her opinion, disastrous—emphasis on cultural achievement and then on mystical illumination. The addresses' references to the earlier artistic or Quietist eras at Saint-Cyr are invariably bitter. For Maintenon, the prudery in the moral education championed by Saint-Cyr in the early eighteenth century is far preferable to the vanity fostered by an artistic education or to the illusions generated by a mystical one.

Second, the addresses to the faculty insist that the education offered at Saint-Cyr must be adapted to the needs of its particular audience: impoverished, provincial, aristocratic women. Ever the pragmatist, Maintenon argues that all education must be suited to the specific vocational horizon of its students. An educational emphasis on science or on mystical contemplation can only alienate pupils who require certain practical virtues and specific domestic skills to survive their straitened futures. Accounting skill trumps fluency in Greek. Temperance takes precedence over wit. It is the vocational destiny of the Saint-Cyr alumna, not a simple aversion to vice, that banishes the educational norm of book-and-lecture and that consecrates virtuous dialogue as the cornerstone of Maintenonian education.

OF THE EDUCATION OF LADIES [2]

"Since God has chosen me to help in the founding of the king's establishment for the education of impoverished noblewomen in his kingdom, I feel an obligation to share with those who will teach them what experience has taught me about the proper methods for a good education. Surely this is one of the most demanding vocations possible. You will scarcely have any free time between your tasks. If you are going to teach children, you must give your entire life to this enterprise.

2. This translation is based on Madame de Maintenon, *Aux Dames de Saint-Louis, Sur l'éducation des demoiselles*, in *LE*, BMV, Ms. P.62, 421–28. This address was first delivered to the faculty in 1686.

"If you only want to develop the pupils' memory a little, they only need a few hours of classroom instruction every day. In fact, it would be unwise to make them work any harder than that. However, if you want to develop their reason, inflame their heart, cultivate their mind, destroy their bad habits—to put it succinctly, if you want to make them love virtue—you will always be working with them. Every moment will have opportunities for this kind of education. You are as necessary for them at recreation as in the classroom. Whenever you leave them to their own devices, they will be the poorer for it.

"However, since it's impossible for one person to guide such a large number of children, it will be necessary to have several schoolmistresses for each class. Now, it's important that all of these teachers act in harmony. They should share the same feelings and the same convictions. They should use the same methods to instill these principles.

"In this work more than any other, you need to forget completely your own interests. Even if you're seeking a modicum of glory through this position, you can only expect to have it indirectly through the success of your students and by the simplest of means.

"When I say that you need to forget yourself, I mean that you must try to make yourself understood and to persuade your students of the value of these principles. We're not looking here for rhetorical eloquence, which can elicit admiration in the listeners. On occasion you should be ready to chat informally with the students. This will help the students to love and trust you. You can acquire an influence over them that will prove beneficial. But not any method will prove helpful in acquiring this influence. Only reasonable methods will prove successful. Only a right intention will merit the blessings of God.

"You should concern yourself less with furnishing their mind than with forming their reason. It's true that this approach provides less occasion for the knowledge and the cleverness of the schoolmistress to shine. A young girl who has memorized a thousand things makes a greater impression on her friends and family than does a girl who simply knows how to exercise her judgment, when to be silent, how to be modest and reserved, how to avoid rushing into showing what she thinks about something.

"Sometimes you should let them express their will so that you may understand their basic dispositions. You can then more accurately teach them the differences between the good, the evil, and the indifferent. You can then proceed to teach them other moral things.

"I think that everyone who will read these words will understand clearly enough what I mean by 'indifferent' things. Nonetheless, since I am trying to be as helpful as possible, I am adding an example that might seem rather banal.

"The uniform, enclosed way of life of the pupils here at Saint-Cyr might seem to offer us less dramatic opportunities to make these moral distinctions than we might have with pupils who are still living in the world. In the latter case the opportunities for showing the stark contrasts are obvious. Still, even here we have the choice to give them one companion over another, to let them walk in one area rather than another, to play one game rather than another. All of these minor choices can let them understand that if they are reasonable, they can be the mistress of themselves in every situation, not only when they want to be.

"I used these previous examples because these choices involve possible moral consequences. A companion might be dangerous, a particular walk might be unwise, a certain game might be inappropriate. But when you refuse them one of these options, I want you, as much as is prudently possible, to tell them the reason why a particular activity is forbidden. I even encourage you to try to grant often the wishes of your pupils, so that when you must refuse them, the refusal will be of a firmness that never cedes to entreaties. You will not believe how easily this way of proceeding facilitates the task of governing students.

"It is good for you to accustom them to never getting their way by importuning the teachers. You must be implacable in dealing with vices. You must punish them either by shame or by punishments as severe as they are rare.

"You should avoid the dangerous attitude of certain people who, out of exaggerated fear of offending God, carefully avoid those occasions where the real inclinations of children can manifest themselves. You cannot have enough knowledge of pupils in order to encourage them to hate vice and to love virtue. You must strengthen them in their pursuit of virtue by giving them principles to help avoid ignorance in this area.

"You must study their dispositions, observe their moods, and examine their little struggles in order to give them a complete education. Experience teaches only too clearly how easily we commit faults without even knowing it. It also shows how many people fall into a life of crime, although by birth they were no worse than many others who led perfectly innocent lives.

"You must teach them how to avoid the occasions of sin. One of the worst is a bad companion.

"You must teach them all the refinements of honor, integrity, restraint, generosity, and humanity. You must draw a picture of virtue as beautiful and as admirable as it actually is.

"Having some brief tales conducive to this end is appropriate and helpful. They both instruct and entertain. Nonetheless, the pupils must be convinced that without religion for a foundation, virtue is not secure. They must also be convinced that God does not tolerate everything and that He disapproves of these pagan and heroic virtues that are only the effects of a prickly pride and of an insatiable thirst for praise. It's not necessary to give long lectures about these issues. It's better to present them as the opportunity arises.

"You should make yourself respected by the children. The only way to achieve this goal is to avoid showing any faults yourself. You wouldn't believe how quick they are to detect any failings. This careful attention to the perfect exterior can be very helpful for your own welfare.

"You should never scold them just because you are in a bad mood. Never give them any reason to think that some times are better than others for obtaining what they want from you.

"You should be indulgent with those who are habitually good, act severely with those who are bad, and avoid being brusque with anyone. By your good humor, you should make them enjoy the presence of their schoolmistresses. In that way they will act in front of their teachers just as they would if they were alone.

"You should share some of the recreation of the pupils. However, you should never use childish language or gestures. On the contrary, you should always try to raise their level of conduct by speaking to them in a reasonable way. As soon as they can speak and hear, the children should be accustomed to reason. The very fact that reason is not opposed to wholesome recreation is one of the reasons why we must permit it.

"External accomplishments, the knowledge of foreign languages, and so many of the other accomplishments that people desire for high-society women have serious disadvantages. Acquiring these skills takes a considerable amount of time that could be more usefully employed. The ladies of the school of Saint-Louis should never be raised in this way, if it can be avoided. Given the fact that they are without wealth, there is no sense in cultivating their mind and their heart in a manner so unadapted to their fortune and to their social position. However, Christianity and reason, which are the two great values we wish to inculcate in our pupils, are as helpful to princesses as to paupers. If our pupils profit from what I want them to learn, they will be more than capable of supporting every good and every misfortune that God will deign to send them."

OF SOLID EDUCATION[3]

Mme de Glapion[4] asked Mme de Maintenon what she meant by this "solid education" she so wanted us to give to the pupils.

Mme de Maintenon said, "I understand it to mean that before and above everything else, you apply yourself to developing the piety, the reason, and the morals of your girls. You inspire in them the love and the practice of all the virtues proper to them now and in the future.

"To do this, you must work night and day to uproot and to plant in these young hearts. This must be done every day by the public and private interviews you have with them. Wisely use the right occasions to inculcate good principles, good counsels, and, even more important, good sentiments and good habits.

"It's not enough, for example, to succeed in having your girls so recollected in church that they don't dare to raise their eyes. It's true that this is useful for teaching them the restraint and the subjection so essential for young people. But don't think that they are somehow more devout than if you had succeeded in planting a real love of piety in their hearts.

"On this subject we might sometimes say to them, 'I'm delighted with your exterior conduct. It's perfect. But only you know truly if you are showing this reverence out of respect for God's presence or if you are doing so out of respect for creatures. If it's the latter, your efforts are rather pointless.'

"Let's imagine that the religious community complained that one group of pupils was disordered and unruly, while their schoolmistress knew that, thanks to God, they had few real faults and that they were truly pious and virtuous. She shouldn't take offense at these criticisms, because we should always strive to be rather than to appear. She should try to remedy any problems that might actually exist.

"Yesterday I was talking on this subject to some of the faculty who were here. I told them that I feared that some of the teachers seemed more upset when their pupils made noise in the corridor than when one day some of the pupils might do something displeasing to God. Only human beings would

---

3. This translation is based on Madame de Maintenon, *Recueil d'un entretien de Madame de Maintenon avec les Religieuses de Saint-Louis, Sur l'éducation solide,* in *LE,* BMV, Ms. P.68, 263–73. Mme de Maintenon so frequently used the term *solide* as a term of approbation that it became associated with her person. Louis XIV nicknamed her *Votre Solidité.*

4. Mme Marie-Madeleine de Glapion des Routis was professed as a Dame de Saint-Louis in 1695 and died at Saint-Cyr in 1729 at the age of fifty-five (*MRSC,* 412). Several times appointed as the superior of the community, Mme de Glapion was a close friend and confidante of Mme de Maintenon.

have been offended by the first type of fault, while God Himself would have been offended by the second.

"One of the teachers told me quite frankly that she could not tolerate the idea that any of her pupils would be found at fault. This was her weakness.

"I told her, 'This is a great fault. Young people, who miss nothing, will easily notice when a teacher is less concerned about establishing virtue in the class than making the pupils appear virtuous in some imaginary world. I can't tell you enough how much I fear that some of you are content just to modify the externals. Your vow of education commits you to raise your pupils in a Christian manner and to accustom them to live a strict moral life. To accomplish this, we must have people who sincerely and wholeheartedly give themselves to the work God has confided to them and who seek nothing for themselves. I don't think that giving yourself wholeheartedly to the pupils just means that you play with them or that you render them some little service. You must provide them with those demanding services that your particular vocation binds you to give.

"Don't avoid getting involved in their games, in their discussions, even in their little disputes. There's so much good to be done everywhere when you want to do it. All of this is part of their education.

"Don't tolerate any fastidiousness or narrowness in their pious practices. Teach them the sacred Gospel in all of its power. Tell them that only the violent will carry away the Kingdom of God;[5] that they must take up their cross and renounce themselves in order to be saved;[6] that they must sincerely pardon those who have offended them; that they must adore God in spirit and in truth, and serve Him in the same way;[7] that they must hold sin in horror, avoid all the occasions of sin, and try wholeheartedly to practice the virtues that Our Lord has counseled.

"Preach to them. Sometimes use the strong and solid maxims of religion. At other times use the maxims of honor and decorum. Even after my death, never stop promoting the importance and the necessity of the simple and solid piety I have been enjoining on you. I have stressed it so often that you may have grown tired of my emphasis on this point.

"Some time ago the duchesse de Bourgogne[8] confided something to me that gave me infinite delight. You know that she was gravely ill. Every-

5. See Matthew 11:12.
6. See Matthew 16:24, Mark 8:34, and Luke 9:23.
7. See John 4:23–24.
8. See above, *Addresses to Students*, note 17.

one was praising the extraordinary effect of the medical remedies that had so quickly taken her out of danger.

"One day she quietly told me, 'I'm convinced that it was Saint Geneviève,[9] rather than the medicines, who healed me. I felt much better as soon as I started a novena to her and I had drunk some water where they had placed some blessed bread of St. Geneviève.'

"I said to her, 'Madame, I'm delighted to find this simplicity of faith, which is rare in the powerful of the world. May God reward this simple and ardent faith with many miraculous healings. Usually these miracles are reserved for simple folk.'

"Recalling some of the miracles in the Gospel, I told her that Our Lord performed them in response to the faith of those who turned to Him. He said to the Canaanite woman, 'Your faith is great!'[10] To another woman, 'May it be done according to your faith!'[11]

"I added, 'Madame, if I saw no signs of piety other than this devotion to Saint Geneviève through her novena and blessed bread, I might fear that we only had superstition here. Although these pious practices are useful and authorized by the Church, they are not essential to the faith. They can even become abusive, when people place all their hope in them and yet neglect their most important duties. Such are those who would not miss saying their rosary for anything in the world, but who have not the slightest problem with blaspheming or with attempting revenge. It's the same with those who voluntarily fast on Saturday but who violate Church law by eating meat on Friday. Some think that they cannot be damned if they just wear a scapular or say the rosary, although they voluntarily remain in a state of sin.

"'It's quite a different matter when these pious practices are accompanied by a life of virtue faithful to all the basic Christian duties. In this case one prefers what is obligatory to these ancillary practices. This is clearly what you do. I notice that you diligently attack your faults, use righteous violence to win your salvation, profit from your Holy Communions, try to control your moods, ask pardon from your ladies-in-waiting when you've been too critical, and, most important, flee sin and try to serve God as well as you can. I gladly acknowledge that your piety has the necessary qualities of a true and solid piety.

9. St. Geneviève is the patron saint of Paris. The Parisian church of Saint Étienne-du-Mont houses her shrine, a popular site of pilgrimage and renowned for its healings. The cult of St. Geneviève was particularly popular in French royal circles.

10. See Matthew 15:22.

11. See Matthew 9:22.

"'Piety which claims to be solid, but which disdains and mocks the pious practices approved by the Church, is a piety of pride. On the contrary, piety which claims only these practices, without fulfilling the most basic duties of religion, is a piety of superstition.'"

Mme de Maintenon added, "My dear daughters, I am telling you all this in order to convince you ever more deeply of the obligation you have to inspire your pupils with the same sentiments. Be careful to avoid letting them develop a haughty piety that dismisses or mocks anything miraculous, without letting them fall into the superstitious narrowness of the unenlightened. They must have a great respect for the devotions approved by the Church, however minor they may seem, but you must always remind them of the essential practices of the faith: the flight from sin, the love of God and of neighbor, and the accomplishment of the duties of one's state in life.

"You must help them to understand that true piety consists in loving God, in thinking about Him, and in asking His help in their various projects. If they are truly pious, they cannot be content limiting their attention to God to the times when they are in church or approaching the sacraments. They must be completely given to God throughout the day by carefully avoiding everything that might displease Him and by doing everything that we know is pleasing to Him."

OF THE DANGER OF PROFANE BOOKS [12]

In his sermon to the pupils he had just confirmed, the Bishop of Chartres [13] had spoken against Christians who delight in reading profane books.

Afterward, Mme de Maintenon said to the Dames de Saint-Louis on this subject, "I think these books are very dangerous, especially for the members of our sex, who are naturally so curious about everything."

Mme de Glapion [14] asked, "What do you mean by profane books? Are these limited only to novels?"

---

12. This translation is based on Madame de Maintenon, *Recueil d'un entretien de Madame de Maintenon aux Religieuses de Saint-Louis; Que les lectures profanes les plus innocentes sont toujours les plus dangereuses,* in *LE,* BMV, Ms. P.65, 421–28. This address was originally delivered to the faculty in 1696.

13. Paul Godet des Marais (1647–1709) served as bishop of Chartres (1692–1709). The spiritual overseer of the academy at Saint-Cyr, in whose diocese it lay, Godet des Marais became a close friend and ally of Maintenon in the struggle against Quietism and Jansenism. He participated in the episcopal committee that condemned the semi-Quietism of Fénelon in 1697 and led a campaign supporting Pope Clement XI's 1705 condemnation of a new variant of Jansenism. Many of his letters of spiritual direction to Maintenon have survived.

14. See above in this section, note 4.

Mme de Maintenon replied, "There are bad books in and of themselves, such as novels, because they only appeal to vanity and to the passions. There are other books that, without being as bad, are still dangerous for young people, because they destroy the taste for pious books or because they puff up the mind. Examples would be books of Roman history, or of universal history, at least those situated in mythic times."

Mme de Blosset[15] said, "But are you then putting these history books in the rank of profane books?"

Mme de Maintenon replied, "I called profane all the books that are not religious, even if they seem innocent, as soon as it is clear that they have no real usefulness. Teach your pupils to be extremely cautious in their reading. They should always prefer their needlework, housework, or the duties of their state in life to it. If they really want to read, make sure they use well-chosen books apt to nourish their faith, to cultivate their judgment, and to guide their morals. A good mind always makes a good use of what is read and somehow turns reading to personal profit. A bad mind abuses it or uses it as a source of pride or of some other vice, which you should be trying to root out in your pupils."

Mme de Rocquemont[16] asked her if we couldn't on occasion use the works of antiquity to show examples of virtue in the ancient philosophers and pagan sages. After all, some of the most religious works, such as Père de Saint-Jure's *La Connaissance de Notre-Seigneur*[17] and the works of Rodriguez,[18] are full of these examples. The same is true of many other similar works.

Mme de Maintenon answered, "I am very afraid that all these grandiose gestures of generosity and heroism will overwhelm their imagination. They will make them as vain and precious as they were at the beginning of this school, when we used this type of matter to instruct them. You saw how everything of this kind that we mixed into their instruction spoiled them. You know how difficult it was to bring them back to the simplicity proper to our sex. There is something pernicious in these types of passages and even more so in entire profane books. They distract the pupils from the beautiful simplicity of the Gospel and from everything that leads to humility, innocence, selflessness, and other Christian virtues.

15. Mme Anne de Blosseville de Blosset was professed as a Dame de Saint-Louis in 1694. She died at Saint-Cyr in 1742 at the age of eighty-five (*MRSC*, 410).

16. Mme Suzanne-Madeleine d'Antony de Roquemont was professed as a Dame de Saint-Louis in 1694. She died at Saint-Cyr in 1730 at the age of sixty-three (*MRSC*, 410).

17. The author is a French Jesuit priest, Jean-Baptiste de Saint-Jure (1588–1657), famous for his devotional works, especially for his commentaries on the life of Jesus.

18. See above, *Addresses to Students*, note 87.

"I do not think I need to say anything else to convince you of the danger of these kinds of readings and passages. Once again, your pupils have an infinitely greater need to learn how to conduct themselves as Christians in the world and how to govern their families wisely than to become scholars or heroines. Women always settle for half-knowledge. The little they know usually makes them vain, disdainful, garrulous, and contemptuous of solid things.

"I am so convinced of the truth of what I'm telling you that this is exactly how I conduct myself with regard to my own niece.[19] I only ask the governess that she make my niece a girl who is good, sweet, pious, generous, and charitable—in other words, a good Christian woman.

"To return to the question of these profane passages, I wouldn't be opposed to the following case: the pupils ask you who Alexander was and you respond simply and without passion that he was a king of Macedonia, a great conqueror, and so on. I could also imagine the following scenario: you have them do a reading that contains some of these pagan details; as they do this reading, you point out in passing the difference between these actions that appear so wonderful and those that are animated by religion and by faith. The former are punished in the other world because of the pride that animates them, while the latter are crowned with an eternal reward.

"The lives of saints and the acts of the martyrs are full of the names of gods, of pagan emperors, and of philosophers. That is not a good reason to avoid them. On the contrary, you should explain in a few words at the right moment who these emperors, these gods, and especially these martyrs are in our history books. Just be careful to encourage your pupils toward the good and toward the hatred of sin by the fear and the love of God. Don't use profane examples from antiquity to do this. Although they are useful for certain occasions, they still tend to excite a certain pride, which then must be destroyed afterward.

"This pride is harder to overcome than the greatest vices. Most people given to God's service must still overcome this. Having carefully decorated the mind, practically turning it into an idol, we then have to renounce it, sacrifice it, and make it submit to the humble doctrine of Jesus Christ.

"Believe me, don't fill your pupils' minds with a lot of books. Flood them with the spirit and the counsels of Our Lord. In truth, they inspire an incomparable grandeur. If your pupils commit a particular fault, tell them, 'How do you harmonize what you said or what you did with the Gospel?' For example, if you must criticize an act of sloth, quote Saint Paul to them. He

19. The niece is Françoise d'Aubigné, the future duchesse de Noailles.

preferred to work with his hands when he preached the Gospel to the nations rather than to be a burden to others.[20]

"This approach to education will not make you popular with high society. But, my daughters, always remember that you are not raising these girls in order to please the world. You are doing this to make them completely virtuous, wise, and reasonable people. I say 'reasonable,' because although they must be led to accept wholeheartedly the exact practice of the Gospel, you must avoid adding anything narrow or petty to it. Don't make up stories, don't turn indifferent things into crimes, don't turn things that are only counsels into a matter of obligation. Always tell them the bald truth and avoid embellishment.

"I think this is the best method for strengthening them in the path of piety. All of the mockery of the skeptics will not be able to shake their faith when they are certain that you have taught them nothing false or extreme.

"As for the books you give them, I want them to be carefully chosen. They must all contain the same spirit, without wandering away from the norm of what all Christians must do in a simple and common life. What you usually have them read on the vowed life, although excellent in itself, doesn't help them too much. They think that these things are only good for the convent. We should fear that some of them who don't want to enter this way of life will abandon all pious practices on this pretext.

"There's another problem when you tell them about sensational and unusual things. After they have spent a good bit of time reading about them, you must spend as much time telling them that these things are to be admired rather than to be imitated. At least, you should make them profit as much as possible from reading about these things. You should guide them to a sense of admiration before the merit of these things, to adore the different ways in which God works with each of His saints, to follow them faithfully when God calls us, and always to submit our inspirations to the lights of God's ministers.

"My dear daughters, you need a piety that is enlightened, balanced, and solid, rather than one that is emotional and theatrical. You must be a solid example of the piety you are tying to form in your pupils! So accustom them to listen to the readings with simplicity, to be edified by what is good, to apply what is proper and useful to their daily lives, and to avoid arguing about what they don't understand or what is not to their taste. Now, it's impossible to stop certain thoughts or reflections occupying our mind, but if they are

20. See 1 Thessalonians 2:9.

contrary to faith or to the respect owed to the operations of God in His saints, we must know how to silence and even to repress them."

Mme de Maintenon added with a smile, "I encourage you to teach the pupils to treat good authors as if they were good friends. You always speak good about them whenever you discuss them. You never say anything bad, or even apparently bad, about them when you talk about them."

Mme de Glapion asked if it were absolutely forbidden to teach the pupils about the history of France.

Mme de Maintenon said, "It's only right to know the princes of one's nation. The pupils need to know enough to avoid mixing up the persons and the successions of our kings with the princes of other empires. It's also important for them to have enough historical knowledge to avoid confusing a Roman emperor with a Chinese or Japanese one, or a Spanish or an English king for the king of Persia or of Siam. But we should do all this without much detail or method. As long as they are not less ignorant than the majority of educated people are on these issues, that is sufficient."

OF THE PROPER CHOICE OF
THEATRICAL PIECES FOR PUPILS [21]

Mme de Maintenon had heard that several young pupils in the "red" class [ages seven to eleven] had changed certain scenes of a sacred tragedy into a farce in order to amuse themselves. She sternly criticized the faculty because, instead of correcting these pupils, the teachers entertained themselves by listening to them.

She said, "You should never give your pupils an education too sophisticated or too theoretical, as we tried to do at the beginning of this school. On the other hand, you shouldn't give them an education that's too servile or too childish. Under the guise of a simplicity that is nothing other than mediocrity, you shouldn't tolerate anything contemptible, such as the piece of tragedy they turned upside down. At Christmas they gave a play where the Blessed Virgin and Saint Joseph entered the stage by banging on doors in order to beg for some lodging.

"Why should our school ever tolerate these ridiculous Nativity plays that mix stupid and risible incidents with the holiest of mysteries? What pos-

---

21. This translation is based on Madame de Maintenon, *Entretien de Madame de Maintenon aux Religieuses de Saint-Louis, Sur le bon choix des pièces qu'elles puissent donner à leurs demoiselles pour leur amusement innocent et sur le danger des livres et des manuscrits qui se pourraient glisser dans la maison,* in *LE,* BMV, Ms. P.67, 733–48.

sible use could there be in having our pupils sing about such things? If it's for recreation, why should they have to amuse themselves at the expense of what is most exalted in our religion? If it's for strengthening their faith, how can you strengthen it by something so frivolous?

"These plays began among the coarsest people. They were first written to teach them the mysteries of faith in a way that would be easy to remember. Later on, trivial, inappropriate, and frankly base things began to be mixed in.

"The purpose of your institute is to educate the nobility of the kingdom. You must inspire your pupils to develop a solid and reasonable piety that can sustain them in the different states of life to which God will call them. Do you honestly think that you are fulfilling the intentions of your founders when you turn the laywomen entrusted to you into stubborn, childish women full of base and vulgar ideas about our religion? How many of them will be shaken when enlightened people mock them about things they received from you as somehow admirable? How many of them will retain all the solid instruction you have given them, if they have mixed this up with these childish indulgences?

"The reason I am so determined about attacking these incidents is that I fear they will become general defects and perpetual faults in the community. As good philosophers argue, you cannot give to others what you yourself do not have. Just how are you going to communicate this righteousness and this solidity I have so often discussed with you if you don't have these virtues yourselves?"

The teachers replied, "We hope that you would communicate these to us. You are our mother and our teacher. You can give us your noble spirit. We ask this everyday when we pray to God."

She replied, "Oh! I do not presume to have any noble spirit. Still, if God has given me some sense of propriety, He is not counting on me alone to communicate it. You know how ardently I want to do this and how determined I have been in talking to you about this. I know your good will. You gladly accept instruction, correction, and reformation. But this docility isn't enough. You have to put this propriety into practice. You talk about my leaving you my spirit. But you have a very different set of tastes than I do, if you enjoy these insipid plays that inspire so little respect for the mysteries of our faith.

"I have never tolerated anyone turning holy things into a game. I've always believed that you must speak about God as God deserves, that is, seriously and respectfully. I would rather that we not speak of God at all than to speak of Him in an improper manner.

"Don't forget that you are raising young laywomen in whom you must inspire a great reverence for everything concerning religion. They should have such a deep veneration for holy things that they would not dare to turn them into matter for amusement. They should only speak about God in a way that raises the mind to God. Their religious speech should be as impeccable as that found in the fine theatrical pieces I have given you.

"You clearly know that I do not even want them to include your consecrated lives in their games by making religious habits or by pretending to profess vows, because I find that such things lack respect. How could I tolerate that they use Sacred History in such a way? We should teach them always to treat serious things with seriousness. You should absolutely remove anything from your pupils' games that imitates the ceremonies of the Church or certain venerable actions typical of convents. Such would be the election of a superior, the exhortation by the bishop at such a ceremony, the holding of a chapter for the reception of a novice, or the chapter of faults."

Mme de Sailly[22] responded, "But in the lives of the saints, authors consider it a good omen that in their childhood games, future saints imitated the ceremonies of the Church, offered sermons, preached, and sang the parts of the Mass."

Mme de Maintenon answered, "We do not know how the saints actually performed these actions. They might have been accompanied by a simplicity and by a piety that made them praiseworthy. The world was much simpler long ago, and people could defend certain practices whose origins were pious and useful.

"For example, Hôtel de Bourgogne[23] was founded to present the Passion of Jesus Christ. They placed a man on the cross, put a sponge full of vinegar to his lips, and in the same way imitated all the other incidents in the Passion of Our Lord. The people watching this performance viewed it with such piety that they melted into tears. But in time this simplicity disappeared. So many abuses began to creep into this play that the authorities had to forbid its performance. Originally built for an edifying purpose, this same Hôtel de Bourgogne is currently used as a theater for the performance of the worst plays.

---

22. Mme Marthe-Thérèse de Sailly was professed as a Dame de Saint-Louis in 1694. She died at Saint-Cyr in 1730 at the age of fifty-five (*MRSC*, 411).

23. Hôtel de Bourgogne was a theater in central Paris, opened in 1548 by the *Confrères de la Passion* for the presentation of plays on the Passion of Christ. The original religious focus faded as the theater was occupied by different theatrical companies: notably the *Comédiens du roi* (1629–80) and the *Comédies-Italiens* (1680–97). The licentious and anti-clerical tone of the comedies performed by these troupes led to the theater's dissolution in 1697 by Louis XIV.

"This illustrates how the best things can be abused and why we must criticize and remove other dangerous things that originally started as very good enterprises. That is why the example of the saints, who in their youth imitated the ceremonies of the Church, cannot be a pretext for you to tolerate the same actions by your pupils. Even if this is not wrong in all cases, we must remain vigilant."

Mme de Bouju[24] asked, "Do you disapprove of the pupils pretending that they are making visits as if they were nuns, just as they often pretend to make visits as if they were adult ladies?"

Mme de Maintenon responded, "No, this game is not bad in and of itself. It's not a real problem if they enjoy pretending that they are in a convent: acting as a teacher or as boarding students, pretending to go the parlor, and so forth. They must, however, avoid mixing the ceremonies of the Church or other religious practices into their play. Then they would risk turning what they should respect the most into objects of ridicule."

She added, "You must remove from their pastimes anything they might abuse. The hard work of education is to turn their games into something useful. If you do not have enough skill to mingle their recreation with this utility, at least you should banish anything that could be dangerous for them.

"I fear, however, that you will not avoid the problems I have been discussing if you continue to have this lamentable passion to seek out new songs, new games, and new shows. Nothing is as dangerous as this craving for novelty. Now, this desire is natural for human beings, especially for the young. But far from nourishing and satisfying this desire, you should try to weaken it by refusing to provide any support for it.

"The whole security of your enterprise is the refusal to innovate. You should be content with the dramatic pieces and the dialogues I have given you. There are enough of them to have sufficient diversity.

"Do you think that the professionals who give public shows change them so often? The tragedies they are performing today are the same ones they performed fifteen years ago. The most they do is to mix in a few new pieces with these old ones, which are always revived. Why should your pupils have a greater problem with this than do society people? Why are you always trying to find something new for them? The most novelty that you should permit them is letting them act out a proverb, on condition that you suppress anything in the performance touching on romantic love or other dangerous passions. The proverb-sketches should also be created spon-

24. Mme Marie-Anne de Bouju de Montgard was professed as a Dame de Saint-Louis in 1694. She died at Saint-Cyr in 1712 at the age of forty (*MRSC*, 411).

taneously, that is, without a written script, because they should not be turned into a formal play."

She added, "Books and manuscripts are an important item in your school. You cannot be strict enough in observing the rule to permit no such item to enter the school unless it has been examined and approved by your superiors. I am not just talking about major books. I am saying that without exception you should not let a single manuscript or printed work pass through the doors without this scrutiny. How can we be consistent if we refuse to read controversial books without the permission of our bishop, but then let pass all these little booklets wrapped in blue paper that usually contain stupid and vulgar things?"

"Do even good books need to pass through this scrutiny?"

"My God! Don't you realize that the ease with which you grant entrance to these little booklets without preliminary approval exposes your pupils to the greatest dangers? If the Jansenists[25] and the Quietists[26] knew this weakness, they would immediately find the secret door to spread their errors. They would flood you with pamphlets containing the maxims, phrases, and songs that they sell practically for nothing. In these minor works they sow their errors with things that seem valuable and against which you are helpless, because you did not suspect anything.

"Do you remember the canticles that Mme de Beaulieu[27] had us sing for the bishop of Meaux[28] during the Quietist period? The bishop called them a bunch of pompous nonsense. They were full of erroneous and pernicious phrases and opinions.

"My dear daughters, in God's name, please be careful. Never let any suspect book or manuscript enter the school without approval, that is, without the preliminary examination and permission of your superiors. Don't let unapproved works sneak in, either through the avenue of educated people, or through that of devout people, or even through that of your servant girls. Never let the latter keep any books that have not been examined and ap-

---

25. On the Jansenists, see the editor's introduction, 18–20.

26. On the Quietist movement, see the editor's introduction, 21.

27. Mlle Marie-Françoise Lefranc de Beaulieu was professed as a Dame de Saint-Louis in 1698. She died at Saint-Cyr in 1741 at the age of sixty-five (*MRSC*, 412).

28. Jacques-Bénigne Bossuet (1627–1704), an ecclesiastic from Dijon, began his rise as a preacher after his arrival in Paris in 1659. Frequently invited to preach at the court, Bossuet was ordained a bishop in 1669 and named to the diocese of Meaux in 1681. A friend of Mme de Maintenon, Bossuet periodically preached at the Saint-Cyr school chapel. He was a close ally of Maintenon during the 1690s struggle against Quietism.

proved. Some people might try to use these servants to pass on works that no one would dare to do by another channel."

Mme de Blosset[29] said that she had seen a pupil with a book containing such works. The pages of the book had originally been used to wrap a package coming from Paris. This pupil then put these pages together and made a little book out of them.

Mme de Maintenon exclaimed, "What! You didn't have enough presence of mind to burn or to destroy these sorts of pages because of the risk that they might fall into the hands of your pupils or that they might damage your entire school? Now this is what I call matter for confession by an officer of the school. If I had done this, I would have said, 'Father, I accuse myself of gross negligence. I let dangerous writings fall into the hands of our pupils. They read a book or a manuscript that I did not have inspected by my superiors. This violated our constitutions, which forbid the reading of any book unapproved by them.'"

All the teachers responded, "Now we are clearly forewarned on this issue."

Mme de Maintenon added, "I want you to transmit to those who will come after you this same fidelity and this same determination to permit nothing suspect in any area to be tolerated by you."

At the end of this interview, Mme de La Rouzière[30] asked what a schoolmistress should do if in her class she witnessed the type of bad play, or song, or game, which Mme de Maintenon had just criticized. Should she just forbid them, hoping that the pupils little by little would just forget about them?

Mme de Maintenon said, "I think that the best strategy would be to tell them simply and candidly, 'My children, I taught you this game, or this song, or this play. I didn't think it was so bad then. However, after giving this issue more thought, I find that this is not very useful for such and such a reason. So I am encouraging you to forget this and to focus on more solid things. In the future I do not intend to tolerate any more such performances.'

"I am very partial to this strict and simple way of proceeding on such issues. Rather than making your pupils dislike you, this frank method will make your pupils respect you all the more. By proceeding in this way, you will give them a fine example of the good faith and the candor they should practice in similar situations. There is nothing as noble as this honesty that

29. See above in this section, note 15.

30. Mme Jeanne-Marie de La Rouzière was professed as a Dame de Saint-Louis in 1695. She died at Saint-Cyr in 1755 at the age of eighty-one (*MRSC*, 411).

refuses to be ashamed of retracting your decision when you were wrong. Even in the world, it is the people of the greatest merit and the finest soul who are more capable of this action than are others. For you, who are bound by your calling to be humble and virtuous and to give all sorts of good examples to your pupils, the obligation is all the greater."

Mme de Berval [31] asked Mme de Maintenon if she was critical of the ceremonial reception that the "red" class had given their headmistress when she returned from her retreat. The pupils had worn special dresses and stood in rows. One of them delivered a flattering address on behalf of all the pupils, while the other pupils sang a song created expressly for this occasion.

Mme de Maintenon replied, "This is a rather innocent way to welcome a headmistress. Still, this sort of ceremony can have its drawbacks. To have the address and the song, someone must write them. This will flatter the one who is the most successful at this sort of thing. Those who are not capable of this sort of skill will feel sad and humiliated, perhaps even disdained. That's why I think it is better to suppress completely these sorts of ceremonies."

---

31. Mme Louise-Catherine Sailly de Berval was professed as a Dame de Saint-Louis in 1694. A close friend of Mme de Maintenon, she occupied a number of key positions in the administration of the school. She held a central role in the transcription and editing of the works of Maintenon. She died at Saint-Cyr in 1738 at the age of sixty-eight (*MRSC,* 410).

SERIES EDITORS'
BIBLIOGRAPHY

PRIMARY SOURCES

Alberti, Leon Battista (1404–72). *The Family in Renaissance Florence.* Trans. Renée Neu Watkins. Columbia: University of South Carolina Press, 1969.

Arenal, Electa, and Stacey Schlau, eds. *Untold Sisters: Hispanic Nuns in Their Own Works.* Trans. Amanda Powell. Albuquerque: University of New Mexico Press, 1989.

Astell, Mary (1666–1731). *The First English Feminist: Reflections on Marriage and Other Writings.* Ed. Bridget Hill. New York: St. Martin's Press, 1986.

Atherton, Margaret, ed. *Women Philosophers of the Early Modern Period.* Indianapolis, IN: Hackett, 1994.

Aughterson, Kate, ed. *Renaissance Woman: Constructions of Femininity in England: A Source Book.* London and New York: Routledge, 1995.

Barbaro, Francesco (1390–1454). *On Wifely Duties.* Trans. Benjamin Kohl. In *The Earthly Republic,* ed. Kohl and R. G. Witt, 179–228. Philadelphia: University of Pennsylvania Press, 1978.

Behn, Aphra. *The Works of Aphra Behn.* 7 vols. Ed. Janet Todd. Columbus: Ohio State University Press, 1992–96.

Boccaccio, Giovanni (1313–75). *Corbaccio, or the Labyrinth of Love.* Trans. Anthony K. Cassell. 2nd rev. ed. Binghamton, NY: Medieval and Renaissance Texts and Studies, 1993.

———. *Famous Women.* Ed. and trans. Virginia Brown. The I Tatti Renaissance Library. Cambridge, MA: Harvard University Press, 2001.

Brown, Sylvia. *Women's Writing in Stuart England: The Mother's Legacies of Dorothy Leigh, Elizabeth Joscelin, and Elizabeth Richardson.* Thrupp, Stroud, Gloceter: Sutton, 1999.

Bruni, Leonardo (1370–1444). "On the Study of Literature (1405) to Lady Battista Malatesta of Montefeltro." In *The Humanism of Leonardo Bruni: Selected Texts.* Trans. Gordon Griffiths, James Hankins, and David Thompson, 240–51. Binghamton, NY: Medieval and Renaissance Texts and Studies, 1987.

Castiglione, Baldassare (1478–1529). *The Book of the Courtier.* Trans. George Bull. New York: Penguin, 1967.

Christine de Pizan (1365–1431). *The Book of the City of Ladies.* Trans. Earl Jeffrey Richards. Foreword by Marina Warner. New York: Persea Books, 1982.

————. *The Treasure of the City of Ladies.* Trans. Sarah Lawson. New York: Viking Penguin, 1985. Also trans. and introd. Charity Cannon Willard. Ed. and introd. Madeleine P. Cosman. New York: Persea Books, 1989.

Clarke, Danielle, ed. *Isabella Whitney, Mary Sidney, and Aemilia Lanyer: Renaissance Women Poets.* New York: Penguin Books, 2000.

Crawford, Patricia, and Laura Gowing, eds. *Women's Worlds in Seventeenth-Century England: A Source Book.* London and New York: Routledge, 2000.

Daybell, James, ed. *Early Modern Women's Letter Writing, 1450–1700.* Houndmills, England, and New York: Palgrave, 2001.

Elizabeth I: Collected Works. Ed. Leah S. Marcus, Janel Mueller, and Mary Beth Rose. Chicago: University of Chicago Press, 2000.

Elyot, Thomas (1490–1546). *Defence of Good Women: The Feminist Controversy of the Renaissance.* Facsimile Reproductions. Ed. Diane Bornstein. New York: Delmar, 1980.

Erasmus, Desiderius (1467–1536). *Erasmus on Women.* Ed. Erika Rummel. Toronto: University of Toronto Press, 1996.

Female and Male Voices in Early Modern England: An Anthology of Renaissance Writing. Ed. Betty S. Travitsky and Anne Lake Prescott. New York: Columbia University Press, 2000.

Ferguson, Moira, ed. *First Feminists: British Women Writers, 1578–1799.* Bloomington: Indiana University Press, 1985.

Galilei, Maria Celeste. *Sister Maria Celeste's Letters to Her Father, Galileo.* Ed. and trans. Rinaldina Russell. Lincoln, NE, and New York: Writers Club Press of Universe.com, 2000.

Gethner, Perry, ed. *The Lunatic Lover and Other Plays by French Women of the Seventeenth and Eighteenth Centuries.* Portsmouth, NH: Heinemann, 1994.

Glückel of Hameln (1646–1724). *The Memoirs of Glückel of Hameln.* Trans. Marvin Lowenthal, with a new introduction by Robert Rosen. New York: Schocken Books, 1977.

Henderson, Katherine Usher, and Barbara F. McManus, eds. *Half Humankind: Contexts and Texts of the Controversy about Women in England, 1540–1640.* Urbana: University of Illinois Press, 1985.

Hoby, Margaret. *The Private Life of an Elizabethan Lady: The Diary of Lady Margaret Hoby 1599–1605.* Phoenix Mill, U.K.: Sutton, 1998.

Humanist Educational Treatises. Ed. and trans. Craig W. Kallendorf. The I Tatti Renaissance Library. Cambridge, MA: Harvard University Press, 2002.

Joscelin, Elizabeth. *The Mothers Legacy to her Unborn Childe.* Ed. Jean LeDrew Metcalfe. Toronto: University of Toronto Press, 2000.

Kaminsky, Amy Katz, ed. *Water Lilies, Flores del Agua: An Anthology of Spanish Women Writers from the Fifteenth through the Nineteenth Century.* Minneapolis: University of Minnesota Press, 1996.

Kempe, Margery (1373–1439). *The Book of Margery Kempe.* Trans. and ed. Lynn Staley. Norton Critical Editions. New York: W. W. Norton, 2001.

King, Margaret L., and Albert Rabil, Jr., eds. *Her Immaculate Hand: Selected Works by and about the Women Humanists of Quattrocento Italy.* 1983. 2nd rev. paperback ed. Binghamton, NY: Medieval and Renaissance Texts and Studies, 1991.

Klein, Joan Larsen, ed. *Daughters, Wives, and Widows: Writings by Men about Women and Marriage in England, 1500–1640.* Urbana: University of Illinois Press, 1992.

Knox, John (1505–72). *The Political Writings of John Knox: The First Blast of the Trumpet against the Monstrous Regiment of Women and Other Selected Works.* Ed. Marvin A. Breslow. Washington: Folger Shakespeare Library, 1985.

Kors, Alan C., and Edward Peters, eds. *Witchcraft in Europe, 400–1700: A Documentary History.* Philadelphia: University of Pennsylvania Press, 2000.

Krämer, Heinrich, and Jacob Sprenger. *Malleus Maleficarum* (ca. 1487). Trans. Montague Summers. London: Pushkin Press, 1928; reprint, New York: Dover, 1971.

Larsen, Anne R., and Colette H. Winn, eds. *Writings by Pre-Revolutionary French Women: From Marie de France to Elizabeth Vigée-Le Brun.* New York and London: Garland, 2000.

Lorris, William de, and Jean de Meun. *The Romance of the Rose.* Trans. Charles Dahlbert. Princeton, NJ: Princeton University Press, 1971; reprint, University Press of New England, 1983.

Marguerite d'Angoulême, Queen of Navarre (1492–1549). *The Heptameron.* Trans. P. A. Chilton. New York: Viking Penguin, 1984.

Mary of Agreda. *The Divine Life of the Most Holy Virgin.* Abridgment of *The Mystical City of God.* Abr. by Fr. Bonaventure Amedeo de Caesarea, M.C. Trans. from French by Abbé Joseph A. Boullan. Rockford, IL: Tan Books, 1997.

Myers, Kathleen A., and Amanda Powell, eds. *A Wild Country out in the Garden: The Spiritual Journals of a Colonial Mexican Nun.* Bloomington: Indiana University Press, 1999.

Teresa of Avila, Saint (1515–82). *The Life of Saint Teresa of Avila, by Herself.* Trans. J. M. Cohen. New York: Viking Penguin, 1957.

Weyer, Johann (1515–88). *Witches, Devils, and Doctors in the Renaissance: Johann Weyer, De praestigiis daemonum.* Ed. George Mora with Benjamin G. Kohl, Erik Midelfort, and Helen Bacon. Trans. John Shea. Binghamton, NY: Medieval and Renaissance Texts and Studies, 1991.

Wilson, Katharina M., ed. *Medieval Women Writers.* Athens: University of Georgia Press, 1984.

———, ed. *Women Writers of the Renaissance and Reformation.* Athens: University of Georgia Press, 1987.

———, and Frank J. Warnke, eds. *Women Writers of the Seventeenth Century.* Athens: University of Georgia Press, 1989.

Wollstonecraft, Mary. *A Vindication of the Rights of Men and a Vindication of the Rights of Women.* Ed. Sylvana Tomaselli. Cambridge: Cambridge University Press, 1995. Also *The Vindications of the Rights of Men, the Rights of Women.* Ed. D. L. Macdonald and Kathleen Scherf. Peterborough, Ontario, Canada: Broadview Press, 1997.

Women Critics, 1660–1820: An Anthology. Ed. the Folger Collective on Early Women Critics. Bloomington: Indiana University Press, 1995.

Women Writers in English, 1350–1850. Series; fifteen vols. published through 1999 (projected thirty-volume series suspended). Oxford University Press.

Wroth, Lady Mary. *The Poems of Lady Mary Wroth.* Ed. Josephine A. Roberts. Baton Rouge: Louisiana State University Press, 1983.

———. *Lady Mary Wroth's "Love's Victory": The Penshurst Manuscript.* Ed. Michael G. Brennan. London: Roxburghe Club, 1988.

———. *The Countess of Montgomery's Urania.* 2 vols. Ed. Josephine A. Roberts. Tempe, AZ: Medieval and Renaissance Texts and Studies, 1995, 1999.

de Zayas, Maria. *The Enchantments of Love: Amorous and Exemplary Novels.* Trans. H. Patsy Boyer. Berkeley and Los Angeles: University of California Press, 1990.

———. *The Disenchantments of Love.* Trans. H. Patsy Boyer. Albany: State University of New York Press, 1997.

SECONDARY SOURCES

Ahlgren, Gillian. *Teresa of Avila and the Politics of Sanctity.* Ithaca, NY: Cornell University Press, 1996.

Akkerman, Tjitske, and Siep Sturman, eds. *Feminist Thought in European History, 1400–2000.* London and New York: Routledge, 1997.

Allen, Sister Prudence, R.S.M. *The Concept of Woman: The Aristotelian Revolution, 750 BC–AD 1250.* Vol. 1. Grand Rapids, MI: William B. Eerdmans, 1997.

———. *The Concept of Woman.* Vol 2. *The Early Humanist Reformation, 1250–1500.* Grand Rapids, MI: William B. Eerdmans, 2002.

Andreadis, Harriette. *Sappho in Early Modern England: Female Same-Sex Literary Erotics, 1550–1714.* Chicago: University of Chicago Press, 2001.

Armon, Shifra. *Picking Wedlock: Women and the Courtship Novel in Spain.* New York: Rowman and Littlefield, 2002.

Backer, Anne Liot. *Precious Women.* New York: Basic Books, 1974.

Ballaster, Ros. *Seductive Forms.* New York : Oxford University Press, 1992.

Barash, Carol. *English Women's Poetry, 1649–1714: Politics, Community, and Linguistic Authority.* New York and Oxford: Oxford University Press, 1996.

Battigelli, Anna. *Margaret Cavendish and the Exiles of the Mind.* Lexington: University of Kentucky Press, 1998.

Beasley, Faith. *Revising Memory: Women's Fiction and Memoirs in Seventeenth-Century France.* New Brunswick, NJ: Rutgers University Press, 1990.

Beilin, Elaine V. *Redeeming Eve: Women Writers of the English Renaissance.* Princeton, NJ: Princeton University Press, 1987.

Benson, Pamela Joseph. *The Invention of Renaissance Woman: The Challenge of Female Independence in the Literature and Thought of Italy and England.* University Park: Pennsylvania State University Press, 1992.

———, and Victoria Kirkham, eds. *Strong Voices, Weak History? Medieval and Renaissance Women in Their Literary Canons: England, France, Italy.* Ann Arbor: University of Michigan Press, 2003.

Bilinkoff, Jodi. *The Avila of Saint Teresa: Religious Reform in a Sixteenth-Century City.* Ithaca, NY: Cornell University Press, 1989.

Bissell, R. Ward. *Artemisia Gentileschi and the Authority of Art.* University Park: Pennsylvania State University Press, 2000.

Blain, Virginia, Isobel Grundy, and Patricia Clements, eds. *The Feminist Companion to Literature in English: Women Writers from the Middle Ages to the Present.* New Haven, CT: Yale University Press, 1990.

Bloch, R. Howard. *Medieval Misogyny and the Invention of Western Romantic Love.* Chicago: University of Chicago Press, 1991.

Bornstein, Daniel, and Roberto Rusconi, eds. *Women and Religion in Medieval and Renaissance Italy.* Trans. Margery J. Schneider. Chicago: University of Chicago Press, 1996.

Brant, Clare, and Diane Purkiss, eds. *Women, Texts and Histories, 1575–1760.* London and New York: Routledge, 1992.

Briggs, Robin. *Witches and Neighbours: The Social and Cultural Context of European Witchcraft.* New York: HarperCollins, 1995; reprint, Viking Penguin, 1996.

Brink, Jean R., ed. *Female Scholars: A Tradition of Learned Women before 1800.* Montréal: Eden Press Women's Publications, 1980.

Brown, Judith C. *Immodest Acts: The Life of a Lesbian Nun in Renaissance Italy.* New York: Oxford University Press, 1986.

———, and Robert C. Davis, eds. *Gender and Society in Renaissance Italy.* London: Addison-Wesley Longman, 1998.

Bynum, Carolyn Walker. *Holy Feast and Holy Fast: The Religious Significance of Food to Medieval Women.* Berkeley and Los Angeles: University of California Press, 1987.

———. *Fragmentation and Redemption: Essays on Gender and the Human Body in Medieval Religion.* New York: Zone Books, 1992.

Cambridge Guide to Women's Writing in English. Ed. Lorna Sage. Cambridge: University Press, 1999.

Cavanagh, Sheila T. *Cherished Torment: The Emotional Geography of Lady Mary Wroth's Urania.* Pittsburgh, PA: Duquesne University Press, 2001.

Cerasano, S. P., and Marion Wynne-Davies, eds. *Readings in Renaissance Women's Drama: Criticism, History, and Performance, 1594–1998.* London and New York: Routledge, 1998.

Cervigni, Dino S., ed. *Women Mystic Writers. Annali d'Italianistica* 13 (1995): entire issue.

———, and Rebecca West, eds. *Women's Voices in Italian Literature. Annali d'Italianistica* 7 (1989): entire issue.

Charlton, Kenneth. *Women, Religion, and Education in Early Modern England.* London and New York: Routledge, 1999.

Chojnacka, Monica. *Working Women in Early Modern Venice.* Baltimore, MD: Johns Hopkins University Press, 2001.

Chojnacki, Stanley. *Women and Men in Renaissance Venice: Twelve Essays on Patrician Society.* Baltimore, MD: Johns Hopkins University Press, 2000.

Cholakian, Patricia Francis. *Rape and Writing in the Heptameron of Marguerite de Navarre.* Carbondale and Edwardsville: Southern Illinois University Press, 1991.

———. *Women and the Politics of Self-Representation in Seventeenth-Century France.* Newark: University of Delaware Press, 2000.

Christine de Pizan: A Casebook. Ed. Barbara K. Altmann and Deborah L. McGrady. New York: Routledge, 2003.

Clogan, Paul Maruice, ed. *Medievali et Humanistica: Literacy and the Lay Reader.* Lanham, MD: Rowman and Littlefield, 2000.

Clubb, Louise George.. *Italian Drama in Shakespeare's Time.* New Haven, CT: Yale University Press, 1989.

Conley, John J., S.J. *The Suspicion of Virtue: Women Philosophers in Neoclassical France.* Ithaca, NY: Cornell University Press, 2002.

Crabb, Ann. *The Strozzi of Florence: Widowhood and Family Solidarity in the Renaissance.* Ann Arbor: University of Michigan Press, 2000.

Cruz, Anne J., and Mary Elizabeth Perry, eds. *Culture and Control in Counter-Reformation Spain.* Minneapolis: University of Minnesota Press, 1992.

Davis, Natalie Zemon. *Society and Culture in Early Modern France.* Stanford, CA: Stanford University Press, 1975, esp. chaps. 3 and 5.

————. *Women on the Margins: Three Seventeenth-Century Lives.* Cambridge, MA: Harvard University Press, 1995.

DeJean, Joan. *Fictions of Sappho, 1546–1937.* Chicago: University of Chicago Press, 1989.

————. *Ancients against Moderns: Culture Wars and the Making of a Fin de Siècle.* Chicago: University of Chicago Press, 1997.

————. *Tender Geographies: Women and the Origins of the Novel in France.* New York: Columbia University Press, 1991.

————. *The Reinvention of Obscenity: Sex, Lies, and Tabloids in Early Modern France.* Chicago: University of Chicago Press, 2002.

Dictionary of Russian Women Writers. Ed. Marina Ledkovsky, Charlotte Rosenthal, and Mary Zirin. Westport, CT: Greenwood Press, 1994.

Dixon, Laurinda S. *Perilous Chastity: Women and Illness in Pre-Enlightenment Art and Medicine.* Ithaca, NY: Cornell University Press, 1995.

Dolan, Frances, E. *Whores of Babylon: Catholicism, Gender, and Seventeenth-Century Print Culture.* Ithaca, NY: Cornell University Press, 1999.

Donovan, Josephine. *Women and the Rise of the Novel, 1405–1726.* New York: St. Martin's Press, 1999.

Encyclopedia of Continental Women Writers. 2 vols. Ed. Katharina Wilson. New York: Garland, 1991.

Erauso, Catalina de. *Lieutenant Nun: Memoir of a Basque Transvestite in the New World.* Trans. Michele Stepto and Gabriel Stepto; foreword by Marjorie Garber. Boston: Beacon Press, 1995.

Erdmann, Axel. *My Gracious Silence: Women in the Mirror of Sixteenth-Century Printing in Western Europe.* Luzern: Gilhofer and Rauschberg, 1999.

Erickson, Amy Louise. *Women and Property in Early Modern England.* London and New York: Routledge, 1993.

Ezell, Margaret J. M. *The Patriarch's Wife: Literary Evidence and the History of the Family.* Chapel Hill: University of North Carolina Press, 1987.

————. *Writing Women's Literary History.* Baltimore, MD: Johns Hopkins University Press, 1993.

————. *Social Authorship and the Advent of Print.* Baltimore, MD: Johns Hopkins University Press, 1999.

Farrell, Michèle Longino. *Performing Motherhood: The Sévigné Correspondence.* Hanover, NH, and London: University Press of New England, 1991.

The Feminist Companion to Literature in English: Women Writers from the Middle Ages to the Present. Ed. Virginia Blain, Isobel Grundy, and Patricia Clements. New Haven, CT: Yale University Press, 1990.

The Feminist Encyclopedia of German Literature. Ed. Friederike Eigler and Susanne Kord. Westport, CT: Greenwood Press, 1997.

Feminist Encyclopedia of Italian Literature. Ed. Rinaldina Russell. Westport, CT: Greenwood Press, 1997.

Ferguson, Margaret W., Maureen Quilligan, and Nancy J. Vickers, eds. *Rewriting the*

Renaissance: The Discourses of Sexual Difference in Early Modern Europe. Chicago: University of Chicago Press, 1987.

Ferraro, Joanne M. *Marriage Wars in Late Renaissance Venice.* Oxford: Oxford University Press, 2001.

Fletcher, Anthony. *Gender, Sex, and Subordination in England 1500–1800.* New Haven, CT: Yale University Press, 1995.

French Women Writers: A Bio-Bibliographical Source Book. Ed. Eva Martin Sartori and Dorothy Wynne Zimmerman. Westport, CT: Greenwood Press, 1991.

Frye, Susan, and Karen Robertson, eds. *Maids and Mistresses, Cousins and Queens: Women's Alliances in Early Modern England.* Oxford: Oxford University Press, 1999.

Gallagher, Catherine. *Nobody's Story: The Vanishing Acts of Women Writers in the Marketplace, 1670–1820.* Berkeley and Los Angeles: University of California Press, 1994.

Garrard, Mary D. *Artemisia Gentileschi: The Image of the Female Hero in Italian Baroque Art.* Princeton, NJ: Princeton University Press, 1989.

Gelbart, Nina Rattner. *The King's Midwife: A History and Mystery of Madame du Coudray.* Berkeley and Los Angeles: University of California Press, 1998.

Glenn, Cheryl. *Rhetoric Retold: Regendering the Tradition from Antiquity through the Renaissance.* Carbondale: Southern Illinois University Press, 1997.

Goffen, Rona. *Titian's Women.* New Haven, CT: Yale University Press, 1997.

Goldberg, Jonathan. *Desiring Women Writing: English Renaissance Examples.* Stanford, CA: Stanford University Press, 1997.

Goldsmith, Elizabeth C. *Exclusive Conversations: The Art of Interaction in Seventeenth-Century France.* Philadelphia: University of Pennsylvania Press, 1988.

———, ed. *Writing the Female Voice.* Boston: Northeastern University Press, 1989.

———, and Dena Goodman, eds. *Going Public: Women and Publishing in Early Modern France.* Ithaca, NY: Cornell University Press, 1995.

Grafton, Anthony, and Lisa Jardine. *From Humanism to the Humanities: Education and the Liberal Arts in Fifteenth-and Sixteenth-Century Europe.* London: Duckworth, 1986.

Greer, Margaret Rich. *Maria de Zayas Tells Baroque Tales of Love and the Cruelty of Men.* University Park: Pennsylvania State University Press, 2000.

Hackett, Helen. *Women and Romance Fiction in the English Renaissance.* Cambridge: Cambridge University Press, 2000.

Hall, Kim F. *Things of Darkness: Economies of Race and Gender in Early Modern England.* Ithaca, NY: Cornell University Press, 1995.

Hampton, Timothy. *Literature and the Nation in the Sixteenth Century: Inventing Renaissance France.* Ithaca, NY: Cornell University Press, 2001.

Hannay, Margaret, ed. *Silent but for the Word.* Kent, OH: Kent State University Press, 1985.

Hardwick, Julie. *The Practice of Patriarchy: Gender and the Politics of Household Authority in Early Modern France.* University Park: Pennsylvania State University Press, 1998.

Harris, Barbara J. *English Aristocratic Women, 1450–1550: Marriage and Family, Property and Careers.* New York: Oxford University Press, 2002.

Harth, Erica. *Ideology and Culture in Seventeenth-Century France.* Ithaca, NY: Cornell University Press, 1983.

———. *Cartesian Women. Versions and Subversions of Rational Discourse in the Old Regime.* Ithaca, NY: Cornell University Press, 1992.

Harvey, Elizabeth D. *Ventriloquized Voices: Feminist Theory and English Renaissance Texts.* London and New York: Routledge, 1992.

Haselkorn, Anne M., and Betty Travitsky, eds. *The Renaissance Englishwoman in Print: Counterbalancing the Canon.* Amherst: University of Massachusetts Press, 1990.

Herlihy, David. "Did Women Have a Renaissance? A Reconsideration." *Medievalia et Humanistica* n.s., 13 (1985): 1–22.

Hill, Bridget. *The Republican Virago: The Life and Times of Catharine Macaulay, Historian.* New York: Oxford University Press, 1992.

A History of Central European Women's Writing. Ed. Celia Hawkesworth. New York: Palgrave Press, 2001.

A History of Women in the West. Vol. 1. *From Ancient Goddesses to Christian Saints.* Ed. Pauline Schmitt Pantel. Vol. 2. *Silences of the Middle Ages.* Ed. Christiane Klapisch-Zuber. Vol. 3. *Renaissance and Enlightenment Paradoxes.* Ed. Natalie Zemon Davis and Arlette Farge. Cambridge, MA: Harvard University Press, 1992–93.

A History of Women's Writing in Russia. Ed. Alele Marie Barker and Jehanne M. Gheith. Cambridge: Cambridge University Press, 2002.

Hobby, Elaine. *Virtue of Necessity: English Women's Writing, 1646–1688.* London: Virago Press, 1988.

Horowitz, Maryanne Cline. "Aristotle and Women." *Journal of the History of Biology* 9 (1976): 183–213.

Howell, Martha. *The Marriage Exchange: Property, Social Place, and Gender in Cities of the Low Countries, 1300–1550.* Chicago: University of Chicago Press, 1998.

Hufton, Olwen H. *The Prospect before Her: A History of Women in Western Europe, 1: 1500–1800.* New York: HarperCollins, 1996.

Hull, Suzanne W. *Chaste, Silent, and Obedient: English Books for Women, 1475–1640.* San Marino, CA: Huntington Library, 1982.

Hunt, Lynn, ed. *The Invention of Pornography: Obscenity and the Origins of Modernity, 1500–1800.* New York: Zone Books, 1996.

Hutner, Heidi, ed. *Rereading Aphra Behn: History, Theory, and Criticism.* Charlottesville: University Press of Virginia, 1993.

Hutson, Lorna, ed. *Feminism and Renaissance Studies.* New York: Oxford University Press, 1999.

Italian Women Writers: A Bio-Bibliographical Sourcebook. Ed. Rinaldina Russell. Westport, CT: Greenwood Press, 1994.

Jaffe, Irma B., with Gernando Colombardo. *Shining Eyes, Cruel Fortune: The Lives and Loves of Italian Renaissance Women Poets.* New York: Fordham University Press, 2002.

James, Susan E. *Kateryn Parr: The Making of a Queen.* Aldershot and Brookfield: Ashgate, 1999.

Jankowski, Theodora A. *Women in Power in the Early Modern Drama.* Urbana: University of Illinois Press, 1992.

Jansen, Katherine Ludwig. *The Making of the Magdalen: Preaching and Popular Devotion in the Later Middle Ages.* Princeton, NJ: Princeton University Press, 2000.

Jed, Stephanie H. *Chaste Thinking: The Rape of Lucretia and the Birth of Humanism.* Bloomington: Indiana University Press, 1989.

Jordan, Constance. *Renaissance Feminism: Literary Texts and Political Models.* Ithaca, NY: Cornell University Press, 1990.

Kagan, Richard L. *Lucrecia's Dreams: Politics and Prophecy in Sixteenth-Century Spain.* Berkeley and Los Angeles: University of California Press, 1990.

Kehler, Dorothea and Laurel Amtower, eds. *The Single Woman in Medieval and Early Modern England: Her Life and Representation*. Tempe, AZ: Medieval and Renaissance Texts and Studies, 2002.

Kelly, Joan. "Did Women Have a Renaissance?" In *Women, History, and Theory*. Chicago: University of Chicago Press, 1984. Also in *Becoming Visible: Women in European History*, ed. Renate Bridenthal, Claudia Koonz, and Susan M. Stuard. 3rd ed. Boston: Houghton Mifflin, 1998.

―――. "Early Feminist Theory and the *Querelle des Femmes*." In *Women, History, and Theory*. Chicago: University of Chicago Press, 1984

Kelso, Ruth. *Doctrine for the Lady of the Renaissance*. Foreword by Katharine M. Rogers. Urbana: University of Illinois Press, 1956, 1978.

King, Carole. *Renaissance Women Patrons: Wives and Widows in Italy, c. 1300–1550*. New York and Manchester, U.K.: Manchester University Press (distributed in the U.S. by St. Martin's Press), 1998.

King, Margaret L. *Women of the Renaissance*. Foreword by Catharine R. Stimpson. Chicago: University of Chicago Press, 1991.

Krontiris, Tina. *Oppositional Voices: Women as Writers and Translators of Literature in the English Renaissance*. London and New York: Routledge, 1992.

Kuehn, Thomas. *Law, Family, and Women: Toward a Legal Anthropology of Renaissance Italy*. Chicago: University of Chicago Press, 1991.

Kunze, Bonnelyn Young. *Margaret Fell and the Rise of Quakerism*. Stanford, CA: Stanford University Press, 1994.

Labalme, Patricia A., ed. *Beyond Their Sex: Learned Women of the European Past*. New York: New York University Press, 1980.

Laqueur, Thomas. *Making Sex: Body and Gender from the Greeks to Freud*. Cambridge, MA: Harvard University Press, 1990.

Larsen, Anne R., and Colette H. Winn, eds. *Renaissance Women Writers: French Texts/American Contexts*. Detroit, MI: Wayne State University Press, 1994.

Lerner, Gerda. *The Creation of Patriarchy*. New York: Oxford University Press, 1986.

―――. *The Creation of Feminist Consciousness, 1000–1870*. New York: Oxford University Press, 1994.

Levin, Carole, and Jeanie Watson, eds. *Ambiguous Realities: Women in the Middle Ages and Renaissance*. Detroit, MI: Wayne State University Press, 1987.

Levin, Carole, et al. *Extraordinary Women of the Medieval and Renaissance World: A Biographical Dictionary*. Westport, CT: Greenwood Press, 2000.

Lewalsky, Barbara Kiefer. *Writing Women in Jacobean England*. Cambridge, MA: Harvard University Press, 1993.

Lewis, Jayne Elizabeth. *Mary Queen of Scots: Romance and Nation*. London: Routledge, 1998.

Lindsey, Karen. *Divorced, Beheaded, Survived: A Feminist Reinterpretation of the Wives of Henry VIII*. Reading, MA: Addison-Wesley, 1995.

Lochrie, Karma. *Margery Kempe and Translations of the Flesh*. Philadelphia: University of Pennsylvania Press, 1992.

Lougee, Carolyn C. *Le Paradis des Femmes: Women, Salons, and Social Stratification in Seventeenth-Century France*. Princeton, NJ: Princeton University Press, 1976.

Love, Harold. *The Culture and Commerce of Texts: Scribal Publication in Seventeenth-Century England*. Amherst: University of Massachusetts Press, 1993.

MacCarthy, Bridget G. *The Female Pen: Women Writers and Novelists, 1621–1818*. Preface by Janet Todd. New York: 1946–47. Reprint, New York University Press, 1994.

Maclean, Ian. *Woman Triumphant: Feminism in French Literature, 1610–1652.* Oxford: Clarendon Press, 1977.

———. *The Renaissance Notion of Woman: A Study of the Fortunes of Scholasticism and Medical Science in European Intellectual Life.* Cambridge: Cambridge University Press, 1980.

Maggi, Armando. *Uttering the Word: The Mystical Performances of Maria Maddalena de' Pazzi, a Renaissance Visionary.* Albany: State University of New York Press, 1998.

Marshall, Sherrin. *Women in Reformation and Counter-Reformation Europe: Public and Private Worlds.* Bloomington: Indiana University Press, 1989.

Matter, E. Ann, and John Coakley, eds. *Creative Women in Medieval and Early Modern Italy.* Philadelphia: University of Pennsylvania Press, 1994. (sequel to Monson; see below)

McLeod, Glenda. *Virtue and Venom: Catalogs of Women from Antiquity to the Renaissance.* Ann Arbor: University of Michigan Press, 1991.

Medwick, Cathleen. *Teresa of Avila: The Progress of a Soul.* New York: Alfred A. Knopf, 2000.

Meek, Christine, ed. *Women in Renaissance and Early Modern Europe.* Dublin-Portland: Four Courts Press, 2000.

Mendelson, Sara, and Patricia Crawford. *Women in Early Modern England, 1550–1720.* Oxford: Clarendon Press, 1998.

Merchant, Carolyn. *The Death of Nature: Women, Ecology, and the Scientific Revolution.* New York: HarperCollins, 1980.

Merrim, Stephanie. *Early Modern Women's Writing and Sor Juana Inés de la Cruz.* Nashville, TN: Vanderbilt University Press, 1999.

Messbarger, Rebecca. *The Century of Women: The Representations of Women in Eighteenth-Century Italian Public Discourse.* Toronto: University of Toronto Press, 2002.

Miller, Nancy K. *The Heroine's Text: Readings in the French and English Novel, 1722–1782.* New York: Columbia University Press, 1980.

Miller, Naomi J. *Changing the Subject: Mary Wroth and Figurations of Gender in Early Modern England.* Lexington, KY: University Press of Kentucky, 1996.

———, and Gary Waller, eds. *Reading Mary Wroth: Representing Alternatives in Early Modern England.* Knoxville, TN: University of Tennessee Press, 1991.

Monson, Craig A., ed. *The Crannied Wall: Women, Religion, and the Arts in Early Modern Europe.* Ann Arbor: University of Michigan Press, 1992.

Musacchio, Jacqueline Marie. *The Art and Ritual of Childbirth in Renaissance Italy.* New Haven, CT: Yale University Press, 1999.

Newman, Barbara. *God and the Goddesses: Vision, Poetry, and Belief in the Middle Ages.* Philadelphia: University of Pennsylvania Press, 2003.

Newman, Karen. *Fashioning Femininity and English Renaissance Drama.* Chicago and London: University of Chicago Press, 1991.

Okin, Susan Moller. *Women in Western Political Thought.* Princeton, NJ: Princeton University Press, 1979.

Ozment, Steven. *The Bürgermeister's Daughter: Scandal in a Sixteenth-Century German Town.* New York: St. Martin's Press, 1995.

Pacheco, Anita, ed. *Early [English] Women Writers: 1600–1720.* New York and London: Longman, 1998.

Pagels, Elaine. *Adam, Eve, and the Serpent.* New York: Harper Collins, 1988.

Panizza, Letizia, ed. *Women in Italian Renaissance Culture and Society.* Oxford: European Humanities Research Centre, 2000.

————, and Sharon Wood, eds. *A History of Women's Writing in Italy.* Cambridge: University Press, 2000.

Parker, Patricia. *Literary Fat Ladies: Rhetoric, Gender, and Property.* London and New York: Methuen, 1987.

Pernoud, Regine, and Marie-Veronique Clin. *Joan of Arc: Her Story.* Rev. and trans. Jeremy DuQuesnay Adams. New York: St. Martin's Press, 1998 (French original, 1986).

Perry, Mary Elizabeth. *Crime and Society in Early Modern Seville.* Hanover, NH: University Press of New England, 1980.

————. *Gender and Disorder in Early Modern Seville.* Princeton, NJ: Princeton University Press, 1990.

Petroff, Elizabeth Alvilda, ed. *Medieval Women's Visionary Literature.* New York: Oxford University Press, 1986.

Perry, Ruth. *The Celebrated Mary Astell: An Early English Feminist.* Chicago: University of Chicago Press, 1986.

Rabil, Albert. *Laura Cereta: Quattrocento Humanist.* Binghamton, NY: Medieval and Renaissance Texts and Studies, 1981.

Ranft, Patricia. *Women in Western Intellectual Culture, 600–1500.* New York: Palgrave, 2002.

Rapley, Elizabeth. *A Social History of the Cloister: Daily Life in the Teaching Monasteries of the Old Regime.* Montreal: McGill-Queen's University Press, 2001.

Raven, James, Helen Small, and Naomi Tadmor, eds. *The Practice and Representation of Reading in England.* Cambridge: University Press, 1996.

Reardon, Colleen. *Holy Concord within Sacred Walls: Nuns and Music in Siena, 1575–1700.* Oxford: Oxford University Press, 2001.

Reiss, Sheryl E., and David G. Wilkins, ed. *Beyond Isabella: Secular Women Patrons of Art in Renaissance Italy.* Kirksville, MO: Turman State University Press, 2001.

Rheubottom, David. *Age, Marriage, and Politics in Fifteenth-Century Ragusa.* Oxford: Oxford University Press, 2000.

Richardson, Brian. *Printing, Writers, and Readers in Renaissance Italy.* Cambridge: University Press, 1999.

Riddle, John M. *Contraception and Abortion from the Ancient World to the Renaissance.* Cambridge, MA: Harvard University Press, 1992.

————. *Eve's Herbs: A History of Contraception and Abortion in the West.* Cambridge, MA: Harvard University Press, 1997.

Rose, Mary Beth. *The Expense of Spirit: Love and Sexuality in English Renaissance Drama.* Ithaca, NY: Cornell University Press, 1988.

————. *Gender and Heroism in Early Modern English Literature.* Chicago: University of Chicago Press, 2002.

————, ed. *Women in the Middle Ages and the Renaissance: Literary and Historical Perspectives.* Syracuse, NY: Syracuse University Press, 1986.

Rosenthal, Margaret F. *The Honest Courtesan: Veronica Franco, Citizen and Writer in Sixteenth-Century Venice.* Foreword by Catharine R. Stimpson. Chicago: University of Chicago Press, 1992.

Sackville-West, Vita. *Daughter of France: The Life of La Grande Mademoiselle.* Garden City, NY: Doubleday, 1959.

Sánchez, Magdalena S. *The Empress, the Queen, and the Nun: Women and Power at the Court of Philip III of Spain.* Baltimore, MD: Johns Hopkins University Press, 1998.

Schiebinger, Londa. *The Mind Has No Sex?: Women in the Origins of Modern Science.* Cambridge, MA: Harvard University Press, 1991.

——. *Nature's Body: Gender in the Making of Modern Science.* Boston: Beacon Press, 1993.

Schutte, Anne Jacobson, Thomas Kuehn, and Silvana Seidel Menchi, eds. *Time, Space, and Women's Lives in Early Modern Europe.* Kirksville, MO: Truman State University Press, 2001.

Schofield, Mary Anne, and Cecilia Macheski, eds. *Fetter'd or Free? British Women Novelists, 1670–1815.* Athens: Ohio University Press, 1986.

Shannon, Laurie. *Sovereign Amity: Figures of Friendship in Shakespearean Contexts.* Chicago: University of Chicago Press, 2002.

Shemek, Deanna. *Ladies Errant: Wayward Women and Social Order in Early Modern Italy.* Durham, NC: Duke University Press, 1998.

Smith, Hilda L. *Reason's Disciples: Seventeenth-Century English Feminists.* Urbana: University of Illinois Press, 1982.

——, ed. *Women Writers and the Early Modern British Political Tradition.* Cambridge: Cambridge University Press, 1998.

Sobel, Dava. *Galileo's Daughter: A Historical Memoir of Science, Faith, and Love.* New York: Penguin Books, 2000.

Sommerville, Margaret R. *Sex and Subjection: Attitudes to Women in Early-Modern Society.* London: Arnold, 1995.

Soufas, Teresa Scott. *Dramas of Distinction: A Study of Plays by Golden Age Women.* Lexington, KY: University Press of Kentucky, 1997.

Spencer, Jane. *The Rise of the Woman Novelist: From Aphra Behn to Jane Austen.* Oxford: Basil Blackwell, 1986.

Spender, Dale. *Mothers of the Novel: One Hundred Good Women Writers before Jane Austen.* London and New York: Routledge, 1986.

Sperling, Jutta Gisela. *Convents and the Body Politic in Late Renaissance Venice.* Foreword by Catharine R. Stimpson. Chicago: University of Chicago Press, 1999.

Steinbrügge, Lieselotte. *The Moral Sex: Woman's Nature in the French Enlightenment.* Trans. Pamela E. Selwyn. New York: Oxford University Press, 1995.

Stephens, Sonya, ed. *A History of Women's Writing in France.* Cambridge: Cambridge University Press, 2000.

Stocker, Margarita. *Judith, Sexual Warrior: Women and Power in Western Culture.* New Haven, CT: Yale University Press, 1998.

Stretton, Timothy. *Women Waging Law in Elizabethan England.* Cambridge: Cambridge University Press, 1998.

Stuard, Susan M. "The Dominion of Gender: Women's Fortunes in the High Middle Ages." In Renate Bridenthal, Claudia Koonz, and Susan M. Stuard, eds. *Becoming Visible: Women in European History,* ed. Renate Bridenthal, Claudia Koonz, and Susan M. Stuard. 3rd ed. Boston: Houghton Mifflin, 1998.

Summit, Jennifer. *Lost Property: The Woman Writer and English Literary History, 1380–1589.* Chicago: University of Chicago Press, 2000.

Surtz, Ronald E. *The Guitar of God: Gender, Power, and Authority in the Visionary World of Mother Juana de la Cruz (1481–1534).* Philadelphia: University of Pennsylvania Press, 1991.

——. *Writing Women in Late Medieval and Early Modern Spain: The Mothers of Saint Teresa of Avila.* Philadelphia: University of Pennsylvania Press, 1995.

Teague, Frances. *Bathsua Makin, Woman of Learning*. Lewisburg, PA: Bucknell University Press, 1999.

Todd, Janet. *The Sign of Angelica: Women, Writing and Fiction, 1660–1800*. New York: Columbia University Press, 1989.

———. *The Secret Life of Aphra Behn*. London, New York, and Sydney: Pandora, 2000.

Valenze, Deborah. *The First Industrial Woman*. New York: Oxford University Press, 1995.

Van Dijk, Susan, Lia van Gemert, and Sheila Ottway, eds. *Writing the History of Women's Writing: Toward an International Approach*. Proceedings of the Colloquium, Amsterdam, 9–11 September. Amsterdam: Royal Netherlands Academy of Arts and Sciences, 2001.

Vickery, Amanda. *The Gentleman's Daughter: Women's Lives in Georgian England*. New Haven, CT: Yale University Press, 1998.

Vollendorf, Lisa, ed. *Recovering Spain's Feminist Tradition*. New York: MLA, 2001.

Waithe, Mary Ellen, ed. *A History of Women Philosophers*. 3 vols. Dordrecht: Martinus Nijhoff, 1987.

Walker, Claire. *Gender and Politics in Early Modern Europe: English Convents in France and the Low Countries*. New York: Palgrave, 2003.

Wall, Wendy. *The Imprint of Gender: Authorship and Publication in the English Renaissance*. Ithaca, NY: Cornell University Press, 1993.

Walsh, William T. *St. Teresa of Avila: A Biography*. Rockford, IL: TAN Books, 1987.

Warner, Marina. *Alone of All Her Sex: The Myth and Cult of the Virgin Mary*. New York: Knopf, 1976.

Warnicke, Retha M. *The Marrying of Anne of Cleves: Royal Protocol in Tudor England*. Cambridge: Cambridge University Press, 2000.

Watt, Diane. *Secretaries of God: Women Prophets in Late Medieval and Early Modern England*. Cambridge, England: D. S. Brewer, 1997.

Weber, Alison. *Teresa of Avila and the Rhetoric of Femininity*. Princeton, NJ: Princeton University Press, 1990.

Welles, Marcia L. *Persephone's Girdle: Narratives of Rape in Seventeenth-Century Spanish Literature*. Nashville, TN: Vanderbilt University Press, 2000.

Whitehead, Barbara J., ed. *Women's Education in Early Modern Europe: A History, 1500–1800*. New York and London: Garland, 1999.

Wiesner, Merry E. *Working Women in Renaissance Germany*. New Brunswick, NJ: Rutgers University Press, 1986.

———. *Women and Gender in Early Modern Europe*. Cambridge: Cambridge University Press, 1993.

Willard, Charity Cannon. *Christine de Pizan: Her Life and Works*. New York: Persea Books, 1984.

Winn, Colette, and Donna Kuizenga, eds. *Women Writers in Pre-Revolutionary France*. New York: Garland, 1997.

Woodbridge, Linda. *Women and the English Renaissance: Literature and the Nature of Womankind, 1540–1620*. Urbana: University of Illinois Press, 1984.

Woods, Susanne. *Lanyer: A Renaissance Woman Poet*. New York: Oxford University Press, 1999.

———, and Margaret P. Hannay, eds. *Teaching Tudor and Stuart Women Writers*. New York: MLA, 2000.

INDEX